Thurman Arnold

Thurman Arnold

A Biography

Spencer Weber Waller

NEW YORK UNIVERSITY PRESS
New York and London

NEW YORK UNIVERSITY PRESS
New York and London
www.nyupress.org

© 2005 by New York University
All rights reserved

Library of Congress Cataloging-in-Publication Data
Waller, Spencer Weber.
Thurman Arnold : a biography / Spencer Weber Waller.
p. cm.
Includes bibliographical references and index.
ISBN-13 : 978-0-8147-9392-3 (cloth : alk. paper)
ISBN-10 : 0-8147-9392-4 (cloth : alk. paper)
1. Arnold, Thurman Wesley, 1891–1969.
2. Lawyers—United States—Biography.
3. Law teachers—United States—Biography.
I. Arnold, Thurman Wesley, 1891–1969. II. Title.
KF373.A7.W35   2005
340'.092—dc22   2005011313

New York University Press books are printed on acid-free paper,
and their binding materials are chosen for strength and durability.

Manufactured in the United States of America
10 9 8 7 6 5 4 3 2 1

For Laura and Jordan
 who wanted me to call the book "Hey Arnold."

Political democracy will not work unless it is founded on industrial democracy. Free and independent political organization cannot survive when free and independent competing business enterprise has disappeared. Organizing against free competition has a logical conclusion. We have seen that overseas.
—Thurman Arnold, September 14, 1939

Contents

Acknowledgments xi

Introduction 1

1   The Spirit of the West   4
2   A Young Lawyer and the War   20
3   Small Town Lawyer and Politician   29
4   An Academic Entrepreneur   39
5   Legal Realist and Firebrand   45
6   Trustbuster   78
7   The Short Unhappy Judgeship of Thurman Arnold   111
8   A Firm Beginning   124
9   Building a Washington Law Firm   151
10   Final Fights   181

Epilogue   199

Appendix A: Cases Decided (Opinion), Concurred, or Dissented by Judge Thurman Arnold   203

Appendix B: Principal Writings of Thurman Arnold   207

Appendix C: Selected Bibliography of Works about Thurman Arnold and His Times   212

Notes   215

Index   251

About the Author   273

All illustrations appear as an insert after p. 180.

Acknowledgments

A project of this nature and scope, especially for a law professor turned amateur biographer, involves the collaboration of an enormous number of people and institutions. At the risk of leaving out any of the number of persons who contributed their inspiration or perspiration to this effort let me thank: Brooklyn Law School for supporting my initial research on this project; Loyola University Chicago School of Law, Dean Nina Appel, the Institute for Consumer Antitrust Studies, Charlene Sneed, my faculty colleagues, and the many colleagues at other law schools who commented on portions of the manuscript; Julia Wentz, the staff of the law library, my research assistants on this project: Rebecca Patterson, Dooyang Kang, Elizabeth Halbert Edwards, Matt Hamilton, Reema Kapur, and Lindsay Frank; the University of Wyoming College of Law and law library, Dean Jerry Parkinson, the American Heritage Center and its gracious staff, the Laramie Plains Museum, Michael Lansing, Mary Burgess, Robin Hill, and John Waggener; Kevin Fredette of the West Virginia University College of Law Library; G. Duane Vieth, Robert Pitofsky, Linda Edwards, the firm of Arnold & Porter, and other current and past partners who offered me their time and recollections; the friends and members of the Arnold family who gave of their time and family memorabilia; and Daniel Ernst, Deborah Gershenowitz, Alison Waldenberg, Anthony Sebok, and Paul Finkelman for their help and advice as I started down the path of legal history and biography. Special thanks go to Laura Matalon and Christopher Leslie who read the draft manuscript in its entirety and improved it immeasurably with their comments and to Laura Kalman who generously provided me with a variety of transcripts and interviews from her prior research on Abe Fortas, allowing me access to the thoughts of many key individuals in the life of Thurman Arnold who are no longer with us.

Introduction

I first learned about Thurman Arnold as a law student studying antitrust law and seeing so many of the landmark cases all stemming from the same five-year period in the late New Deal when Arnold headed the Antitrust Division of the Justice Department. Later I worked briefly in the Antitrust Division in the same majestic building on Pennsylvania Avenue where Arnold had presided from the office on the fifth floor and where his successors still work today. Even outside of work, it was hard for me to escape the presence of Thurman Arnold as I lived equidistant from the Thurman Arnold building, then located at 21st and M streets and the former site of the Arnold & Porter firm in the townhouse at 19th and N streets.

Later in private practice and law teaching, I learned much more about the importance of Thurman Arnold in terms of the history of antitrust but knew little about him as a person and the many other aspects of his lengthy and distinguished career. My interest in the legal realist movement led me to Arnold's academic writing and career. Being assigned to teach civil procedure led me to a marvelous book called *The Buffalo Creek Disaster*, which told the story of a pro bono suit by a team of lawyers from Arnold & Porter following a lethal flood in the coal country in West Virginia. The author was Gerald Stern, a younger lawyer at Arnold & Porter, who admired Arnold deeply and peppered his book with frequent anecdotes about Arnold. Here I learned for the first time the importance of Arnold's western upbringing in turn-of-the-century Laramie, Wyoming, and his exploits as a small-town lawyer and politician before he burst onto the national scene. Still later, I heard about Arnold the civil libertarian in the 1950s, handling critical pro bono cases in the dark days of the McCarthy era. Everything I stumbled across showed me that Thurman Arnold was not just an important figure of our history but an extremely interesting character far different from the modern button-down legal world.

All of these snippets formed a kaleidoscopic, but incomplete, portrait of Arnold and whetted my appetite for more. I looked for a biography of Arnold but could find none, although Arnold was discussed in all the biographies of his contemporaries and throughout the many histories of the New Deal. I enjoyed the biographical sketch in *Voltaire and the Cowboy*, the volume of Arnold's correspondence edited by Eugene Gressley, but was frustrated that there was not more. I left my pursuit of the real Arnold unfulfilled and returned to the more mundane tasks of teaching classes and writing law review articles.

Some months later, it hit me that I should write the biography both to learn and to tell the story that I had been seeking. It was a relief to turn from the purely academic to doing the oral history and archival research until a more complete portrait of Arnold began to emerge. Being both a beginner and an amateur at legal history was daunting, but people were simply eager to talk about Arnold, his genius, and his impact on their lives and the world at large. Friends, family, former colleagues, and even surviving students brought him back to life for the hours we spoke so I could see along with them why Arnold was both one of the most important and fascinating figures of the twentieth-century legal world and why Laramie, Wyoming, was crucial to the telling of that story.

In a world where most people are famous for one thing, Arnold stood out in many endeavors making him in essence the decathlon champion of American law. He was an eminent practitioner, law dean, law professor, legal realist, best-selling author, the creator of modern antitrust law, one of the key players of the New Deal, federal appellate judge, defender of civil liberties and free speech, and one of the creators of the prototype of the modern Washington law firm.

Aside from his accomplishments, he was one of the warmest human beings of his time. With his creativity, wit, and dislike of pomposity, he possessed the unique ability to both skewer the establishment and at the same time participate in it without anyone objecting too strenuously to the seeming contradiction.

In addition to being a unique, vital, funny human being who was front and center at the great public events and debates of our country for more than four decades, Arnold was one of handful of the great liberals of the twentieth century who made his mark at the center of power but who grew up at the periphery and never forgot what it meant to be subject to the whims of distant masters. Arnold made the promotion of economic competition, free speech, and opposition to the misuse of unchecked private and public power the cornerstone of his life's work in all the different phases that his restless intellect pursued. This is the story of that journey.

1

The Spirit of the West

To understand the life and work of Thurman Arnold, you have to know something about Laramie, Wyoming. Parts of Wyoming passed to the United States from France in 1803 as part of the Louisiana Purchase and the rest through later treaties with Spain, Great Britain, and Mexico.[1] Although a few French traders and explorers visited the territory in the eighteenth century, and white American explorers claimed to have passed through these lands fleeing Indians as early as 1807, the first official exploration on behalf of the U.S. government was a three-day journey led by Charles Fremont in 1843. The Laramie plains in the southeast corner of the present state of Wyoming were the site of a fur-trading post and supply depot as early as 1834. An army garrison, Fort Sanders, was eventually established on the same site near the Laramie River in 1849. Fort Sanders served as the county seat and protected the fledgling Overland Trail and Telegraph companies.

The city of Laramie sprang up in anticipation of the coming of the Union Pacific railroad. The Union Pacific's track reached Laramie moving westward from Cheyenne in the spring of 1868 on its way to unite with the Central Pacific track at Promontory Point, Utah, in 1869 to form the first transcontinental railroad. The week before the railroad arrived, the Union Pacific began to sell land lots in Laramie that it had received in grants from the United States. The buyers were mostly the couple of hundred people who had been camping on the site that the railroad had platted for the town. Within a week, four hundred lots were sold, and within two weeks, five hundred "buildings" had been erected.[2]

Portable warehouses and railroad bunk cars were quickly replaced with a railroad terminal, a land office, tents, simple stores, a location for a hotel, pastures for grazing animals, and struggling farms. On May 10, the first passenger train arrived carrying all manner of settlers and the merchandise of frontier life in post–Civil War America. As Wyoming historian T. A. Larson notes, Wyoming was the first part of the West where a majority of the settlers came by rail rather than wagon. The first white child was born on June 21. Throughout 1868, Laramie remained the division headquarters for Union Pacific construction, virtually assuring its future, unlike some of the later railroad towns that quickly vanished from the scene.[3]

The town was situated on the high plains of southern Wyoming. Desolate and flat, there were a few hills to the east, and more than thirty miles to the south and west lay the pine tree-laden Medicine Bow mountains. In between lay outcroppings of red rock, scrub, and pasture land, few if any trees, and a sense of the sufferance of nature with the puny attempts of the men and women of Laramie to make a home. As one travel guide put it, "In the vast open spaces of Wyoming, the sky takes on its own importance, sometimes making the land seem like an afterthought."[4] Most who saw southern Wyoming by train thought it a "barren wasteland."[5] While summers were pleasant with cool evenings, few could have looked forward to the winters when the prospect of subzero temperatures, howling winds, and blinding snows meant probable death to anyone foolish enough to venture far beyond the few streets of the fragile new town.

The town, such as it was, grew almost entirely on the east and north side of the Union Pacific tracks. Tents were quickly replaced with shanties and other temporary, usually floorless, houses. Although a mayor was quickly elected, the provisional government was weak, and the first summer was a lawless one. The first mayor was a saloon keeper elected with support of the gambling houses, brothels, and bars. The administration appointed as its first marshal a man who had just left Cheyenne after being acquitted of murder. The railroad, and the army with it, pulled out in July as part of the relentless march of the iron rails to Rawlins and westward to the historic Golden Spike in Utah. By 1870 the population of Laramie had dropped to a mere 828.[6]

Once the army was gone, the initial crime wave in Laramie began almost immediately. There was little sense of order or civil society until October, when the three worst town desperadoes were captured and hanged by a posse of armed citizens, and more than a hundred hoodlums and harlots were shipped out of town on all the available railroad cars. Despite this helpful series of events, law and order did not come quickly, and Laramie remained subject to federal court rule until 1874.[7]

Throughout the 1880s, Wyoming recreated itself as the cowboy state. As the wars with the native American Indian tribes ended, the cattle industry grew, spreading from the southern tier throughout the state. The weather, soil, and climate, which was so unfavorable to agriculture, proved splendid for the open grazing of livestock. The Wyoming cowboys were first occupied with the grand trail drives of cattle, which the expansion of the railroad put to an end, and then later as ranch hands. Only partially consistent with the image of the gunslinger and outlaw created by writers[8] and later the movies, the Wyoming cowboy nonetheless played a key role in the development of the immensely important livestock industry that characterized the Wyoming economy prior to the twentieth-century energy boom.[9] Their more typical tasks in the post-trail drive era included the round-ups in the spring, the branding of the young cattle, the neutering of bulls, dehorning, taking care of sick cattle, and eventually the physical upkeep of the ranches as they became fenced in. Unfortunately, the cattle boom ended prematurely due to overexpansion and the terrible winter of 1886–1887. While the industry survived, it no longer thrived.[10]

In Laramie, the more everyday aspects of a Western small town quickly developed. The first schools and churches were built in 1869, and the Union Pacific built a critically important iron mill for its rails in the 1870s. A courthouse was erected in 1871, and the Wyoming penitentiary was built on the less desirable side of the tracks in 1873. A fire department, municipal water supply, hospital, courts, parochial schools, libraries, and a myriad of businesses followed in the coming years. In addition to the Union Pacific mill, by 1887 Laramie could boast of a brickyard, glass factory, tannery, flour mill, chemical works, and a cigar factory that turned out a brand of perfectos called "Woman's Rights." The end of Laramie's days as a true frontier town is best symbolized by two events in 1882: first the opera house opened, and then Fort Sanders closed due to lack of business following the end of the Indian wars. The first mansion was built in 1885, less than a decade from when hogs and cattle had the run of the dirt streets.[11]

Laramie was also defined by its competition with Cheyenne for the capital, the center of power, and the distribution of government spending in early Wyoming. Cheyenne was the initial capital largely because it was developed earlier as a railroad town and because it was the closest town to Nebraska, the former capital of the Dakota territory from which Wyoming was created. Because it was the capital, Cheyenne became the center of the territorial Republican party after the popularity of the Republican party grew following the assassination of Lincoln and the end of the Civil War.

Laramie lost several attempts to relocate the state capital away from Cheyenne. The closest it came was in 1873 when the Wyoming House passed a bill moving the capital by a 7-6 vote. This caused the Cheyenne members of the upper house, the Council, to boycott the session lest a quorum be found. There is at least a suggestion that the legislators were absent more as a result of vicious hangovers from a particularly impressive party for government officials the night before at the home of Judge Joseph Cary.[12] The remaining legislators declared the seats of their colleagues vacant and proceeded to enact a variety of legislation, including relocating the capital to Laramie, only to be defeated when the Republican governor refused to sign any of the bills enacted by the rump council. Laramie eventually settled for the establishment of the University of Wyoming as a consolation prize following the legislative session of 1886. To convey an idea of the stakes involved, Cheyenne received $150,000 as the capital and Laramie a mere $50,000 for hosting the university.[13]

Laramie was also the center of the Democratic party in the more populous southern half of the state. The Democrats had dominated Wyoming politics at the territorial level in the early days but soon took a back seat to the Republican machine created by Frederick Warren, also the head of the failed Cattle Trust of the 1880s.[14] The Republicans became identified with the Union Pacific Railroad, still the preeminent force in Wyoming economy and politics, and the powerful Wyoming Stock Growers Association of cattle owners. Laramie and the Democratic party thus became the center of the antimonopoly movement in Wyoming.[15] However, Laramie remained the second city of Wyoming to Cheyenne in terms of population, wealth, and influence.

Even in the early days, both Laramie and Wyoming were more than the Wild West of novelists Owen Wister and Zane Grey. The territorial government of Wyoming was created in April 1869 with a Republican territorial governor and other territorial officials appointed by President Ulysses S. Grant. By November 1869, the all Democratic nine-member upper chamber and twelve-member lower chamber Wyoming territorial legislature granted women the right to vote and sit on juries, the first such decisions in the United States or its territories. The legislature also enacted a law forbidding discrimination in pay for teachers on the basis of sex. In December, women received the right to hold property, and in 1870 the first woman justice of the peace was appointed by the pro-suffrage territorial Republican governor. Women in Wyoming began to sit on grand and petit juries in 1870, and women cast their first votes in the election of September 1870.[16]

These bold decisions were not a sign of either nineteenth- or twentieth-century liberalism,[17] but rather an attempt to attract additional population to a territory that had barely 8,000 people and fewer than 1,000 women. Nevertheless, it was also a sign of the openness and tolerance that characterized the West, and particularly the Laramie that produced Thurman Arnold and his unique and irreverent perspective on law, power, and society.

Thurman Arnold's grandfather, Franklin Luther Arnold, came to Wyoming as a Presbyterian missionary in the early 1870s. In addition to being the first Presbyterian minister in the state, Franklin Arnold assisted in the initial survey of what became Yellowstone National Park. Born in Parma, New York, he was raised in Ohio as part of the great migration to the Western Reserve of Ohio in the 1820s. Following the death of his father at age twelve, Franklin became a school teacher at the tender age of sixteen. He later attended what is now Oberlin College and became a minister.[18]

While in Africa as a missionary, he met and married Thurman's grandmother, Maria Ramsauer, a native of Oldenburg, Germany.[19] As Thurman Arnold writes in his autobiography,

> My Arnold grandfather and my Ramsauer grandmother became acquainted and married under peculiar circumstances. When . . . Franklin arrived in Africa as a missionary, he found Johannes Ramsauer's son there seriously ill. He wrote a letter to the young man's parents in Oldenberg [sic], Germany, telling them that they had better send someone out to care for him. His sister came out, but the journey in those days was very long, and before she arrived her brother had died. . . . Later they were married, and remained in Africa as missionaries.[20]

Franklin and Maria had two children in Africa and decided to come to the United States, where Franklin wanted to work as a missionary in the West. On the way home, they visited Maria's parents in Germany who would not hear of bringing the children to the United States. They were people of wealth and prominence and would not countenance allowing their grandchildren to be brought up in the wilds of the American West.

The two children remained behind and were raised in Germany,[21] and by the early 1870s Franklin and Maria made their way to Wyoming to continue a missionary life. After a time in Laramie, Franklin continued his ministry ever further west, first in Evanston, Wyoming, and later Salt Lake City, Utah, where he continued to correspond regularly with his extended family back in Laramie.

Four more children were born in the United States. The third child was born in 1860. Constantine Peter Arnold, Thurman's father, was named after the Grand Duke Peter Constantine. Despite this noble moniker, Arnold's father detested his full Christian name, and went by C. P. as an adult. Franklin and Maria's poverty prevented them from ever seeing their eldest children in Germany again, and C. P. waited until he was forty years old to meet his older brothers for the first time.

C. P. Arnold graduated as valedictorian of Wabash College in Indiana and returned home to Laramie to become a prominent attorney involved in local Democratic politics. The Arnolds were one of five families that then defined Laramie society.[22] In addition to his law practice, C. P. was a ranch owner, scholar, author, geologist, and poet over the course of his long life.

C. P. was a flowery orator in the style of the day. According to a family friend, "He never just said something, he always claimed something."[23] The *Laramie Daily Bugle* described him as "iridescent in oratory and invincible in argument." He stumped for the Democratic party candidates in local and state-wide elections, normally unsuccessfully as the Republican party began to assert its control over state politics. In 1898, he lost the election for the Wyoming congressional seat as a Democrat running on the fading Free Silver ticket. C. P. lost to former Congressman Frank W. Mondell by a vote count of 10,762 to 8,466.[24]

Even in the late 1890s, Wyoming politics had not entirely outgrown its Wild West past. As one observer described the Mondell campaign, "During the campaign in those days there were always a great many 'doubtful voters,' and it sometimes required several quarts of liquor and an unlimited number of cigars to convince them."[25]

In addition to his law practice, C. P. owned what became known as the Millbrook ranch outside of town and participated prominently in the array of growing social and cultural events as Laramie developed as a city. Later in life, he became the first president of the Wyoming State Bar Association and was viewed for the last several decades of his life as the "dean" of the Albany County bar.

July 1890 produced the two great events that proved so influential in the life of Thurman Arnold. First, Congress overwhelmingly passed the Sherman Antitrust Act, which President Benjamin Harrison promptly signed on July 2. On July 10, President Harrison signed the bill making Wyoming the forty-fourth state in the Union, despite continuing controversies over whether Wyoming met the population and other requirements for statehood.[26]

On June 2, 1891, Thurman Arnold was born in the Arnold family home at 812 Grand Avenue, which his father had built the previous year. At the time, it was on the outskirts of Laramie, with little between it and the Old Main university building several blocks away. It was a Victorian house with a stiff formal feel on both the outside and inside and parlor rooms complete with horsehair furniture.

As a boy, Thurman remembers his grandfather Franklin as a kindly, tall, and stately man, about six feet two inches tall with a long white beard, who habitually wore a frock coat and a high silk hat. He celebrated the Sabbath from 6 p.m. on Saturday evening through Monday morning and tolerated no games or amusements during this extended day of rest. He particularly disliked card playing of all kinds, except for a self-invented game called "Flinch," which Franklin explained could not bring on the kind of gambling addiction that card playing normally led to because no gambler knew how to play it.[27]

The Laramie of the turn of the century was a small town, part of the high plains that stretched in every direction, and only one short generation away from its founding. As late as 1904, Laramie had a notorious lynching of a black prisoner who had escaped from the penitentiary. Arnold noted about that year: "In my day in 1904 on Sunday it seemed that half the population went to Church and the other half got drunk in the eight or ten saloons on Front Street."[28]

Arnold remembered seeing the houses of prostitution down by Front Street, a reminder of the railroad camp town that Laramie once had been. When Arnold was a boy, Tom Horn was a hero as the hired gun of the Wyoming Cattleman's Association to rid the county of rustlers. Horn eventually was executed following his conviction for murder in a celebrated trial in Cheyenne. Like all young people at the time, Thurman Arnold avidly followed the trial, not only because Tom Horn was a true folk hero but also because his father represented one of the prominent ranchers involved in the case. Another local hero was Bill Nye, the legendary humorist and editor of the *Laramie Daily Bugle*.[29]

Although Laramie had a telephone exchange beginning in 1882, cars were not prevalent until 1910. Arnold's father was convinced that the horseless buggy was a mere fad and did not succumb to the new fashion himself until 1915. Thurman, like most of the boys in Laramie, had a pony and an affinity for the open land surrounding this thin slice of civilization.

Outside of Laramie was cattle country. The cattle roamed unfenced, and the illegal fencing of federal lands remained a hot political issue for decades to come. Spring brought old-fashioned roundups, cowboys, and campfires. Arnold took long two-day trips to the mountains by pack animal or all-day trips on the rickety Laramie, Hans Peak, and Pacific railroad. He worked summers raking hay or wrangling horses. Arnold was nearly thrown from his horse one morning when he saw five elephants on the Laramie plains that had broken free from the circus stranded in Laramie the day before.[30]

Arnold attended high school at the University of Wyoming which in those days functioned primarily as a college preparatory academy rather than a true university. Originally, the university was comprised of one lone building. Roosters and cattle could be seen and heard in the not-too-distant surroundings.[31] The students amused themselves by leaving a cow in the second floor public rooms of the university building for the administration to remove the next day. When security improved, the students merely deposited the reluctant bovine on the back porch of the university president's home.

Arnold wrote little of the education he received in Wyoming, but his high school days and his freshman year in college in Laramie were the beginning of a life-long affiliation with the university. What Arnold remembered was the Reserve Officers' Training Corps (ROTC) training where he was taught close order drill using a wooden gun assigned to him because of his youth (twelve) and his small size. True to the Wyoming tradition of gender equality, the women students trained as well, thereby doubling the potential contribution to the national defense.

Upon graduation, just shy of his sixteenth birthday, Thurman Arnold enrolled at his father's alma mater, Wabash College in Indiana, and left Laramie for the first time in his young life. The Laramie that Thurman Arnold knew from his childhood left an indelible impression. Later in life as a Brahmin of the Washington, D.C., bar, he wrote: "I will never get over my love for that wild semiarid country."[32]

At Wabash, Arnold excelled academically at such subjects as Greek drama, German, rhetoric, and inorganic chemistry, but he stayed only one year.[33] He appeared to detest his time at Wabash and never referred to his time there as a student until late in life.[34] Even then, he omitted any reference to his time at Wabash in his autobiography, claiming only to have attended Princeton as an undergraduate.

Arnold in fact entered Princeton in 1908 with sophomore standing from the credits he had accumulated at Wyoming and Wabash. Arnold's Princeton was a far cry from the distinguished Ivy League institution of today. Princeton had only become a university in 1896. Until then, Princeton had been known as the College of New Jersey, which dated back to colonial times. It served primarily as a finishing school for the intellectually mediocre scions of the eastern establishment. That image began to change under the leadership of Woodrow Wilson, who became president of the university in 1903, but a complete transformation was a long time away.[35] Even in the first decade of the 1900s when F. Scott Fitzgerald briefly attended Princeton, it remained "the pleasantest country club in America."[36]

Princeton was not a happy experience socially or intellectually for young Thurman. Although he excelled academically and eventually earned Phi Beta Kappa, he always felt like a Western cowboy in an Ivy League setting. Neither Laramie, nor rural Indiana, were any real preparation for the social mores of one of the bedrock institutions of the eastern establishment. In Arnold's words, "My Western clothes, mannerisms, and speech did not fit. I was immediately classed as a queer character. I was not admitted to any club; indeed I was never admitted to anything at Princeton. . . . My years at Princeton were chiefly remarkable for their loneliness." He told family members more succinctly that Princeton had been "miserable." In particular, he was never invited to join the eating clubs of Princeton, then the principal social institutions of the university, and he spoke with bitterness and hurt about this exclusion throughout his life.[37]

The academics were dull and stifling. Arnold recalls virtually every course being taught in a vacuum, unconnected to the culture or civilization in which the required Greek and Latin texts were created. The same was true for philosophy, which interested Arnold, but consisted of learning the formulas of the famous philosophers and searching for abstract systems of timeless truth. Arnold recalled fondly only one course, a course on the Constitution taught by E. S. Corwin. Otherwise, nothing "had any relevance to the development of the social institutions that existed outside the college walls."[38]

The only extracurricular activity that Arnold appeared to have participated in was the *Nassau Literary Magazine*. A full decade before F. Scott Fitzgerald would make Princeton famous as a birthplace of writers, Arnold penned less memorable essays on Chesterton, Twain, and "Why Women Marry." Perhaps emulating his father, he was an amateur poet as well, a habit that he used later in life to author more satirical verse about events and people he found annoying. At Princeton, his offerings were the more deadly serious "The Wanderlust" and "London."

Arnold captured at least a bit of his feelings of homesickness for the West in the stilted language of his other published poem, "The Prairie":

> O tawney stretch of never ending plain,
> Dissolving far away into the blue
> Of Hills that vie with heaven's paler hue,
> Long may your winds stir up their dirty train,
> Driving the desert clouds that bring no rain,
> Before man with his plow shall harness you.
> But no! Soon ends the coyote's wild refrain,
> And fences check the antelope's swift flight,
> Soon vanishes the prairie's sterner mood,
> Robbed of its freedom's secret, solitude,
> And every where man's dwelling meets our sight,
> Save only when that soft enchantress, night,
> Over the past and vanished wild doth brood.

In the late summer of 1910, Arnold made a modest version of the grand tour of Europe by visiting his Uncle Gottfried in Hamburg and traveling to England, France, Switzerland, Italy, and Holland along the way.[39] After graduation in the spring of 1911, Arnold spent the summer in Laramie and returned east once again in the fall, this time as a law student at Harvard.

At Harvard Law School Arnold found he had greater interest in the law classes than in the stifling classicism of Princeton. In comparison to Princeton, the professors seemed "intellectual giants." Arnold liked "the narrow logic of the law, the building of legal principle on the solid basis of a long line of precedents, and the analysis of cases in class by the Socratic method."[40] Unlike Princeton, it was fun and hard work.

The Harvard Law School of Arnold's day shared one characteristic with Princeton—an emphasis on abstract reason and conceptual thinking about principles, rather than linking the subjects to the needs of the society in which those principles applied. Harvard Law School remained a bastion of conservatism, despite having hired Roscoe Pound as a professor, who became famous for his brand of sociological jurisprudence linking law with certain of the social sciences and the need to consider policy and societal issues in formulating legal rules. The bulk of the law school faculty taught a style and theory of the law more closely tied to either the nineteenth-century natural law tradition or that of legal formalism associated with its prior dean Christopher Columbus Langdell.[41] Pound himself grew more conservative on issues of jurisprudence and legal education over time and became one of the fiercest opponents of the Legal Realists associated with Harvard's principal rivals, the Yale and Columbia law schools.[42]

Arnold lampooned the dominant style of Harvard in a poem about Conflicts of Law, a course which was taught by Joseph Beale. Beale was the Reporter for the *First Restatement of Conflicts of Law* promulgated by the American Law Institute, one of the stars of the Harvard faculty, and generally viewed as the high priest of the formalism preached by Dean Langdell. Conflicts of law dealt with cases in which parties were from two or more states or countries or where parties from one state had some dispute centered in another state, and the courts hearing the dispute had to determine which state's or country's law would be applied to determine liability. Beale was famous for advocating a series of fixed rules that determined which jurisdiction's laws applied to any particular dispute. Beale's rules were slightly different depending on whether the case involved torts, contracts, property, marriage, etc., but they were utterly indifferent to any of the real world consequences the choice of law made to the outcome of the case in the real world.[43]

To capture the spirit of this rarified conceptualism, Arnold returned to poetry and wrote as a law student in a more whimsical vein:

> CONFLICT OF LAWS with its peppery seasoning,
> Of pliable, scarcely reliable reasoning
> Dealing with weird and impossible things,
> Such as marriage and domicil, bastards and kings,

All about courts without jurisdiction,
Handing out misery, pain and affliction,
Making defendant, for reasons confusing,
Unfounded, ill-grounded, but always amusing,
Liable one place but not in another
Son of his father, but not of his mother,
Married in Sweden, but only a lover in
Pious dominions of Great Britains sovereign.
Blithely upsetting all we've been taught,
Rendering futile our methods of thought,
Till Reason, tottering down from her throne,
And Common Sense, sitting, neglected, alone,
Cry out despairingly, "Why do you hate us?
Give us once more our legitimate status."
Ah, Students, bewildered, don't grasp at such straws,
But join in the chorus of Conflict of Laws.

Chorus

Beale, Beale, wonderful Beale,
Not even in verse can we tell how we feel,
When our efforts so strenuous,
    To overthrow,
    Your reasoning tenuous,
    Simply won't go.
    For the law is a system of
    wheels within wheels
    Invented by Sayres and Thayers and Beales
    With each little wheel
    So exactly adjusted,
    That if it goes haywire
    The whole thing is busted.
    So Hail to Profanity,
    Goodbye to Sanity,
Lost if you stop to consider or pause.
On with the frantic, romantic, pedantic,
Effusive, abusive, illusive, conclusive
Evasive, persuasive Conflict of Laws.[44]

There is no reason to believe Arnold was in any way a full-blown legal realist as a student. The legal realist intellectual movement was just beginning to brew and would not take shape until Arnold was a practicing lawyer and elected official back in Laramie in the 1920s. There he would have had little time or inclination to participate in what was largely a battle of contending law review articles about the future of legal education and the nature of law and judging. But Arnold nevertheless chaffed as a student under the older system and was ready, willing, and able to challenge the former orthodoxy when he later entered the academic arena as a law professor.

Outside the classroom, Arnold found only partial social acceptance during law school. While he made lifelong friends, and in the process acquired his love of cigars, he also joked with a touch of bitterness throughout his career about his relatively low grades early in law school and his failure to make the *Harvard Law Review*,[45] the professional version of the social exclusion he had felt at Princeton.

Arnold had a limited amount of money from his parents but nothing on a par with his wealthier classmates. He could not afford the customary souvenir Harvard spoons as Christmas gifts for the few young ladies he knew. He felt awkward attending the Christmas season dances in Stamford, Connecticut, and elsewhere along the Boston–New York corridor because he danced like "an awful dud."[46] In fairness, Arnold simply wasn't interested in some of the usual social bonds of the student world. Sports was one of those accepted activities that left Arnold cold. With only a little tongue in cheek, he wrote his father in 1912:

> [L]ittle is happening in Boston except the world's series [sic] in baseball, which has just been won by Boston. It is absolutely wonderful how these fool people go crazy over the antics of the hired thugs on the baseball field. Then none of them come from Boston, nor do I see what credit their winning reflects on Boston, but an average of 40,000 people pay exorbitant prices to see them play, and go absolutely crazy when they win. They have just got thru giving them triumphal processions, led by the mayor, and the prominent citizens, and have taken them to Faneuil Hall to worship them. Politics, death, and salvation take a second place to them. Boston is the champion of the world. They have won the world's series, so-called I suppose because of the interest that it excites in Afghanistan and points east. A strange person is the baseball fan.[47]

Although Arnold attended the Harvard and Princeton football game while visiting his younger brother Carl, then a Princeton undergraduate, it elicited little more than indifference.[48]

All was not studious attention to the law however. Once, in the middle of finals, following a particularly grueling Torts exam, Arnold went with a group of friends to Revere Beach to swim, eat, ride the roller coaster, and clear the mind. Unfortunately, he also had his pocket picked and had to pawn his Phi Beta Kappa key in order to get enough money to return to Cambridge.[49] Arnold also took advantage of some of his social contacts from Princeton, and those of his father, and attended a number of dinners and parties along the Boston–New York corridor. The rough-and-ready boy of the West was receiving a smattering of East Coast polish in the process.

Opera was one of the more sophisticated activities that interested Arnold. Over one Christmas break he attended three operas. In one of those productions he had a small on-stage role in order to save the price of admission. In his operatic debut, Thurman Arnold appeared with the great Enrico Caruso, although Arnold's role consisted of leading a mule across the stage without any speaking or singing lines. Arnold was captivated by Caruso and told his mother that Caruso had "the most marvelous voice in the world, so wonderful that even the untrained ear can easily tell the difference between him and any other singer. It was worth the bother of putting on my elaborate costume to hear him sing so close by."[50]

Operas, dances, and beach parties were the exception to three years of academic grind. Arnold pledged to his mother that he would be working ten hours a day, six days a week. Despondently, he wrote her that "I have given up hope of getting an A, except by some lucky chance, but if I do get a B I do not think I am fitted for the law."[51] At his most despondent, Arnold questioned spending the extra money on a round trip train ticket back home for the summer since he didn't know whether he would be returning to Harvard the next fall.[52]

Law school also meant a chance to work in the legal clinic and handle actual cases. In his letters home, Arnold wrote of working on divorce cases where the parties were too poor to pay the filing fees and a dispute over wages due to a maid where the employer ultimately settled by paying $6 of the $12.50 allegedly owed.[53] As pitiful as these cases were, they represented Arnold's first taste of the real practice of law, and they stuck in his mind over the years far more than most of the classes he took. They also proved to be an exaggerated, but grimly accurate, predictor of his own early years as a lawyer.

Graduation meant finding a job. Arnold turned down both an offer with a respected Boston firm as well as the chance to return home to Laramie. Professor Thayer had told Thurman that he shouldn't practice in Boston because of the flood of Harvard graduates entering the market every year and that opportunities in Chicago were much better. For a time, he equivocated to himself and his father, "I am inclined to think that perhaps I have time to try a year in a large office, even though I eventually may come back to Laramie."[54] Trying out different formulations to justify himself to his father, Arnold wrote a short time later:

> The reasons governing me in this are not entirely the fact that Laramie is a place of rather limited opportunity so far as the law is concerned, but to go home seems like drifting with the current and taking the easiest course out. I will simply go into a place made for me, and there will be little incentive to get down and do any real hard work. There will be no push of necessity, and I feel that I had better get out and see what I can do.[55]

As Arnold continued to justify himself and seek his father's approval, he offered these prophetic words for his later career:

> I can't help feeling that I am foolish sometimes because I have decided not to start in Laramie, but the idea of living there all my life does not appeal to me. *I have ambitions to become a big lawyer in a big city*—very likely improbable of realization, for of course I know that the chances are, taking it as matter of probability, or average, that I will become no such thing.

He continued in all apparent sincerity and with only a hint of his now trademark sarcasm:

> I represent a huge investment of over ten thousand dollars. Part of the money has been well spent. A good deal has been foolishly spent. But it can't be recovered now in any action known to the Common Law. But the chief thing that I have to thank you for is for yourself. Very many fellows that I know have richer fathers, but none that I happen to run across have fathers of whom they can feel so proud, and to whom they

can look up to as an example to emulate in every way, not only because of unusual abilities and success, but because of qualities of mind and heart, power of expression, imagination, and character.[56]

In the end, based on little more than the recommendations of a professor and a friend, and armed with some letters of introduction from his father, Arnold chose Chicago to make his mark as a practicing attorney.

2

A Young Lawyer and the War

Upon moving to Chicago, Arnold made the rounds of the larger law firms seeking an associate position. He visited some twenty-five firms and received two tentative offers and one definite offer carrying the "staggering salary of $5 a week." He wrote his mother that the outlook was discouraging and most firms advised that he go home to Laramie. He became quite discouraged because of the bitter competition and his perceived need to eventually make $10,000 a year in Chicago rather than $5,000 in a smaller market like Laramie.[1]

Arnold did, however, have advantages most middle-of-the-class Harvard graduates did not, namely his father. C. P. Arnold had acquaintances and clients throughout the country dealing with land purchases from the Department of the Interior, the railroads, and other legal work that opened doors for his son. In Chicago these included the president of the department store Carson, Pirie Scott & Co. and the president of Western Electric.[2]

Those career advantages did not necessarily extend to living arrangements. Once gainfully employed, Arnold moved from the downtown LaSalle Hotel and took a room at the Wilson Avenue YMCA on the North Side of the city. It was twenty minutes from the Loop, Chicago's downtown business district near the elevated subway train, or "L." Rent was $13 a month for a tiny room, and Arnold also had to scrape together another $15 for the membership fee for the YMCA. With the YMCA pool and gym, Arnold pronounced himself satisfied with his temporary quarters.[3]

He eventually accepted an offer with a relatively large and prestigious corporate law firm, Adams, Follansbee, Hawley & Shorey, which was located on LaSalle Street, the Wall Street of Chicago. Arnold received the offer in part as a result of family contacts. The firm had four partners, one counsel, and five associates, including Arnold. Among the partners,

George Follansbee was himself a Harvard Law graduate and served as president of the Chicago Bar Association in 1898. When Arnold joined the firm in 1914, Mitchell Follansbee, also a partner, was the current president of the Chicago Bar Association and taught Illinois Practice at Northwestern University Law School.[4]

This was a modestly unusual choice for a Harvard law graduate of 1914. Unlike the native midwesterners who attended Harvard and returned to Chicago, or who were drawn to the de facto capital of the American Midwest, Arnold had no ties to the region or the city. He also had other options, including an offer from an eminently respectable Boston firm. Moreover, there was always the option of returning to Laramie and joining his father in his increasingly lucrative practice. At roughly the same point in time, C. P. Arnold was elected president of the newly formed Wyoming State Bar Association in 1915. Although returning to Laramie was never far from his mind, Arnold persevered in the Windy City.

At the firm, the work was hard and largely routine. His early work was not that different from his work at the Harvard Legal Aid Society—collections, divorces, minor criminal matters, and probate.[5]

Perhaps due to the amount and the monotony of his workload, Arnold's correspondence to his parents slowed dramatically. He took time to write in the middle of the October bar exam in Springfield, Illinois, mostly to complain about the state capital, where he was taking the exam, as "an indescribable mid-Victorian architectural monstrosity" and the "depressing lack of intelligence" of the Jewish students taking the bar with him.[6] This was an uncharacteristic and immature remark for a normally open-minded man who went on to found one of the great Washington, D.C., firms with Abe Fortas, a Jewish fellow name partner.

Back at the firm, his only interesting case was the bankruptcy of a large Wisconsin lumber company in which Arnold investigated fraud claims on behalf of certain creditors. Otherwise, Arnold notes in his letters home that his work was quite routine and comparable to what he could have expected back in Laramie: defending clients charged with bigamy, losing a criminal trial, and getting small clients of his own from friends.[7] Of greater interest was the work he did for the Reo Automobile company where a friend had become general counsel.[8] On the social side, on the advice of his boss, Arnold joined the City Club despite the $20 annual dues. In his limited spare time, he taught English to Italian immigrants at the Chicago Commons and took Latin classes at a local college.[9] In November 1915, he received a raise to the lofty sum of $70 a month.[10]

Despite, or perhaps because of, the pay scale, Arnold and two fellow associates left the Follansbee firm in 1916 and formed their own partnership, O'Bryan, Waite & Arnold. It would be the first of three firms in Arnold's lifetime that bore his name. O'Bryan, Waite & Arnold took well-furnished offices about a block from their old firm in the New York Life Building, a handsome turn-of-the-century fourteen-story terra-cotta elevator building at 39 S. LaSalle, which still stands today in the heart of the Loop. The building boasted a grand two-sided marble staircase and housed a variety of small law firms, accountants, and other service firms.

The first week of the new firm involved moving and the second in sending out announcements. Arnold sent announcements of the creation of the new firm to over five hundred friends, colleagues, and strangers in the Chicago area and prevailed on his father to send the formal announcement to his many contacts in Wyoming.

The next weeks and months involved long hours of work typically of no greater import than at the old firm. His distant father could send no clients, but he offered instead only the vaguely comforting advice that every lawyer has the experience of working long hours and getting no money for it.[11] The Follansbee firm, and another firm where the new partners had contacts, sustained the new enterprise with what amounted to the subcontracting of legal research which the new entrepreneurs eagerly tackled for a fee of $1 an hour.[12]

Arnold assisted other lawyers at trial, took over smaller files from them, and took on contingency fee cases involving personal injury, libel, and tax protests. At one point, the firm even represented a potential buyer for the Cleveland Indians baseball club, who in the end proved to have no discernable money. To supplement his income, Arnold taught law school at night for a year using slides prepared by his father. Most humiliating was the need for Arnold's request to his father to post a surety bond where his own negligence would have prevented his client's right of appeal had the bond (then beyond Arnold's means) not been posted.[13]

Letters home resembled accounting ledgers with lists of monthly cash receipts, accounts receivables, and the occasional profit.[14] In April 1916, Arnold had his picture published in the *Chicago Daily News,* then the leading afternoon paper. That month, the firm took in a record $301.85 in fees and turned its first profit.[15] In June, while thanking C. P. for a $5 gift, he complained to his father: "Have not made any money this month, except for a few dollars, and that prospects of taking any in are not bright."[16] Arnold's mother would chip in as well with the occasional $5 and $10 gift, plus pajamas and underwear, which never went unthanked.[17]

All of this was in the shadow of World War I and America's ultimate decision to join the conflict. Arnold himself had flirted with the "childish notion" of becoming an ambulance driver in France.[18] In June 1916, just as prospects were looking up at the law firm, Arnold was called up to join the Illinois National Guard in an artillery unit which included an inordinate number of the sons of prominent Chicago families.[19] According to Arnold, the unit had "quite a social register, there was a long waiting list to get in."[20]

Arnold was first posted to Fort Sheridan, about thirty miles north of Chicago where he initially drove a team of horses in a twelve-hour 130,000-man military parade.[21] A summer visit home to Laramie was cancelled when Arnold's unit was mobilized to patrol the Mexican border as part of General Pershing's attempt to capture Pancho Villa as punishment for his raids into New Mexico.[22]

Arnold was one of 25,000 troops in a shadeless camp under the 105-degree sun. He was assigned as a first class gunner but never saw action. Instead, he spent a large part of his time digging latrines with picks and shovels. What Arnold took away from this experience was that "if you were called out on a pick-and-shovel detail, you should select a pick instead of a shovel. That was owing to my discovery that you shovel practically all the time where as a pick can be used only at intervals." Beyond latrine duty, Arnold vividly recalled a four-day march by all 25,000 troops from San Antonio to Dallas, Texas, and back again, suggesting a certain lack of purpose and poor staff organization.[23]

By September, he was in Laramie vacationing with his family and giving a public address arranged by his father under the title of "The Man from Mexico."[24] Later in the fall, Arnold was back at the law firm. In December, he wrote his father, "Poverty still lurks in every corner."[25] February 1917 brought a slight profit, and March produced a $125 profit per partner and a more optimistic note that "business for the future looks better than it ever did before."[26]

Arnold's career in the Chicago bar effectively ended with America's entry into World War I. His partners were gracious about Arnold's leaves for military service, but by May 1917 he was gone for good. At the same time, Arnold's younger brother Carl also volunteered for the Army, leaving Princeton for three months of reserve training at Ft. Meyers, Virginia.

Arnold originally considered the reserves and passed the officer's reserve test early on, but he was upset that no position was available for him. This meant that if he went to officers' training school he would have to pay his own expenses and hope for later reimbursement from Congress. He tried to enlist in the Marines, believing this to be his best shot at an officer's commission, but failed the physical due to a heart murmur.

Wyoming Senator Frederick Warren and Congressman Frank Mondell wrote letters seeking to get both Arnold boys officers' commissions. Ironically, Congressman Mondell was the candidate who had defeated C. P. Arnold in the 1898 election for Congress, and Senator Warren was the head of the Wyoming Republican machine, but both nonetheless sought to help the offspring of their prominent Democratic acquaintance. By May 9, the commission came through, and President Wilson appointed Thurman a second lieutenant in the Field Artillery Section of the Army Reserve Corps.

Arnold trained as an artillery officer at Fort Sheridan. Unlike his earlier stint with General Pershing, this was hard technical professional soldiering. He had to master everything to calculate where shells would land, including the type of gun and shell, positioning, trajectory, mathematics, temperature, barometric pressure, and the other factors that could mean the difference between a hit, miss, or the disaster of friendly fire. He yearned for the chance to get to France to train with the actual guns he would be commanding in battle.

Arnold's entry into the war also precipitated his marriage to the former Frances Longan. Frances, who liked to be known as Miss Frances, was a descendant of the founders of Virginia, which was a source of great pride to her and her family. In more recent generations, the Longans were prominent bankers, lawyers, and politicians in and around Sedalia, Missouri. Her father was a well known and respected state court judge.

Frances's older sister, Agnes, had gone to Chicago to study opera. Agnes then studied in Paris on two occasions, returning for good to Chicago in 1914 on the eve of World War I to live with her sister Frances.

Frances was a year older than Arnold. She attended Hollins College in Virginia and had spent three years in schools in Switzerland and France. She was also "the black sheep of the family." She neither worked nor went to school after college. Instead, "she lived with her sister and had a good time." Frances always joked that if she had to, she could "always teach French." Although she was in fact quite fluent, her accent was terrible and somewhat of a family joke.[27]

Agnes's boyfriend, and later husband, met Thurman at the Jane Adams Hull House and introduced him to Frances. According to Frances's niece, she was "witty, had many boyfriends, but was not a great beauty," and Thurman wooed her in part by teasing Frances that "she was the dumbest thing around but that he had never met anyone as pretty."[28]

The wedding of his Chicago roommate produced a similar desire on Arnold's part. In a puckish, but not particularly romantic way of putting it, he told his mother in June 1917 about the effects of the war on his plans to marry: "It is the best time to get married. You don't have to support your wife or even live with her. It will be considered all right just to visit her occasionally. This is almost ideal and too good a chance to be missed."[29] Despite the sarcasm, Arnold's partners reported to C. P. Arnold that Thurman really was "head over heels in love" with Frances.[30]

Thurman was in New York, on the verge of being shipped overseas, when he summoned Frances to join him and get married before his ship sailed. Frances came on the train. She did not tell her family but confessed to her niece years later that eloping was "very scary." On the train, Frances met Ima Hogg, the daughter of legendary Texas Governor James Hogg. Ima took Frances under her wing and found her a place to stay in New York while she attempted to track down Thurman, who had gone to visit army friends at their training camp. In true Arnold fashion, he managed to leave his wallet and all his money in a railroad car during the trip. Frances had to pay for the entire ceremony, except for some money Arnold was able to borrow from friends.[31]

No family members were present for the early September church ceremony, and Thurman's parents did not even know of the hurried nuptials until they received a letter from the Slossons, family friends of the Arnolds, who were the only witnesses to the marriage that would last more than fifty years. Preston Slosson, the editor of the *New York Independent* and father of one of Thurman's close friends, wrote a short note saying Thurman never looked better, and by the way, was now a married man. Mr. Slosson closed by telling C. P. that Mrs. Slosson would be sending a note describing the wedding in detail.[32]

Mrs. Slosson was a somewhat better correspondent and wrote a lengthier letter the next day. Frances told her at the ceremony that "I want to marry him before he goes to France, because if he should be crippled he might refuse to let me when he comes back and that would break my heart. I want the right to care for him if he should need me." Mrs. Slosson noted for the parents back home in Laramie that "Frances isn't pretty but she has vivacity and charm and is deeply in love with Thurman."

Frances's parents apparently found out about the elopement and wedding in an even more unexpected fashion. According to an anecdote both Frances and Thurman frequently told later in life, an officious telegraph operator back in Sedalia tried to reach Judge Longan, Frances's father. Mrs. Longan asked if there was bad news and the operator hesitated, replying: "I don't know how the news will affect you, but. . . ." Exasperated, Mrs. Longan said, "Well, go ahead and tell me about it, because the Judge has gone to the office, and I have to know sooner or later." The operator then said: 'Well, it seems that Frances has gotten married." According to family legend, Mother Longan took to her bed for three weeks before recovering from the shock and the affront to the family code of conduct.[33] It was however, the beginning of a close and loving relationship between Frances and Thurman's parents, particularly his father, with whom Frances corresponded tenderly over the years when she and Thurman had returned to the East Coast.

The bride and groom meanwhile spent a brief overnight honeymoon in nearby Long Beach on Long Island, and Thurman sailed for Europe six days later.[34] Given her mother's reaction to the news of the elopement, a return to Missouri was not in the offing. Instead, Frances went to Virginia to stay with close friends from Hollins and to Georgia to visit family until the end of the war.

Lieutenant Arnold was posted in England until crossing the channel to join the troops in France. By October, Arnold wrote his bride that London was deserted and no one was happy. He reported that everyone was relying on the United States to win the war. In talking to a British soldier, Thurman mentioned how many young boys wanted to come over and join the fight. The more experienced Brit merely said, "The poor ignorant youngsters." On a more personal level, Thurman told Frances, "I keep thinking how brave and game you were to come on and marry me and how deeply and tenderly grateful I am to you for giving me the greatest happiness of my life." He also told his father how wonderful, charming, and brave Frances was.[35]

On the eve of his eight-hour crossing of the channel to France, he wrote home in one of his most emotional letters:

England seems scarcely recognizable to me. Everyone is in mourning, and a sort of grim unhappy determination hangs over the whole place. No regular trains run, railroad stations are deserted, and the hotels have an atmosphere of gloom. Everything in England begins and ends with war, and the return of soldiers [are] a constant unhappy reminder of what it is costing. The convalescent hospitals here are by no means a pleasant sight.

America never can feel the war as England feels it now. It is too big. Never can America so exhaust her supply of young men as England has done, because there are not enough ships to get them all over.[36]

Arnold's company arrived in France in November 1917, and he trained at firing ranges until the end of the year. He made arrangements with his mother to help support Frances out of the income from family property.[37] Besides training, he had dinners with the other Princeton graduates in the service and pleaded with his mother to send cigars, pajamas, socks, chocolate, coffee, sugar, and pipe tobacco.[38]

Arnold's letters home remained gloomy once he left for the front in February 1918. While not the war poetry of Rupert Brooks or the prose of an Erich Maria Remarque, Arnold's letters show a noticeably more subdued and less sarcastic young man seeing the dangers of the real world for the first time. The cold and wet were his constant companions and his normal complaints, along with the lack of cigars or pipe tobacco.[39]

Arnold's company traveled behind the front, seeing and occupying the villages that the Germans had abandoned in the waning days of the war. They stayed in German bunkers that the Central Powers' troops had so carefully and sturdily built. The French and American officers would dine on fine china in the remains of burnt-out buildings and stumble back to their quarters quite drunk, hoping that there would be no night-time action.[40] While food was scarce, looted champagne was plentiful.[41]

Thurman's job was to get the shells to the guns for night shelling. Most days at the front were spent digging holes with picks. The troops would only drop their picks and run for cover when fired upon. Most of the soldiers did not mind the occasional off-target shell so they could stop digging. Most nights when the guns were quiet, Thurman would just smoke and watch the planes flying overhead on their way to or from their missions. After only six months, Arnold observed,

> The war seems an endless business. Both sides lodged in almost impregnable positions, shooting millions of dollars of ammunition, consuming incredible quantities of supplies and accomplishing nothing—not even in a military way. Seems normal method of existence almost. Except one gets so weary of the cold, the lack of civilized comforts, and the endless ruins everywhere.[42]

In August 1918, Arnold was ordered back to the United States to help train a new division about to sail for France. The Armistice was then signed in November, and Arnold remained stateside until his eventual discharge.

While Arnold faced no immediate personal danger in France, the war had a lifelong impact on him. Like many men of his generation, World War I was the defining moment of his youth. Youth in Arnold's case was more relative as he was 27, about to turn 28, when he entered full-time service. However, as a result of the war, Arnold was always "profoundly patriotic."[43] He maintained his reserve commission for years after. Those who judged him by the liberal causes he supported and his work against the excesses of McCarthyism, were often quite surprised by his support for U.S. foreign policy goals including anti-Communism. Later in life, his defense of the Vietnam War and objections to the anti-war movement can best be explained by a support for the president as the representative of the country in foreign affairs and the frustration of an old soldier with those of a younger generation who refused to do their duty.

Arnold had one final soldierly duty in Laramie after the war was over. Now Captain Arnold, he, along with First Lieutenant Samuel H. Knight and Ralph E. McWhinnie, a University of Wyoming student, toured Wyoming in a small tank promoting the sale of Victory Bonds. This unlikely threesome, with the student acting as the manager of the group, transported the tank from town to town on a railroad flatcar, demonstrated such feats as climbing in, on, or over large excavations and piles of bricks, and offered rides in or on the tank to new bond buyers.[44] Then "Soldier" Arnold once again became "Lawyer" Arnold. Thurman and Frances moved to Laramie, and he joined C. P. in the Laramie law practice that was the destiny he had sought to avoid by going to Chicago in the first place.

3

Small Town Lawyer and Politician

Arnold came home to Laramie with Frances in 1919. The Arnolds rented a home on Third Street in Laramie while they built a home on the corner of Fifteenth and Garfield, one block from the expanding University of Wyoming. The house was designed by Fred Porter, a prominent Cheyenne architect. The home, which still stands today with numerous renovations and modernizations, is more East Coast than western in style, resembling an elongated New England cottage.

He and Frances also homesteaded on the family ranch outside town for nearly two years. Gene Gressley, the editor of Arnold's voluminous correspondence, suggests that this arrangement where the young Arnolds homesteaded property that in truth belonged to the father was basically a fraud,[1] but does not indicate who was defrauding whom of what. T. A. Larson, in his landmark history of Wyoming, provides a clue in discussing the $2000 property tax exemption enacted to reward veterans of the Civil, Spanish-American, and the First World War,[2] which Thurman clearly qualified for, but C. P. Arnold did not. As Frances wrote years later to Robert Woodruff, the chairman of Coca-Cola, reflecting back on those times,

> We homesteaded on an acreage father wanted to fence in into his ranch holdings. . . . In those days military service could be counted on your homestead allotment. . . . Thurman used to say I almost put him in jail for violating the Homestead Act in telling . . . notables on *the Hill* of how his father persuaded us to *file* so he could fence in his ranch lands![3]

Nevertheless Thurman and Frances spent the necessary time at the ranch with their infant son, Thurman Jr., in a rough cabin occasionally cut off from town by the harsh winters, an image which delighted many in their later years in encountering the Frances Arnold of Washington, D.C., a society hostess in elegant gowns and historic gracious homes.

Once the Arnolds were back living in town in their new home on Fifteenth Street, they threw themselves into socializing with friends and families. Frances was an active member of the bridge club, occasionally luring Thurman to attend as well. As Laramie socialites, they attended church functions, drama, musicales, family picnics at C. P.'s ranch, and were frequently mentioned in the gossip and social columns of the town newspapers, the *Boomerang* and the *Republican*.[4]

Unfortunately, Arnold's timing in returning home was poor from an economic prospective. The general prosperity of the 1920s never made it to Laramie. Its remote location and failing agriculture, ranching, and banking industries meant that the Great Depression for Wyoming effectively lasted from 1920 to the start of World War II.[5]

Arnold was a partner in the firm of Arnold, Patterson & Arnold in a generously sized second-story office in Laramie's fledgling downtown, a short walk away from the train depot where the Union Pacific had pulled into town creating Laramie a mere fifty-one years before. But law was only one of his pursuits.

Almost immediately, Arnold entered politics in 1920 and was elected for a term as the sole Democratic member of the Wyoming House of Representatives. Arnold came in third in a field of six candidates and would not have been elected but for the recent redistricting that gave Albany County four seats in an expanded lower chamber. To while away the hours of being the ultimate powerless outsider in a small clubby Republican part-time legislature, Arnold entertained himself and exasperated his fellow Representatives with a variety of antics. During a series of long-winded speeches culminating in the carefully planned election of the speaker of the house, Arnold interjected himself by announcing from the floor,

> Mr. Speaker, the Democratic party caucused last night, and when the name Thurman Arnold was mentioned, it threw its hat up in the air and cheered for fifteen minutes. I, therefore, wish to put his name in nomination for speaker of the House.

He sat down only to rise again quickly to second the nomination saying: "I have known Thurman Arnold for most of my life, and would trust him as far as I would myself." As chaos reigned, Arnold rose for a third time and announced, "Mr. Speaker, some irresponsible Democrat has put my name in nomination and I wish to withdraw it."[6]

On the more serious side, the legislature did manage to pass a series of bills cracking down on prostitution, which had never really vanished from its origins in the frontier days of the state. Arnold drafted and helped secure passage of a bill that imposed strict penalties on those whose property was used to further prostitution, gambling, and alcohol.[7]

The state-wide depression led to a struggle over the budget and calls for fiscal retrenchment. A pay raise for legislators failed. The budget for the University of Wyoming was slashed by one quarter, and the percentage of revenues the university received from oil lands was cut in half, both over the spirited opposition of Arnold. More generally, reform efforts to introduce an income tax, a department of agriculture, arbitration of industrial disputes, an eight-hour work day for women, and the creation of a single livestock board all stalled without resulting in legislation, despite having the backing of the Republican governor. The legislature also spent time on amendments to the corporation laws, the need to build a larger prison (since the state then had 250 cells and 301 prisoners), and the need to increase the number of teachers.[8]

It is fairly surprising that the legislature could even accomplish this much. The 16th Legislative Session met in Cheyenne from January 11, 1921, until February 20, 1921. Arnold sat on five committees—Judiciary, Ways and Means, Railroads, Federal Relations, and Engrossing—but as a Democrat, chaired none. All of these assignments were relevant to Arnold's later work in academia and Washington, D.C., particularly the Engrossing Committee, which was named after an English common law term meaning the unlawful cornering of a market. This was, in all likelihood, Arnold's first exposure to the antitrust issues with which he would later make his lasting mark.

When his term expired, Arnold returned to full-time legal practice until his election in 1922 as mayor of Laramie. He was elected by a majority of exactly forty-four votes over Frank Blair, his Republican opponent, an employee of the local Standard Oil of Indiana refinery. In his campaign, Arnold distinguished himself from his opponent and fed the whispering campaign that Blair was the tool of the "Eastern Establishment" with his vow: "I represent no corporation whose interest by way of taxation or otherwise conflicts with the interests of the city." More concretely, he promised to remove a fish hatchery that was polluting local waters, continuing a sewer construction program, erecting a new viaduct over the rail yards, and, in general, to practice economy in city government.[9]

Arnold also ran on a temperance platform that was decidedly against his own personal predilections. He pledged to make Laramie a truly dry town in line with the growing prohibitionist sentiment that culminated in the ratification of the 18th Amendment to the United States Constitution and went into effect in 1920. Much to the confusion and consternation of both his friends and foes, he actually did his best to enforce this pledge once in office and made it a hallmark of his administration, along with his a drive for good government and an informed citizenry in the Progressive tradition.[10]

Being mayor of Laramie in the 1920s was hardly a full-time job, nor was it particularly remunerative, paying $25 a month. It did, however, mean that Arnold was at the beck and call of his constituents. Shortly after taking office, Arnold received a call from an irate lady who insisted that the mayor do something about cats squalling on her back fence for the past three nights. Arnold assured her that he would take care of the problem and promptly forgot about the matter. A week later, the woman called back to congratulate the Mayor for taking care of "those noisy cats." Arnold graciously replied: "Don't give it a thought, madam, except I wish you would remember it when I next run for office."[11]

Years later, the *Saturday Evening Post* described perhaps the oddest moment of his mayoralty:

> One morning, when he had his feet on the mayoral desk, a big cigar in his mouth and not a care on his mind, his office was frighteningly invaded by two matronly ladies in semi-Roman costume, bearing spears. They belonged to a fancy-dress fraternal organization then holding a convention in Laramie. . . . They were indignant, for the convention was losing patience, awaiting an address of welcome from Laramie's forgetful chief executive. Without further ado they bore Arnold off to the convention hall, pausing at the door only long enough to go through a complicated knocking procedure. As the door swung open Arnold beheld an aisle lined with double ranks of more matronly ladies, also in semi-Roman costume, also bearing spears. The ladies crossed their weapons, bridging the aisle. Arnold quite dazed, marched beneath spears to the platform. Just as he mounted the steps, inspiration came.

"Sisters of the Centurion," he began, "I welcome you to the city of Laramie. As mayor of this city, I bring you only a very short message, but I think it is one you will understand." (With the utmost earnestness): "The trouble with modern civilization is that we are getting away from fundamentals." The Sisters cheered Arnold to the rafters.[12]

Being mayor also called for action on a series of important but hardly glamorous matters. During Arnold's term, the city paved Grand Avenue, the boulevard leading from the train station through the downtown and then passing the university on the left and the home where Arnold was born on the right. And, as promised, Mayor Arnold indeed separated the fish hatchery from the water supply.

As a practicing lawyer, Arnold specialized, along with his father, in the iron triangle of Wyoming legal practice—land, energy, and ranching—precisely the areas hardest hit by the on-going depression. Most matters were about land, transferring it, dealing with what was growing on it, or, increasingly, the mineral rights below it. Land in Wyoming came from either the U.S. government, the Union Pacific Railroad, or both, and virtually all land titles could be traced back to the federal government within less than a hundred years. Besides property and real estate cases, the firm handled a variety of estate planning and probate work including cases involving German and Dutch clients with property in the United States.

Arnold's general business practice fell prey to two forces he could hardly control. The first was the irascible and eccentric nature of his father, the senior partner of the firm. Although a pillar of the community, C. P. had the reputation of being a benevolent tyrant who would throw clients out of the office when he disagreed with them.[13] The second irresistible force was what Arnold eventually termed the economic colonization of the West by large national (primarily Eastern) corporations. For example, the Federal Trade Commission estimated in 1921 that Standard Oil of Indiana owned 97 percent of the oil in Wyoming.[14]

Some of the locally owned businesses were driven out of business by their national competitors, some just couldn't keep up, and still others were acquired. Arnold lost such important clients as a local oil refinery, a plaster mill, and the movie theater. Even in the best case scenario where the business was acquired as an ongoing concern, the former owners became mere managers and decisions were made far away, usually at corporate headquarters on the East Coast. The loss of the legal business of these firms was only one symptom of how the events of the 1920s moved the power to control one's daily life far away from the community to national businesses indifferent to the local consequences of their decisions. It was a lesson that Arnold never forgot. In his autobiography, Arnold described the process as "plain murder of small business, but nobody seemed to mind."[15]

Arnold also represented dozens of individuals in their more personal problems. One of the classic Thurman Arnold stories is best recounted by Gerald Stern, one of his young associates at Arnold & Porter in Washington, D.C., who was forever impressed by its lessons of perseverance, creativity, and humor on behalf of a doctor friend of Arnold's:

> *Doctor*: Thurman, I've got a problem.
> *Thurman*: What is it?
> *Doctor*: I just received three ties in the mail, three neck ties which are very pretty.
> *Thurman*: What's the problem?
> *Doctor*: There was a letter with the ties—they said if I liked the ties I should send $3 to them, and if I didn't like the ties I should return them.
> *Thurman*: What's the problem?
> *Doctor*: I like the ties.
> *Thurman*: Fine, what's the problem?
> *Doctor*: I don't want to send them $3.
> *Thurman*: Ooooh. I see. Well, just keep the ties. You don't have to do anything.
> *Doctor*: You mean, I don't have to send $3 to them?
> *Thurman*: No, don't worry about it.
> The doctor left, very relieved. Two weeks later he returned, very upset.
> *Doctor*: Thurman, I just received a letter from the tie company. They say they want me to send them the $3, since it appears to them I have kept the ties.
> *Thurman*: Don't worry Doc, I know just what to do.
> Thurman then dictated the following letter:

Gentlemen: The Doctor did receive the three ties which you sent to him. As you have guessed, he is delighted with them and has kept them. Everyone here in Laramie has complimented the Doctor on his beautiful ties. They appear to be well worth the $3 you mention in your letter.

> Please find enclosed a pill. The Doctor has prescribed this pill here in Laramie for many years for all the ailments of the body—lumbago, back-ache, arthritis, neuritis, neuralgia, sinus, what-have-you. It is a superb pill, cured hundreds of people here in Laramie down through the years. The pill is worth the $5 the Doctor charges for it.
>
> Accordingly, please send us $2 which is the balance. You now owe us.

The doctor left, excited and happy. Two weeks later he returned, out of breath and even more agitated than before.

Doctor: Thurman, I just went down to the post office. They had a registered package for me to pick up. It was from the tie company. They've returned the pill. Their letter says they don't want it. And they want their $3.

Thurman: Well, now. We do have a problem. I know what we shall do. I'll dictate another letter.

So Thurman sent this letter:

> Gentlemen: We are very distressed to learn you did not want the miraculous pill the Doctor sent to you. It truly is a wonderful pill. Cures all sorts of ailments. But we accept your decision not to use the pill.
>
> This morning the Doctor went to the post office to pick up the package you sent him.
>
> Here in Laramie such a trip is considered a house call. The Doctor charges $10 for house calls. Please send us the $7 you now owe us.

That was the last time the doctor heard from the tie company.[16]

Like any other small-town general practitioner, Arnold also litigated a bit. Most of Thurman's cases were local affairs in the state courts for which there are no reported decisions. However, he made occasional trips to Cheyenne for appearances in the federal court or the Wyoming Supreme Court. In all, he handled three reported cases in the Wyoming Supreme Court, each of which involved the challenge to the expenditure of state funds because of some alleged irregularity. Two of the cases, decided on the same day, involved the state treasurer's duties to credit monies to the state education fund from the lease of school lands for oil and gas exploration.[17]

The final case challenged the allotment of funds from the "Militia Contingency Fund" for non-military purposes.[18] The state legislature appropriated $50,000 for the payment of expenses of the Wyoming National Guard. When the funds were drawn down but not replenished, Arnold, representing the adjutant general of the Guard, sued. He argued that new funds had to be deposited in the account through a continuing appropriation. Arnold's co-counsel was the future senator of Wyoming, Joseph O'Mahoney, a valuable ally for Thurman in his later Washington days.

The state auditor challenged any payments from the $50,000 fund as beyond the scope of what the legislature had intended. He further argued that the original statute had not authorized a continuing appropriation and that any such continuing appropriation without subsequent legislative action would be unconstitutional under the Wyoming state constitution.

The court did the expected, and probably sensible thing and held that the legislature had intended the original appropriation to cover all the expenses of the Guard but that there was no evidence that it had intended to authorize a continuing appropriation.[19] These cases, though hardly earthshaking, show a pattern that Arnold would follow for most of his life in being, or representing, the gadfly challenging the actions of the government or the powerful interests with keys to the corridors of power.

While in Laramie, Arnold and Frances started their family. Their first son, Thurman Jr., was born in 1919, and their second son, George, soon followed in 1921. Thurman's brother Carl returned to Laramie after his own military service and also joined the family law practice. The time in Laramie was also the beginning of a close and loving relationship between Frances and Thurman's parents, particularly the otherwise irascible C. P.

Arnold also played a critical role in the founding of the University of Wyoming College of Law. Anyone in Wyoming wanting to study law beyond apprenticing in an office had to go out of state for their legal education because there was no in-state law school. Enough of the Harvard experience had rubbed off on Arnold that he wanted to establish an affordable state law school, but one that would draw on the Harvard model as much as possible.

The first law students at Wyoming began in 1920 in what had been the science hall of the university. A grand total of fourteen students comprised the classes of 1920, 1921, and 1922. The initial faculty was drawn from local judges and practitioners, including Arnold, who taught Torts and Property as an adjunct in the early years of the school. He also helped establish the Potter Law Club, named for the Wyoming chief justice, a strong supporter of the school. The Potter Club was a combination social club, moot court society, and speaker's bureau for the law school modeled on a mélange of Arnold's own experiences at Harvard. The Arnold law firm let the students use their library as did the firm of the other main teacher during that first year of the law school.[20]

Thurman began an Arnold family connection to the law school that continues to this day. His brother Carl attended the law school, and after a year of post-graduate studies at Yale, joined the Wyoming law faculty full-time in 1928. His speciality was constitutional law. Carl was selected as dean in 1933 and served in that capacity until his untimely death in 1941. Throughout this period, the school expanded its facilities, its faculty, and its library but never had a class size that exceeded twelve.

The small collegial school with high standards that Thurman founded, and Carl nurtured, continued with input from the Arnold family in the next generation as well. Thurman's son George also served on the faculty as the first director of the school's legal clinic beginning in 1970, and Thurman's grandson George Jr. graduated from the school in 1977.

Despite all of these deep and organic connections to Laramie, the Arnolds ultimately left in 1927, never to return except as visitors until Frances unexpectedly came back as a widow in the early 1970s. Events beyond the continuing depression and the destruction of the local economic base combined to prevent Thurman Arnold from staying and following his father's path as dean of the Laramie bar.

While still mayor, Arnold lost a humiliating election for prosecuting attorney in 1924, coming in fourth in a field of four. Arnold attributed his loss to his appointment while mayor of a Catholic as police chief at a time of anti-Catholic activity and the increasing influence of the Ku Klux Klan movement and its anti-Catholic bias.[21] Regardless of the reason, the loss hurt him deeply and effectively brought his political career in Laramie to an end.

The final event pushing Arnold back East was more fortuitous. A Harvard law school classmate, Dave Howard from West Virginia, retained Thurman in 1926 with respect to some oil leases in Wyoming. Howard also served on a committee to select a new dean for the West Virginia University College of Law and invited Arnold to interview for the position. Dean Roscoe Pound of the Harvard Law School had remembered Thurman as a law student and also recommended him for the vacant deanship at West Virginia. In a sign of the informality of the times (or perhaps the dominance of Harvard Law School), Arnold was hired after a brief interview and broke the news to his family that he wanted to try something new.

At a farewell lunch with his wife and parents, he was serenaded by the local Lions Club with a rousing rendition of "For He's a Jolly Good Fellow." Frances was so moved that she wept in the arms of the waitress. The town was so affected by the sudden and unexpected decision of Arnold to relocate that fifty cars accompanied the Arnolds all the way to the Great Divide in the Rockies on their way east.[22]

Arnold frequently referred to his Laramie days in his later correspondence and his speeches. A particularly heartfelt example was in his 1943 commencement address at the University of Wyoming where he described Wyoming as having

> . . . an individuality and a ruggedness and a charm that no other state possesses. Those of us who leave it will always feel the pull to come back. It has a beauty that is only fully revealed to those who have lived here. And I like to think that its winds and its winters produce an independence of action and thought that those who live in the hard life of cities and of more organized communities never know.[23]

Arnold also wrote later in life, "How we hated to leave that wonderful combination of rolling plains and blue, snow-capped mountains." The Arnolds may have left Laramie physically for good in 1927, but neither Thurman nor Frances ever fully left emotionally and each felt the tug of Laramie as home for the rest of their lives.

4

An Academic Entrepreneur

Arnold's time as the dean of the West Virginia University College of Law is the least discussed aspect of his life and work. Arnold himself devotes exactly one line of his autobiography to this period.[1] However, Arnold's first brush with full-time teaching and administration proved critical to his development as a scholar and a player in legal academia. It also laid the groundwork for his introduction to the legal realist movement and his more literal introduction to his first professional mentor other than his father, professor and later dean, Charles Clark of Yale.

When Arnold arrived as dean at West Virginia University, the College of Law had only five faculty members besides himself, a tiny student body, and a total annual budget of $61,000, which rose only slightly during his tenure. Since the faculty was small, the teaching loads were heavy and most of the faculty were generalists, teaching many different and seemingly unrelated courses.

Dean Arnold was no exception. He taught every semester that he was at Morgantown. He taught criminal law and domestic relations to the first-year students and sales of personal property and trusts to the second-year students. After his first year as dean, Arnold cut back, limiting himself to criminal law and trusts. One summer, Arnold offered a special honors independent research course in interstate commerce and procedure. This was a relatively light load in comparison to his colleagues without administrative duties who normally taught six courses over the school year, thus leaving relatively less time for research and scholarship.[2]

It was in fact a fairly distinguished faculty, which meant that West Virginia was being raided by more prestigious schools and left Arnold to rebuild the faculty on the fly. While Arnold was dean, Harold Havighurst left for Northwestern University. Later on, David Cavers left, ending up at Duke, and Jeff Fordham left as well, eventually becoming dean of the University of Pennsylvania Law School.

Despite the small size of the school and the heavy teaching loads, most modern law deans would recognize and sympathize with Arnold's daily routine. He spent the majority of his time out of the classroom absorbed in budgeting, covering the curriculum, staffing issues, recruiting new faculty, offensive and defensive struggles with the university, contacts with the local bar, finding new revenue streams, improving contacts with the alumni, and attempting to upgrade the faculty and improve scholarly productivity.

Dean Arnold worked on requiring three full years of college as a prerequisite for law school, in part to solve the problem of the "overcrowded bar," in part to eliminate the one-third failure rate of students after their first year of law school, and in part to help improve West Virginia's reputation and distinguish it from even so-called national schools that required less college experience for their entering law students. He also hoped that such a requirement would help bring students to the law school who had a broader view of law as a social institution, in keeping with Arnold's emerging legal realist perspective.

Arnold coupled this strategy with a plan to reduce tuition. West Virginia was one of the most expensive law schools in the country, trailing only Harvard, Pennsylvania, and a handful of other elite schools. Its tuition was more than double that of most state schools, and thus it failed to attract many out-of-state students, even those from neighboring states contemplating legal careers in West Virginia. Arnold used classical economics in his annual report to University President John Turner, arguing that the tuition reduction would increase enrollments and total revenue and would be particularly needed to offset any anticipated decline in enrollment due to the new three-year college requirement.[3]

Arnold outlined his vision for a new type of law school but tried to make it a realistic one for a small state law school in a relatively isolated location. He wrote his university president that the challenge for a state law school

> ... has two aspects. On the one hand it must be more than a mere trade school because it is part of a University. To justify the expenditure of the taxpayers' money it must be interested in the law as a social agency, even though such interest is of no practical importance from the standpoint of a particular individual struggling to build up a practice under existing conditions in a small town. On the other hand in its interest in the law as a social agency the state law school should not attempt to imitate the

national law school by trying to do the things which the national law school can do better. It serves a particular state. In so far [as] it is interested in the cultivation of law as a legal science it should attempt to be a clearing house for the legal ideas of the state in which it functions rather than for the country as a whole.[4]

He also focused on practical issues such as the pressing need for a new dorm and a more modern curriculum. Law students previously were scattered in various fraternities. A dedicated law dorm would help to increase camaraderie among law students as part of the educational experience. To approach the always delicate issue of curricular reform, he appointed a joint committee of faculty and practicing lawyers to examine the issue.

In his few years at West Virginia, Arnold was a whirlwind. He reorganized the law review, created a moot court for students modeled on his own experiences at Harvard, created honors seminars, allowed credit for student research under faculty direction, hired one practicing lawyer a year as a special lecturer, and used his contacts to bring the legal luminaries of the day such as Leon Green of Northwestern, Walter Wheeler Cook of Johns Hopkins, Charles Clark of Yale, and others to the West Virginia campus either as speakers or as summer faculty.

Arnold's continuing friendship with his former Harvard Law School classmate David Howard proved to be of great importance in cementing good relations between the law school and the practicing bar and in obtaining critical funding for the law review and other projects. Through Howard's support, the state bar supplied as much as $1500 a year to the law school, a welcome addition to the precarious state funding in the Depression years. Howard also came to Morgantown as a lecturer and summer teacher at the law school, as did Arnold's brother Carl, who was now teaching full-time at Wyoming. On the personal side, Howard performed legal work for Arnold family interests and Wyoming clients in the energy field, directed investment opportunities to Arnold, and even referred occasional legal work to Arnold, which provided a welcome supplement to his academic salary. Only Howard's tragic death in a traffic accident in 1931 cut short this deepening personal and professional friendship.

The deanship also gave Arnold the chance to ride out the beginning of the Great Depression on a dean's salary that reached $7500 a year. Even this salary wasn't enough for grand living, and the Arnolds nevertheless suffered the effects of the Depression years like most Americans. Thurman had bought almost $10,000 in stocks and oil and gas interests at the height of the market in 1929, all of which were completely worthless by the end of 1932. Ranching interests obtained as legal fees from his Laramie practice days were similarly wiped out in value. As a result, money was tight despite the generous dean's salary. Arnold made due for his family by rearranging loans, pressing his other investments for even greater returns, and postponing expenses and payments where possible.

In addition, he began his own legal scholarship involving empirical research about procedure and the courts[5] and undertook a major project in cooperation with the West Virginia Bar Association to produce a codification and revision of West Virginia procedure.[6] Arnold also published an astonishing number of short case notes and book reviews on such diverse topics as contempt of court, constitutional law, construction law, competition in public services, rate making, suretyship, trial practice, banking, bankruptcy, appellate procedure, the jury system, criminal law, and oil and gas law, all in the *West Virginia Law Quarterly* and the state bar journal.[7]

Arnold devoted a great deal of time and energy to modernizing and codifying West Virginia procedure, following the lead of what he viewed as the more progressive, reform-minded states such as Connecticut. Arnold first proposed the formation of a judicial council that would have representatives of the bench, bar, and the law faculty to review the rules of procedures and court administration. This expert body would be free from politics and well qualified to gather and analyze the mass of laws and statistics beyond the interest or experience of any legislature.[8] The council would also create and periodically update procedural rules for the courts freed from the politics and delays of the legislative process. More controversially, Arnold also strongly implied that the legislature lacked the basic knowledge to do the job an expert and disinterested council of experts could do. He then proposed that the law school act as a research bureau for the state bar, investigating legal problems of state-wide interest.[9] Over the summers, Arnold was only partially successful in involving his faculty in creating similar projects such as restating and analyzing the other laws of West Virginia along the lines of the work of the American Law Institute.[10]

During these years, Arnold continued to work on legal matters related to older business back in Laramie and on occasion undertook legal work in his part of the state for David Howard. Despite his turn from full-time law practice, Arnold deprecated his own skills as an academic. He wrote in 1929 to Fred Nussbaum, a professor at Wyoming and lifelong friend: "As for me I have become a promoter. Scholarship doesn't seem particularly to be my line. I'm too lazy."[11] Colleagues at West Virginia described him more charitably and more characteristically as a "crusader against false gods" and as the "most unforgettable character" they had encountered.[12]

As part of the procedural reform process, Arnold began cultivating the contacts that led him to join the Yale faculty on a permanent basis by 1930. His work on procedure brought him to the attention of Professor Charles Clark, soon to be the dean of Yale Law School, who was pursuing a similar project in Connecticut. Arnold's project was squarely within the tradition of the wing of legal realists at Yale who saw in the social sciences and statistics the opportunity to reform law to meet the needs of modern society and to make the law in action match the law on the books.[13] Impressed with Arnold and his mission, Clark took the unprecedented step of funding a summer legal research institute at West Virginia with Yale resources. For his part, Arnold worked under Clark's general direction as part of the pre-testing of a larger study of the federal judiciary and urged Clark to expand the program to other schools.[14]

This mutual admiration society resulted in Arnold spending the summer of 1928 as a visitor at Yale where he taught Trial Practice. Arnold was in good company with a distinguished summer faculty that also consisted of legal realist icon Karl Llewellyn of Columbia and evidence guru Dean Charles T. McCormick of North Carolina. It was a high honor for Arnold to be included in such distinguished company so early in his academic career and even more so since the summer program at Yale was small and ran a "considerable" financial deficit.[15]

Most unusual for a sitting dean, Arnold also spent the fall 1930 semester as a visitor at Yale as well. It was the custom of Yale to have a visitor from another school who would return to his regular position at the end of the term. Arnold was a natural in view of his close working relationship and growing social friendship with Clark. President Turner of West Virginia reluctantly granted Arnold his leave because of the prestige of Yale and the hopeful boost to West Virginia on the condition that Arnold stay in Morgantown for registration and "keep general control of budget," including dealing with the legislature if necessary.[16] For a time, Arnold hemmed and hawed about the offer to continue his visit in New Haven, worried about salary issues, the costs of housing in New Haven, and the ability to sublet his West Virginia house. Although he was always willing to absorb some costs for the opportunity Yale presented, in the end he didn't have to. Dean Clark offered a slight salary increase to defray the additional expenses, and President Turner generously offered to cover transportation to and from Morgantown so Arnold could better stay in touch during his year away.[17]

It was a busy year in New Haven with Arnold combining his teaching and scholarship duties at Yale with a long-distance deanship back in West Virginia. He dealt with the resignation of the librarian, the defection of a key faculty member to another law school, and salary issues for the rest of the faculty, and he squashed an ill-conceived plan by the president to require the law school to offer a business law survey course for engineering students.[18]

At the end of 1930, an unexpected faculty vacancy led Yale to offer Arnold a permanent position. Arnold accepted the offer of a permanent faculty post from now Dean Clark and faced the awkward task of informing the president of West Virginia University that he would not be returning to Morgantown, except to assist in selecting his successor and to inform his former colleagues at the law school. The president took the slightly unexpected news well, cordially congratulated Arnold, and graciously opined that there was "little hope of duplicating Dean Arnold."[19]

As busy as he was, Arnold never severed his close relationship with Laramie during his years in West Virginia. His correspondence is full of responses to his father's requests for information and occasional help on those cases that had been pending when he left for West Virginia. Arnold still had investments and bank accounts, although increasingly precarious and few, in Laramie. His family and many friends were now reduced to pen pals whom he could only see on the occasional holiday visit. As a result he felt increasingly isolated in Morgantown, writing: "I have been lonely here the past year. Out of the entire community I have not made one intimate friend."[20] Frances described Arnold's colleagues at the university as "old, doddering and very conservative."[21] This was the precise opposite of the new colleagues Arnold was to have for the rest of his academic career at Yale.

5

Legal Realist and Firebrand

At Yale, Arnold was like a kid in a candy store. He was free from the constraints of being dean at a small law school in one of the poorest states now further hard-hit by the Depression. He was now at a major Ivy League institution and continued to be sought after, rejecting offers to join the faculty at Harvard Law School and to be the dean at the University of Wisconsin Law School. As a result of this competition for his services, Yale matched the offer from Harvard, resulting in a new salary of $10,000.[1] At his new permanent home at Yale he was surrounded by some of the most intellectually exciting law professors and social scientists in the country, led by his mentor and now dean, Charles Clark, and including Arthur Corbin, William Douglas, Walton Hamilton, Leon Green, and Underhill Moore.[2]

Yale in the 1930s had become the center of the legal realist movement that had begun the decade before at Columbia. The realist mission focused on reexamining legal rules that the previous generation of professors and judges had deemed natural and predetermined from a set of enduring principles that could be derived through logic and legal reasoning. Anything considered "formalist" and "conceptual" or anything that derived legal rights in a vacuum from the needs of society was a target for critique and ridicule.

A principal target was the pivotal distinction between "private" and "public" spheres that animated much of legal analysis and served to limit the power of government to address questions of justice and power in the marketplace. A leading realist, Karl Llewellyn, focused on reforming contract and commercial law to reflect the custom and usage of the parties rather than the hoary maxims of contract law that law students had been reading in turgid treatises. Other targets of the realists were conceptions of private property that were thought to be natural, pre-societal, and divorced from the government power that maintained their very existence.

Similarly, Leon Green focused on tort law and sought to demonstrate that formalistic elements of tort law such as duty, breach, and proximate causation were all just useless abstractions that obscured the central role of legal duties derived from societal needs.[3]

Another important, but largely unfulfilled, part of the realist project was the reformation of legal education away from the legal science approach that Christopher Columbus Langdell had introduced at Harvard Law School in the late nineteenth century. Langdell viewed the law library as the laboratory of law and the case law as the experimental results that law students should study to derive the immutable principles of law in each field and to determine the fundamental unity of law between fields.[4]

The realists disagreed with every aspect of this syllogistic view of law and legal education and further resented the prestige that Harvard had gained from this approach. While some of the rivalry degenerated into a continuation of ancient Ivy League rivalries best left to undergraduates, the Yale and Columbia realists did have a profoundly different vision of the goal and content of legal education. The casebooks used by the realists soon included relatively little case law and increasing amounts of notes, essays, economics, history, sociology, psychology, criminology, journalism, and other ephemera that placed law in its past and contemporary social context.

The traditional law school curriculum was similarly attacked to strip it of its formalist, conceptual, and doctrinal components and to reconstruct it along "functional" lines. Thus, William Douglas combined material about corporate law, finance, and bankruptcy into books and courses built around the concept of corporate reorganization. In another famous example, Leon Green's torts casebook contained no chapters on duty, breach, proximate cause, or any of the standard doctrines of tort law. Instead it arranged the cases in terms of the settings in which they arose: cases about railroads; cases about telegraphs; cases about airplanes, and others. Even the famous *Palsgraf* case could only be found buried in a later edition of the casebook in the section on railroads and frequently was not even assigned except as an object of ridicule.[5]

The realists sorted into two basic approaches with Arnold straddling both camps and eventually rejecting both approaches. One group of the realists focused on applying the insights of social sciences to legal problems.[6] The second group focused on the indeterminacy of legal rules and expressed a growing skepticism that either legal rules or facts constrained the formulation or exercise of power through law and legal institutions.[7]

Arnold dabbled with both approaches at different times in his academic career. His earliest work at West Virginia and during his initial time at Yale was the closest to the social science wing of the realists, but Arnold quickly lost interest saying that the collection of statistics was mostly "bunk."[8] As he described in his autobiography, Arnold worked with Douglas on an empirical study of the Connecticut courts, funded by the Rockefeller Foundation:

> We . . . proceeded to count everything that happened in courts in Connecticut. We found the exact number of demurrers and every other kind of pleading that had been filed over the course of a year. We counted the time it took to finish the cases. We learned how many cases were decided for the plaintiff and how many for the defendant. In addition, we counted everything else that we or anyone else could think of. All this information was transferred to cards with holes punched in them and run through the trusty Holorith [sic] machine. The result was the most fascinating body of legal statistics that has been collected in this century. They had only one flaw. Nobody then and nobody yet has ever been able to think of what to do with them.[9]

He also worked closely with Douglas on an empirical study of enforcement of prohibition commonly referred to as the Wickersham Study. His disenchantment with statistical work grew when he and Douglas received only one request for the two hundred reprints of the study they had ordered.[10]

Since Arnold was recruited to Yale because of his past empirical work and his interest in continuing that work with Clark and Douglas, some commentators have raised the issue of whether Arnold's early interest in empirical court studies was merely "opportunism." Professor John Henry Schlegel finds Arnold's initial interest genuine, but he uncharitably credits his waning enthusiasm to a short intellectual attention span that could ultimately only be satisfied by the pace of private practice. Professor Schlegel's extensive research into the failure of the empirical wing of the realist project more properly suggests that Arnold merely lost interest somewhat earlier than the rest of his colleagues, who also abandoned such work, drifted off into more interesting and fertile lines of research, or left academia for the New Deal or practice. Arnold's dismissal of such research as merely "counting cars" was no more deprecating than most critics of this line of work including the great Karl Llewellyn who dismissed similar projects by saying, "I read the results, but I never dug out what most of the counting was good for."[11] In all likelihood, Arnold abandoned these projects because he was convinced they were worthless.

In place of more empirical studies, profound skepticism came naturally to Arnold and became a pivotal part of his early articles. By the time that Arnold had completed the two books that made him famous, his interest in law and psychology had led him in an entirely original direction in exploring the purely symbolic functions of law, a direction that was ultimately as critical of his friends in the realist camp as of the usual targets of realist ire.[12]

Part of Arnold's originality is shown in his areas of interest more than just his approach. He simply was interested in things that most of the realists ignored. Arnold focused on government regulation of the economy and the working of bureaucracies and administrative agencies, while most of his Yale colleagues continued to focus on the courts and the common law. Arnold's friend William Douglas was one of the few colleagues who shared Arnold's passion for the regulatory side of law.

Another of Arnold's differences was his background. He and Douglas were conspicuous Westerners in an elite eastern institution. Whatever the existing differences and rivalries between Harvard and Yale, they paled in comparison with the gulf in backgrounds between Arnold and most of his colleagues. He entered academia older and from a vastly different career path than his fellow professors. He shared their elite educational background, but almost none shared either his practice experience or political service.

As a teacher, Arnold was memorable, if not always effective. He taught Trials and Appeals, Evidence, advanced research courses on Trusts and Law Administration, as well as a series of interdisciplinary seminars on law and psychology that became the basis for his scholarship and his eventual reputation in the outside world. His evidence and procedure classes had as many as 140 students, and his seminars and smaller courses fluctuated between fifteen and forty.

Victor Kramer, one of Arnold's students and later his partner in private practice, recalls his first memory of Arnold as a professor in 1936 as watching him tug at his underwear while wearing clothes filled with tobacco ash and the previous day's food. Legendary federal Judge Gerhard Gessell remembers his first impression of Arnold as a teacher "covered with cigar ashes, looking as though he had just gotten out of bed in his clothes, and somewhat bewildered and shaggy." However, Norman Diamond also one of his students and later partners, recalls Arnold as "the greatest showman I've ever seen in any class" and the only teacher whose class students would attend even in the midst of the writing competition for the *Yale Law Journal* because "it was too much fun, it was better than a Broadway show."[13]

Arnold would deconstruct both the fashionable nonsense of the day and the hoary old maxims of the law to lay bare their symbolism and to put things in plain English even if it meant losing the majesty of the law or the power of the government. For Arnold, "neither rain nor snow nor dark of night shall deter the postman from his appointed rounds" meant that "mail shall be delivered even in bad weather." Arnold would sometimes pose a question from the court record of a case and ask, "What was the objection?" Before the student could respond, he would bellow "It doesn't matter. Use a loud voice and sound convincing. Maybe the judge doesn't know either."[14]

Arnold frequently brought his dog Duffy to class and even told the law school registrar who tried to stop him on one occasion: "Dammit, I'll not only take my dog inside, but I'll bring a pony next time." Arnold frequently threatened to call on Duffy if the class did not shape up to his liking.[15]

He was never without a cigar or pipe. His teaching style was free association, and sometimes the words and ideas came so quickly that he became tongue-tied or appeared incoherent. On occasion he would throw a handkerchief or similar object on the floor and shout at the students to get it into evidence.

As Washington, D.C., reporters Joseph Alsop and Robert Kintner wrote years later,

> Another of his peculiarities was a habit of drawing a Thurberish horse on the blackboard, declaring that it represented legal jurisdiction, and explaining that "jurisdiction is only a thing you get somewhere with." The students sang: "Jurisdiction is a horse, or this we learn in Arnold's course," and when in classes on the Psychology of Judicial Institutions, they called them "the cave of the winds." Some students were repelled, some fascinated by Arnold.[16]

Arnold influenced the Yale curriculum in ways beyond the classroom as well. To get students involved in the reality of law, rather than its abstract principles, Arnold introduced the Moot Court of Appeals for first-year students, now known as the Thurman Arnold Moot Court. In this then revolutionary (but now routine) exercise, students were given the records of actual trials and instructed to prepare the briefs and present the oral arguments on appeal to a "court" consisting of professors and occasionally practitioners and real judges.

Arnold frequently presided over these arguments and injected his usual levity into the situation. On one occasion, a student defended his argument with a series of case citations from various Southern states in the early 1860s. Arnold was moved to exclaim: "What in the hell are you anyway—a civil war veteran?"[17]

Although he was a self-taught rather than a professionally trained scholar, Arnold quickly made up for lost time. He moved beyond the shorter practice-oriented articles he had published in West Virginia into lengthier, more theoretical articles on criminal law, trust law, the work of the American Law Institute, the symbolic values of trials and jurisprudence, and a continuing series of book reviews on eclectic topics, all published in the leading student-edited law reviews of his time, including Harvard, Columbia, and Yale.[18] He abandoned the largely buttoned-down descriptive style of his shorter works in the *West Virginia Law Quarterly* for a slash-and-burn style filled with wit and irony (but not many footnotes) that was consistent with the legal realists around him in challenging the arid formalism of the prior generation.[19] In one article Arnold simply turned over one of the footnotes to a colleague who wrote a paragraph criticizing a point raised by Arnold in the text!

Most of Arnold's early Yale articles were broadly consistent with the debunking tradition of the realist movement, but he already displayed important differences from most of his colleagues. For one thing, he was both funnier and a livelier writer than most lifelong academics. He also was more interested in psychology and the symbolic or mythic value of law than most of his colleagues. He shared with most realists an abhorrence for abstract concepts and the view that the law was inconsistent, if not incoherent, as to any individual doctrine or set of doctrines.[20] However, Arnold broke ranks in seeing a socially useful value in that inconsistency in allowing the law to arrive at good results, even at the price of theoretical inconsistency.[21]

Arnold tied together and expanded his early Yale work in his 1935 book *The Symbols of Government*.[22] The idea for the book came out of the seminar on law and psychology that Arnold had co-taught with the psychologist Edward Robinson. Robinson published his own book *Law and Lawyers* at virtually the same time, but it was Arnold who received the bulk of the attention.[23] While much of *Symbols* was a revision of his previous articles on trials and jurisprudence, these chapters were tied together with new work and by an astonishingly breezy and genuinely funny writing style that made Arnold famous, and for the first time a true peer to his Yale law school colleagues.

Arnold announced his aim in the preface:

> By the symbols of government we mean both the ceremonies and the theories of social institutions. Ordinarily, these ceremonies and theories are collected and studied, not as symbols, but as the fundamental principles of the separate sciences of law, economics, political theory, ethics, and theology. In this book we propose to examine law and economics, not as a collection of truths, but as symbolic thinking and conduct which condition the behavior of men in groups.[24]

Arnold sought to portray the social sciences as stationary and their principles as a bar to progress in contrast to the natural and medical sciences, which sought to solve problems and not enunciate eternal principles. He argued that government itself has not been as stationary as the thinking about government has been. He applauded changes in the care of the aged and the sick, public health, and relief for the poor, but noted, "Yet principles and rational ideas of government, instead of making easier the introduction of new techniques in sanitation or housing have only served to make it harder. *Principles have been obstacles, and not aids.*"[25]

He argued that no human institution could possibly follow any consistent or systematic set of principles:

> [R]ational or moral principles are useless as explanations, or bases for prediction, but they are of the utmost utility in moving groups of people, and that a symbol which is a fundamental philosophy, as religion, or an eternal truth in the mind of one man, may be a very useful tool in the hands of another, who wishes to exercise social control.[26]

For Arnold, symbols were the *point* of the system. He wrote: "Almost all human conduct is symbolic. Almost all institutional habits are symbols." He argued that institutions should be treated as people subject to psychological forces and distractions. For example, there was little if any difference between a court, a bureau, and a commission other than the difference in our attitudes toward these three institutions and the way those differences were reflected in the self conception of the individuals acting in those roles.[27]

He then explored the concept of legal theory itself. Arnold pressed the view that law was one of the few disciplines that was obsessed with internal consistency and the derivation of immutable principles rather than solving the problems within its purview. The need for a coherent theory about law (what Arnold called the mysteries of jurisprudence) instead of just using law to solve problems was the barrier to achieving anything of substance in the real world.

Viewed in its symbolic role though, the need to rationalize and systematize stems from the function of law "not so much to guide society but to comfort it." Arnold was equally critical of the failure of both the old guard and Arnold's fellow legal realists to recognize this symbolic function of law. If anything, Arnold is more dismissive of the realists than the reactionaries for opposing progress in the name of principle. For Arnold, "the realist is ordinarily a man who is emotionally conscious of the discrepancy between the behavior of the world and the way it talks about that behavior. He is not, however, conscious of the fact that talking and writing is just as much a form of behavior as eating." Moreover, "no realist or skeptic ever quite escapes the influences of the symbols of his time, because most of his conduct and the conditions under which he maintains his own prestige are based on those symbols." Finally, "It is child's play for the realist to show that law is not what it pretends to be. . . . Yet the legal realist falls into grave error when he believes this to be a defect in the law. From any objective point of view the escape of the law from reality constitutes not its weakness but its greatest strength. Legal institutions must constantly reconcile ideological conflicts, just as individuals reconcile them by shoving inconsistencies back into a sort of institutional subconscious mind." Realism in law schools tends to become "only the same old jurisprudence with a new terminology" and the "same old courses with new names."[28]

Symbols thus represented a fundamental break with most of the realist tradition. Arnold had already abandoned the empirical work that sought to link law and social science. He now also abandoned the rule and fact skeptic approach to law in favor of his psychological and symbolic approach to law as a form of public ceremony.[29]

In Arnold's view, law played the same role as theology did in the previous century. Both required acceptance on faith of a moral and logical rule of law above men and even governments. Both are based on mystical faith and are "dramatized by ceremonies which bear a marked similarity all over the world, from primitive to modern times, marked by reverence, color, particular dress, and parades." Both sought to rationalize fixed rules that nonetheless produce outcomes that good should be rewarded and the wicked should be punished. Both too often argued the illogical and indefensible proposition that "more benevolent results in the long run are achieved by refusing benevolent principles in particular cases." Since no system can withstand such contradictions, both institutions sacrifice symbolic consistency to follow both impulses at the same time—the courts combining law and equity and theology with visions of God as both (but separately) Lord and Redeemer. In a particularly deft turn, Arnold ended this section with a comparison over the then hotly contested struggle in civil procedure over the degree of detail required in a complaint (fact pleading versus notice pleading) and the equally controversial struggle between the proponents of the lengthier Episcopal liturgy and those favoring the simpler Presbyterian prayers.[30]

Arnold then turned to economics. Economics, like jurisprudence, represented an attitude toward conduct that simultaneously strives to be logical and to reconcile inconsistent institutions and conflicting ideals. Economics also posited eternal laws that imposed limitations on man-made laws to attempt social justice. Economics, however, excluded the moral element of law and religion and attempted to confine its world to the "unfettered operation of human greed." The abstract man that economics adopts was an automaton but an important construct that justified keeping law out of any field deemed to be the province of economics. According to this view, when human law sought to regulate economic activity in contradiction to the immutable laws of the market, it was unnatural and doomed to failure. Even good results were written off as short-term aberrations. Arnold concluded from all this that "it is better to suffer under a sound principle than to thrive under an unsound one."[31]

The institutional safety valves that reconcile utterly contradictory maxims and impulses are present in economics as well as law and religion. Rules that governments must balance their budgets collide with the imperative that public works are a good investment in times of distress, and further collide with the theory that the government should not interfere with business. To satisfy all three criteria at once, a portion of the budget is balanced, a portion is spent on public works through government corporations, but only on things that aren't needed, all in order to satisfy the theory that government should not enter into business, which consists of producing the things people do need.[32]

All of the theorizing was really a prelude to Arnold's real topic: demolishing the critics of the New Deal who challenged the pragmatic experimentation of the Roosevelt Administration on the grounds that it violated the maxims and theories of good government, due process of law, or sound economics. Arnold recognized that to be successful the New Deal required immediate action that had to bear at least a superficial resemblance to the old forms and symbols lest either a revolution or total reaction ensue. Thus, the dole to the needy had to be temporary, not large, and made to look like productive employment. Similarly, public works projects had to be clothed in the rhetoric of creating character, priming the pump, or stabilizing industry rather than in terms of providing work to the unemployed or developing new infrastructure for the country. The symbolic effect of public works became more important than their practical need and then became vulnerable to attacks based on practicality and common sense. He lamented about how much more could have been accomplished if poverty, unemployment, and lack of production were attacked with the same fervor as the rebuilding of the Philippines, in which the United States was "investing" in an underutilized productive asset rather than "spending" the money on the poor and the downtrodden.[33]

As a result, most of the New Deal legislation suffered from conflicting ideological forces and enjoyed only limited real world success, including the National Recovery Administration (NRA), the labor laws, tax policy, and the Securities Exchange Act. Arnold was more impressed with the "practical common sense" of the Agricultural Adjustment Act and the Social Security Act. But when the Supreme Court declared the most important pieces of the New Deal unconstitutional, it denied government the freedom to improvise and grow that is routinely granted to business enterprises. Good results (or at least their potential) were again sacrificed on the alter of consistency to ancient principles and their symbols.[34] What Arnold admired most was muddling through and not consistency to abstract principle.

What followed next was a digression through the symbolic importance of the criminal trial, largely derived from Arnold's previous writing.[35] For Arnold, trials, particularly criminal trials, were not as efficient as arbitration or administrative tribunals, but they represented "a set of ideals among which efficiency is of only minor importance." While the civil trial is most important to businessmen who need a feeling of security from the encroachments of the government, the criminal trial embodies both the dignity of the state as an enforcer of the law and the dignity of the individual who is an avowed opponent of the state.[36]

These contradictory ideals can only coexist when society itself is reasonably secure, and thus they disappear in times of war, revolution, and crisis. The ideal of a fair trial and the ideal of law enforcement are merely two forms of myths and drama that preserve diametric inconsistencies but nonetheless have a real meaning in our emotional lives.[37]

In Arnold's words,

> It is of course true that all the machinery surrounding the ideal of a fair trial has its social cost in delays, technicalities, and injustices in the judicial process. It is equally true in times of public fear and intolerance this machinery is seldom strong enough to prevent the conviction of weak and harmless persons. Yet the cultural effect of these failures on mass psychology is probably worth everything it costs because of its contribution to the ultimate survival of a great humanitarian ideal.[38]

Observing the trial as a ceremony, Arnold viewed the role of the jury as managing the many inconsistencies built into the system by absorbing criticism of the unsatisfactory results in the trial of particular cases and thus deflecting criticism against the judicial system itself.[39]

In contrast to the ideal of the fair trial was the equally important ideal of law enforcement. Law enforcement represented the ideal of a set of principles that are applied neutrally and logically without regard for the station or circumstances of the defendant or the accused. This principle clashes with principles of fair trial and individualized justice. Arnold pointed to the insanity defense and other expert testimony on psychology as the way these conflicting principles were presented to juries, who can then acquit if they so choose without jeopardizing either ideal and yet purporting to follow both.[40]

Thus, the government could prosecute Al Capone for income tax evasion rather than the unprovable bootlegging and racketeering, while freeing other bootleggers because of an illegal search. These were each examples of vindicating the prestige of the government in enforcing the law while celebrating the memory of individual freedom from law enforcement. The abstract ideal of pure law enforcement appeared to Arnold most prevalent in areas of the law where the laws not only were not enforced but could not be, such as Prohibition.[41]

The various challenges to the New Deal leading up to the Supreme Court's invalidation of the National Industrial Recovery Act (NIRA) in *Schechter Poultry* represented a similar contest between viewing the Constitution as a restriction on tyranny and bureaucracy without actually interfering with the exercise of national power. For years the country labored under an improvised system of New Deal legislation that had no definitive Constitutional interpretation. For Arnold, this was merely a dramatic illustration of the day-to-day nature of the judicial system: "Courts owe their prestige to the idea that they are constantly making the law more and more certain. They owe their power to the fact that they never clarify total situations."[42] The civil trial functioned primarily as a modern form of trial by combat as a symbol of individual freedom from active interference by the government, preserving conservative traditions in the face of new regulatory legislation. Thus the New Deal could be enacted, the Courts could avoid passing on its legality while it was tested in the real world and prevaricate on its legality when forced to opine, and once liberals and conservative alike began to despise it, rule that it was unconstitutional without saying what other laws were or might be constitutional.[43]

Arnold's substantive critique was that the necessity of enforcing regulation through the contested civil trial prevented a wide variety of governmental experimentation that was routinely accepted as necessary in the private sector. For the Supreme Court, he recommended,

> In the celebration of legal and economic theories, the Court should be equipped only with prayer books and collections of familiar quotations. In the protection of those seeking a fair trial it should be armed with a sword which it dared to use with courage. Here is a function for which the grand old ceremony of trial by combat is eminently fitted. It should be used for such purposes rather than as an instrument for hit-or-miss conservative social planning.[44]

Arnold's criticism of piecemeal judicial review reflected his experience in the New Deal and particularly the Agricultural Adjustment Administration. While judicial review at times tied up the implementation of the New Deal and sowed confusion as to its legal status and legitimacy, it also provided necessary breathing room for it to be implemented in the first place. Arnold's stance as detached observer in *Symbols* contrasted with his simultaneous role as an advocate in the New Deal itself. Arnold the scholar advocated a system in which the constitutionality of the Agricultural Adjustment Act (AAA), the NRA, and even the New Deal as a whole (which incorporated thousands of individual measures) could be tested swiftly and in its entirety. In practice, he was unable to implement what he preached in the early days of the AAA. There he was forced to avoid at all costs a definitive court ruling on the constitutionality of the act. Despite personally pushing for faster and broader judicial review of the AAA, Arnold was successful in bringing true test cases only when Abe Fortas, Jerome Frank, and the higher-ups in the AAA were convinced there was a safe case that would not be overturned.[45]

Arnold saved his best for next to last. In the chapter "Courts versus Bureaucracy," Arnold deals with the worship of courts as protector of liberties and the dismissal of bureaucracy as tyranny. While each was treated differently in law and in society, for Arnold they were merely part of a continuum of ways of dealing with social problems and disputes. Symbolically, the inefficiencies of courts are revered as "procedure" and "precedent," while the very same techniques of agencies are reviled as "red tape." When judges were forced into bad decisions, it stemmed from adherence to grander neutral principles that uphold, rather than diminish, the prestige of the judiciary as an institution. When bureaus or commissions err, they have no such institutional prestige or principles to fall back on, and their esteem falls even lower in the public eye. If anything, "bureaucracy" is a potent negative symbol to be opposed, even at the price of opposing a genuine humanitarian agenda that the public would otherwise support.[46]

Arnold found this all quite absurd given the complex and utterly unreviewable regulation of vast aspects of American life by *private enterprise,* which never raised a fraction of the outrage generated by the mildest sort of administrative regulation undertaken by the New Deal. This attitude "destroys the confidence of officials in their ability to take practical action unless they are able to escape into some other atmosphere. If they call themselves a corporation, or a political party, or any familiar symbol which permits freedom of action, their difficulties disappear."[47]

In the final chapter, "A Philosophy for Politicians," Arnold abandoned the device of the detached ironic observer and advocated a new pragmatic way to describe and operate government for the benefit of society without following abstract self-contradictory ideals. Unlike the rest of *Symbols,* it is earnest in tone and quite jarringly different from the vast majority of the book that it follows. Arnold offered a particularly unfortunate metaphor in stating that "from a humanitarian point of view the best government is that which we find in an insane asylum" because the physicians in charge seek to make the inmates as comfortable as possible regardless of moral desserts and do not concern themselves with the separate sciences of law, economics, or sociology. Despite this poor choice of words, Arnold sought a pragmatic role for government so it could experiment when necessary to address social needs with the same freedom that private enterprise uses in managing large and small business without having to resort to subterfuges of incorporating public entities to manage particular enterprises or delegating governmental functions to political parties or political machines. But in the end, all Arnold proposed was the axiom that the man who works only for himself with only marginal room for the humanitarian be replaced with a new social philosophy that man works only for his fellow man with only incidental room for personal gain.[48]

He ends with the quite startlingly incongruent conclusion that

> the writer has faith that a new public attitude toward the ideals of law and economics is slowly appearing to create an atmosphere where the fanatical alignments between opposing political principles may disappear and a competent, practical, opportunistic governing class may rise to power. Whether such a hope is well founded or not, it is impossible to say, but to that end this book is dedicated.[49]

It was as if a brilliantly engaging and complex movie ends with a jarring, happy ending tying up all the impossible loose ends or just concludes because the studio refused to advance further funds to the director.

Nonetheless, with a handful of aphorisms and some extremely piquant writing, Arnold managed to undermine both the conservative and the liberal fight over the role of law and the strengths or defects of the New Deal. The conservative was silly to seek a consistency in the law where none exists. The liberal (and realist) was equally silly to point out the obvious inconsistency in the law as a fundamental criticism. Both missed the symbolic point of law of allowing change while wrapping that change in the comforting (however false) notion of consistency to eternal principles.

Arnold's message was gleefully revolutionary but hardly likely to endear him to his earnest colleagues in the realist movement who had spent the better part of fifteen years thinking they were making substantive progress by exposing the contradictions of the American law and the indeterminacy of legal rules and the real explanation for how courts made decisions.

Symbols gave Arnold immediate stature in both legal and New Deal circles. It was reviewed in nearly twenty law reviews and countless more general journals and newspapers. Most of the reviews were short and merely described the work, but, surprisingly, a number of the leading lights supporting the realist movement weighed in with thoughtful essays in praise of Arnold.

Karl Llewellyn, the de facto dean of the realists, wrote that "no more striking, original, or significant contribution to jurisprudence has appeared during the last ten years."[50] Similar glowing encomiums came from key figures in the legal realist and New Deal camps. Harold Laski praised Arnold as a thinker equal to Felix Frankfurter, Oliver Wendell Holmes, Charles Clark, Benjamin Cardozo, Morris Cohen, Max Lerner, and Louis Brandeis in "renewing the foundations of modern jurisprudence."[51] The aforementioned Morris Cohen called it "a stimulating and brilliant book, full of acute and liberating observations which deserve to be widely disseminated."[52] Virtually every observer praised Arnold's irony, satire, wit, and writing style that made the book scintillating rather than the deadly dull tome which the subject matter would suggest.

Most who praised the book viewed Arnold as working in the realist tradition and in most cases concluded that Arnold had made a major contribution to the realist agenda.[53] This is an odd conclusion, given that Arnold throughout *Symbols* attacks the realists as well as the formalists for their respective defense and attack of the substance of abstract legal principles while not recognizing the symbolic importance of legal principles and institutions that could not possibly stand for the literal truth of what they purported to uphold. Only two reviews pointed out that Arnold did not completely embrace the agenda of the realists or referred to him as a neo-realist.[54]

All was not praise however. Max Radin concluded in an otherwise positive review that Arnold had "exaggerated both the force of the impulse to be logical and its function."[55] Morris Cohen and others noted that Arnold was not particularly rigorous in defining what he meant by the natural or social sciences and the nature of their methodologies.[56]

The critics had a point. *The Symbols of Government* lacks an organic consistency and structure that makes it a bit of a shaggy dog story, frequently brilliant but lacking a consistent thesis and ending with more of a prayer than a path to the pragmatic, progressive government for which Arnold yearned. At best, it has a "unity of mood" as Felix Cohen noted.[57] Julius Stone was somewhat less kind in noting that

> it is a pity that Mr. Arnold has attempted to make a coherent book out of essays in a mode of thought which does not lend itself to coherent presentation. The result is to hide jewels of both wit and perception against a background of tinsel smartness and banality.[58]

Some of the critics were as over-the-top as Arnold could be. One reviewer accused Arnold of simply abandoning the Constitution when it suited his purpose.[59] Another attributed to him "only a hazy idea" of what the social sciences are and said that the whole purpose of the book was "to defend the experimentation under the New Deal in this country and under Fascism, Nazism, and Communism abroad."[60] One review called him indebted to the "patron saint of Fascism."[61] Only the protean nature of Arnold's argument could both get under the skin of ideologically opposed readers and simultaneously conjure up images of such contradictory models. In so doing, such critics largely confirmed Arnold's arguments about the power of symbols and principles and the deeply ingrained psychological need for false logical consistency in analyzing questions about the proper role of governments.

Symbols was, in the end, the work of a brilliant amateur armchair anthropologist of law with an engaging writing style that was thrilling in places but tended to gloss over logical flaws in some of the arguments. But it was, after all, a work dedicated to exposing the flaws of sterile logical argument in the key fields of inquiry affecting the political economy of the times. It accomplished the seemingly impossible task of aligning Arnold with both the realists and their opponents. In relying primarily on psychology in analyzing symbols, Arnold made common cause with the social science branch of legal realism. Arnold's gleeful exploding of myth after myth also put him deeply into the rule-skeptic branch of the realists. But at the same time, he argued that both branches of realism were wrong in closely examining the substance of law, economics, and sociology, and in failing to use (rather than discredit) those symbols to achieve meaningful pragmatic change in the real world.

The Symbols of Government also had an unlikely impact on a young man far removed from legal academia. Future Attorney General Nicholas Katzenbach was a nineteen-year-old Princeton undergraduate when he enlisted in the Army Air Force following the attack on Pearl Harbor. Katzenbach flew nineteen B-25 bombing missions as a navigator when his bomber was hit and crashed into the ocean. He and the rest of the crew were captured by the Italians and eventually sent as prisoners of war to the German POW camp featured in the Steve McQueen movie *The Great Escape*. While Katzenbach did not join in the escape itself, he helped hide the dirt as the POWs dug their elaborate tunnel.[62]

During his two years of captivity, he mostly read the hundreds of books that the YMCA had sent to the POWs. He read Plato, Shakespeare, Galsworthy, Locke, Herodotus, and Thurman Arnold. The YMCA shipment coincidentally included both *The Symbols of Government* and Arnold's later book, *The Folklore of Capitalism*. Katzenbach was particularly moved by *The Symbols of Government*. He had no prior exposure to semantics and years later recalled that *Symbols* "revealed a great deal that I had never thought about." He reread the book several times and kept it by his bed. When the German guards roused all the prisoners in the middle of the night and force-marched them in a bitter snow storm out of the camp to the west to avoid the advancing Russian Army, Katzenbach took only his clothes and his dog-eared copy of Arnold's book.[63]

The next year Arnold published his casebook on trials and appeals, which he co-authored with his Yale colleague Fleming James, most famous later as the father of no-fault automobile insurance.[64] The casebook, like *Symbols,* fully reflected Arnold's intellectual playfulness and eccentricities. Like *Symbols,* it began on a note of ironic detachment:

> [M]uch of the material in this book deals with underlying attitudes and phobias which the writers consider must be understood and taken into account by the trial attorney. This does not mean we are opposed to legal reform. It only means that we consider the attitude of detached observation more suitable for purposes of *understanding* the situation,

whether that understanding be used for general reform or for the narrower objectives of advancing the cause of a particular client.[65]

Like most realist casebooks it was arranged along so-called functionalist lines. The authors included not only edited federal and state court decisions on procedure, but also liberal helpings of jurisprudence, federal jurisdiction, conflict of laws, and administrative law. Chapter headings, rather than being organized conceptually, or even chronologically in the life of a case, included "The Mystical Conception of a Court"; "The Time, Place and Subject Matter of Judicial Decision"; and "The Ritual of the Commencement of a Suit." Leading cases were occasionally included, but so too were utterly indefensible cases, primarily so that Arnold and James could ridicule them. Beyond cases and notes, the book was full of references and excerpts from law reviews, textbooks, unpublished manuscripts, book reviews, ancient writings, code provisions, and even newspaper and magazine articles.

The book was well received and respectfully reviewed. The highest compliment was offered by one reviewer who admiringly noted: "If this be a 'case-book,' it is enough to make Professor Langdell turn in his grave."[66] Laura Kalman in her intellectual history of legal realism at Yale noted: "Of all the realist casebooks, Arnold and James's was the only one that did what a realist casebook might have been expected to do: satirize the law."[67]

Only the occasional and modest royalty from West Publishing suggests that it was ever used by anyone other than James and Arnold. The largest royalty they received was $600 in 1947. More typical payments were in the range of $10 to $30 for a six-month period.

Arnold's impish ways expressed themselves as a faculty colleague in addition to his teaching and scholarship. He sided with his colleagues in the routine rejection of faculty candidates educated at Harvard or too attracted to the mere doctrine of law. He typically dominated faculty conversations at the lunch table to the exasperation of his colleagues who eventually found themselves agreeing with opinions they had dismissed as nonsense at the beginning of the discussion. He routinely sided with the younger and more liberal colleagues who sought to add non-lawyer social scientists to the faculty. However, there were limits even to the resources of Yale, especially during the depression, as well as constraints imposed by teaching at a law school and not a pure research institution. Despite being one of the acknowledged leaders of the faculty, Arnold failed in 1934 to convince the faculty to hire the political scientist Max Lerner.[68]

In 1933, he pushed, along with Bill Douglas, for a faculty appointment for Abe Fortas as a teaching fellow. Fortas had been one of Yale's most brilliant, yet abrasive, students. Fortas graduated in 1932 after serving as editor-in-chief of the *Yale Law Journal,* taking first prize for his student article for the *Journal* the previous year, and earning several other prestigious prizes and scholarships. Thus began a complex lifelong intellectual, if not social, friendship that lasted through Fortas's rise through the ranks of the New Deal, the formation of their eventual law partnership, and Fortas's spectacular rise and fall as lawyer, adviser, and confidant of Lyndon Johnson and eventually Supreme Court Justice until Arnold's death in 1969.

The faculty presided over a variety of other matters beyond the life of the mind, including certain student disciplinary offenses. On one occasion, two of the then all-male student body were brought before the faculty facing expulsion for having brought two Broadway chorus girls to their rooms. Their defense was in essence that nothing untoward had happened and that the four of them had passed the evening and early morning listening to records and playing cards. Arnold rose in mock indignation and spoke to the faculty:

> All the evidence is in. The campus policemen examined the suite of rooms where all this occurred and have assured us that nothing untoward went on; a Victrola and records were in the center of the room; cards were on the floor; there was no evidence of any wrongdoing. Everything is exactly as the boys represented.
>
> Now, gentlemen, we have a case here of two perfectly normal, healthy young men. They escort to their dormitory rooms at near midnight two lovely young ladies from the Paramount Chorus. They remain there for an hour and a half. And what do they do? They play Tchaikovsky's NUTCRACKER SUITE. That's what they do, and that's ALL they do. In light of this, I say again that we don't really need these boys at Yale, and I say this not because of what they DID do but because of what they DIDN'T do!!!

Suitably embarrassed, the faculty took no further action in the matter. One of the grateful young men later became a distinguished lawyer and corporate counsel in Texas and reminded Arnold of the story thirty years later as a senior member of the bar.[69]

Like many of his Yale colleagues, Arnold dabbled in the New Deal, spending his summers in Washington, D.C., and taking various leaves to work on projects for the Roosevelt administration. While many of his colleagues such as Douglas, Fortas, and a growing list of others quickly entered the government on a full-time basis, Arnold did not. Instead, he initially combined extensive part-time governmental service with his teaching, scholarship, and home life in New Haven. He began by working on the enforcement and constitutionality of the marketing orders issued by the Agricultural Adjustment Act with Jerome Frank and Fortas and preparing a plan for farm relief with fellow Yale professor Wesley Sturges.[70]

During different summers, Arnold assisted in the administration of the Philippines, working under eventual Supreme Court Justice Frank Murphy on a program to establish a quota on sugar production and then moved to the Securities Exchange Commission as a trial examiner under Douglas on issues of corporate reorganizations. While on sabbatical in 1937, he briefed and argued a series of tax cases for the Justice Department in the Supreme Court, winning three of his four cases.[71] He was forced to turn down full-time appointments to the National Labor Relations Board and the Securities Exchange Commission because of an inability to obtain the necessary leave from Yale.[72] Arnold concluded his part-time brain trust work serving in the Antitrust Division of the Justice Department under future Supreme Court Justice Robert Jackson.

Although he was frequently away from home, life in New Haven was beginning to take on a stability that Arnold had not truly experienced since he had left his parents' home for college. There was little money in the bank at first, but the financial situation quickly stabilized. Thurman and Frances had borrowed money on a subsidized basis from the university to buy their home on Willow Street, where they were neighbors with Bill Douglas. To the great irritation of Frances, the two became great drinking buddies and poker pals.

In his autobiography, Douglas tells one of many stories of the Rabelaisian adventures of Thurman Arnold. On a night when the Arnolds were giving a dinner party, Douglas and Arnold continued an office conversation over drinks at Douglas's home to the point where Arnold was over an hour late for his own party. Douglas and Arnold argued jovially over who would handle Frances. In the words of Douglas, "As Thurman reached the door, Frances appeared. With her left hand she seized him by the collar. With her right she took him by the seat of the pants, and literally threw him into the street. Shaking her fist, she shouted: 'And I'll do the same to you, Bill Douglas.'" Douglas and Arnold then finished off the remainder of a fifth of bourbon and went driving along the sidewalks of New Haven in search of more "friendly people" and "friendly attitudes." They knocked on more than a dozen doors urging better relations among the citizens of New Haven until Frances finally tracked them down following phone calls from most of the wives of the homes visited by the revelers. Relations inside the Arnold home and between Frances and Douglas were distinctly frosty for several weeks despite both apologies and flowers.[73]

Douglas, Arnold, and others played a variety of games and pranks when they weren't hard at work on their writings, New Deal projects, classes, and general faculty business. Douglas, Arnold, and Sturges had a contest where the players earned increasingly higher points depending on whether they were cited in law review articles, speeches, newspapers, actually quoted, or featured in a picture. Douglas, Arnold, and a very young Abe Fortas also formed the New Haven Hunt Club, whose meetings consisted of night time rambles in the great outdoors with sacks, flashlights, and ample liquor in search of snipes and other nonexistent wildlife.[74]

In both his serious and more frivolous endeavors, Arnold was beginning to form the intellectual, political, and social friendships that would last into the 1960s and the corridors of power in Washington, D.C. In both New Haven and Washington, Arnold befriended William Douglas, Charles Clark, Walton Hamilton, Abe Fortas, Jerome Frank, and to a lesser extent Felix Frankfurter, one of the few Harvard men that Arnold viewed as a progressive and New Deal supporter. These friendships, formed through teaching, advocacy for the New Deal, common intellectual cause, or simply drunken excess, would last a lifetime and serve him well.

The Folklore of Capitalism, Arnold's last book as a member of the Yale faculty, proved to be his legacy.[75] *Folklore* began with a repetition and extension of the arguments of *Symbols*. It focused on why so much light and heat was expended on choosing between capitalism, fascism, and communism as systems of government. Arnold argued in familiar fashion that people neither choose a system of government as a matter of free will nor live with a fully formed philosophy regardless of its real world consequences. All governments, regardless of so-called ideology, seek pragmatic solutions to the daily problems of distributing goods and services at the cost of ideological incoherence. All governments professed a creed but contained a variety of conflicting institutions and principles to allow them to function in the real world despite the many contradictions. The creeds that governments and people espouse resemble the true faiths espoused by religions and generate "automatic religious opposition to new forms of organizations." Governments, like churches, are not judged on the effectiveness as organizations but on the purity of their creeds."[76]

However, the question remains, how do men choose their creeds? According to Arnold, they don't, but instead become bound by loyalties and enthusiasms to existing organizations. From this point of view, capitalism (and any other creed) is falsely believed to have a meaning and is studied, apart from the living organizations to which it is attached.[77]

Every government creed must represent all the contradictory ideals of a people if it is to be accepted by them. In America, this came down to the contrasting myths of the business man and the government bureaucrat, the personification of corporations, and the language of private property in an age of the large organization. The businessman was an individual (and his corporation was an individual as well) beholden to no one and nothing except the Constitution. Despite the fact that private organizations dominate most people's lives through the provision of necessary goods, services, credit, and even basic security for the future, the accepted wisdom did not think about business organizations as "government" in any sense. Thus, business held a "complete and autocratic" control over the lives of millions, but government was forced to move through sub rosa political machines when it wanted to accomplish something in the real world.[78]

The actual government was not to be trusted. Bureaucrats were petty tyrants and the destroyers of the rule of law. Congressmen were politicians who could not be trusted to act pursuant to sound principles. Since organizations tend to assume the character of their own mythology, government was no career for an up-and-comer; it could not be trusted to do its own hiring and had to be controlled by civil service laws. Only the myths of business and money allowed business to act pragmatically without violating its own creed. As a result, business solved problems, and government action, even if identical to that undertaken by business, would be condemned as leading to bad tendencies and violations of first principles regardless of its real world effect.[79]

New myths arise only as new classes gain power with new heroes of their own. Yet, the existing myths continue to exert influence. Few businessmen remained as true independent actors in the American economy of the late 1930s. They had been replaced by complex corporate organizations run by armies of functionaries. Even as a new class of engineers, salesman, managers, and social workers actually ran the country, the mythology required them to portray themselves as serving the old order rather than replacing it.[80]

Folklore was no longer folklore when recognized as such. By exposing the unconscious myths, Arnold could then demystify the prevailing wisdom and hopefully enable the government to address the problems of the day. For the folklore of the day was unrelentingly hostile to the new role of the government arising out of the New Deal and the Great Depression. The folklore of 1937 was to encourage the type of organization called business or industry and discourage the type known as government. It supported bold confident decisions by business, even if wasteful, but condemned government action as destructive. The folklore of the day was more interested in saving posterity from evil creeds than in solving the day-to-day distribution of food, housing, and clothing to the needy.[81]

Arnold analogized these issues with medieval opposition to the medicinal value of quinine because it did nothing to address the prevailing theories of medicine that traced all ills to an imbalance of the humors: "Measures like child labor, conservation of oil, or regulation of agriculture had to be considered without relation to the immediate benefits to children, oil or agriculture. Future tendencies were regarded as far more important than immediate effects and danger to posterity seemed more real than danger to existing persons."[82]

The greatest myth was that of private property. The debate over government policy was frequently phrased in the language of personally owned private property, "when as a matter of fact the things which were described were neither private, nor property, nor personally owned." Even in 1937, what most people had was not physical property at all, except for their furniture or their car, and even then it was more a right of use of complex items whose construction, finance, and repair were dependent on the assistance of large impersonal organizations.[83] Arnold stated,

The other things the writer "owns" are all claims to rank and privilege in an organizational hierarchy. He is a professor at Yale Law School and hopes that Yale will feed and lodge him. He has a piece of paper from an insurance company which he hopes will induce that organization to take care of his wife if he dies. He has other pieces of paper from other organizations operating buildings and railroads and manufacturing plants which give him precarious privileges in those industrial governments. Wealth today consists in nothing any one individual can use. The standards of wealth are simply current expectations of how the individual stands with the rulers of industrial baronies coupled with a guess as to the strength of those principalities. . . .[84]

Had there been a realization that these organizations were not dealing with private property, it would have been obvious that the remedy lay in giving control to men with a different sense of responsibility. . . . [Those who rose] to power and rank . . . were more interested in the manipulation of financial symbols than in transportation, or housing, or the actual production and distribution of any sort of goods. Position and rank obtained in this fiscal world had carried no social obligation because they were subject to the rules which governed the accumulation of private property.[85]

Arnold's view of private property was both based on his own experiences (and those of countless Americans in the depression) and prescient for the future. Much of Arnold's wealth had in fact vanished in the depression as stocks, oil and gas rights, and interests in ranching operations back in Wyoming became worthless. It was Arnold's status at Yale that had allowed him to "buy" a house, which was only possible because of Yale's assistance in the financing and its guarantee of his livelihood. Arnold's status as a tenured professor of law was a guarantee that he would continue to earn a living when he ceased to work in government. Even that would be taken away from him when he was stripped of his tenure after it was clear that he would not return to Yale anytime soon when serving from 1938 onward as head of the Antitrust Division.

The idea of status and entitlements as the only real form of property in a modern complex economy was a concept far ahead of his time. This notion was clearly understood by Arnold's later protégé Charles Reich in his own groundbreaking work *The New Property*[86] and anyone with a 401(K) account in the post-Enron economy.

Had Arnold stopped there, he would have introduced his previous ideas to a broader public but not much more. In one letter he even described *Folklore of Capitalism* as a repetition of *Symbols of Government* with different examples.[87] However, the later chapters in fact made *Folklore* its own unique work.

Two key chapters discussed the personification of the corporation and the effect of the antitrust laws. In Arnold's view, vast corporate organizations were treated as if they were individuals, freeing them from the "restrictions of theology" that otherwise prevented experimentation as in the case of governments. Moreover, the personification of the corporation required granting the highest degree of constitutional protection to business and perversely made anyone struggling for the liberties of actual individuals highly suspect. Thus, Felix Frankfurter was ostracized at Harvard during his fight for Sacco and Vanzetti because it interfered with Harvard's endowment drive with its wealthy, more conservative alums. Roger Baldwin, the head of the American Civil Liberties Union (ACLU), was actually imprisoned for his work on behalf of individual freedoms. These were merely illustrations of "how the personification of the great corporation actually worked to monopolize the mantle of protection designed for the individual."[88]

Arnold then ridiculed the antitrust laws as empty symbolic vehicles designed to assuage popular fears of bigness and power without actually constraining the behavior of the modern business corporation. If the popular creed called for competition among small businesses treated as individuals but the economy required large industrial organizations capable of efficient large scale production, then it "became necessary to develop a procedure which constantly attacked bigness on rational legal and economic grounds, and at the same time never really interfered with combinations."[89]

Thus came antitrust, which for Arnold was both the perfect ritual of the folklore of capitalism and symbol of the modern American government. The continuing belief in antitrust law convinced those who cared "either that large combinations did not actually exist, or else that if they did exist, they were about to be done away with just as soon as right-thinking men were elected to office." Instead of having any real-world effect, "[t]rust busting therefore became one of the great moral issues of the day, while at the same time great combinations thrived and escaped regulation." Arnold viewed antitrust as about as likely to affect corporate power as the laws against prostitution would suppress that ancient trade or that political reform would dismantle the political machine.[90]

If the enemies were Carnegies and Rockefellers, they could be attacked through antitrust laws that prohibited bad conduct by bad men and meted out appropriate punishment primarily through criminal prosecution. However, when the economy demanded sophisticated corporate entities more difficult to personify as the work of a single owner or leader, antitrust began to play a different role:

> In this atmosphere the antitrust laws were the answer of a society which unconsciously felt the need of great organizations and at the same time had to deny them a place in the moral and logical ideology of the social structure. They were part of the struggle of a creed of rugged individualism to adapt itself to what was becoming a highly organized society.[91]

Those who invoked antitrust were crusaders, or essentially ministers of the gospel of the nineteenth century, preaching to a congregation that had no intention or ability to follow their minister's precepts but felt better having heard an impassioned sermon to their liking. The actual result of antitrust "was to promote the growth of great industrial organizations by deflecting the attacks on them into purely moral and ceremonial channels." Even worse, the antitrust laws became "the greatest protection to uncontrolled business dictatorships" and eliminated any impulse toward more practical and effective forms of supervision of economic organizations whether through taxation or regulation. Politicians could make careers on invoking antitrust but could not make a difference. Arnold cited Teddy Roosevelt's reputation as the great trustbuster and, in a move he quickly regretted, the 1930s populist Senator William Borah.[92]

Arnold found that antitrust did have one unlikely impact. By personifying corporations, the individuals comprising the great corporations that evolved came to perceive themselves as moral and gentlemanly in their dealings and abandoned some of the more brutal anticompetitive techniques that led to the rise of antitrust in the first place. This, however, did not lead to increased competition but merely to the suppression of competition by different techniques less amenable to antitrust challenge such as the manipulation of securities, patent pools, and price leadership.[93]

Arnold followed the discussion of antitrust with similarly insightful but scathing descriptions of the rituals of corporate reorganization and the rise of private taxation at the same time as the condemnation of public taxation. For corporate reorganization law, the purpose was to prove that when corporations cannot pay their debts they must surrender their property to their creditors like any other individual and permit a practical treatment of a political problem without violating this folklore.[94]

Arnold began his chapters on private and public "taxation" with the mock Dickensian chapter abstract: "In which it is shown how taxation by industrial organizations is a pleasanter way of paying tribute than taxation by government." Corporations levied money from individuals in heavier and more draconian manners than traditional taxation through "investment" and "purchasing" but were spared the condemnation for their actions through the fiction that such levies were "voluntary."

To Arnold, this was nonsense. Payments for rent, heat, and transportation were no less involuntary payments than taxes for police protection, libraries, and parks, except as to the degree of public control over the expenditures. But most Americans viewed the former as voluntary and the latter involuntary and hence undesirable. Somehow prices were "something a person could pay or not pay as he chose." Only the "taxes" levied by public utilities as admitted monopolists looked more like traditional governmental taxes and seemed to justify in the public's mind a greater role for governmental control.[95]

There is a kind of thrilling recklessness in Arnold's writing as he blurs the line between public and private with a dizzying array of examples: the corporation that issues bonds and uses the proceeds like a sovereign government; the stock exchange exercising the power to print money like a government; companies deducting a portion of an employee's paycheck to buy stock to create claims against the corporation in their old age, which the government was forced to ape to win acceptance of social security; the Ford Motor company simply shipping cars to their dealers and requiring payment on pain of surrendering their franchise; securities firms forcing customers to take the sour issues if they wanted access to the sweeter deals; and the raising of prices through producer combination (cartels) to charge all that the traffic would bear.[96]

In contrast, the true governmental equivalents were condemned as unsound and judged by their failures, while the industrial organization was judged by its successes. A corporation could spend more than its income in a particular year and still balance its budget on the theory that it was acquiring "assets" in return for its expenditures. The government could not use the same techniques because it was not supposed to own any property and it merely spent (or wasted) tax dollars but did not invest.

Thus, private schools could capitalize their organization and make money; but public schools could not because it cannot be conceived that the government sells education in the manner of a private organization. Only through the fiction of a government corporation could the government operate assets in the normal sense of the term and then only if the government did not "make money" that threatened interference with private business. One notable exception was the town of Coral Gables, Florida, which funded millions in improvements by issuing what appeared to be private bonds that ultimately went unpaid, but the improvements remained. This proved, to Arnold at least, that public governments invested in exactly the same manner as their private industrial counterparts.[97]

Arnold eventually ends the parade of examples to conclude,

> [T]he central idea was that "government" does not spend its "own" money. It can have no assets. It cannot use corporate methods of balancing its budgets. These were all incidents of the prevalent belief in the essential benevolence of private government.[98]

Less benevolently, he continues,

> The notion is that nobody "pays" for the mistakes of private organizations, except the investors, the laborers, and the purchasers, and that their loss is not a tax but is something due to their own fault for investing in, working for, and purchasing from the particular organizations. In the case of governmental organizations, every mistake is a tax on posterity.[99]

Arnold concludes with chapters entitled "The Social Philosophy of Tomorrow" and "Some Principles of Political Dynamics." He ends more effectively than in *Symbols* but still with somewhat of a whimper compared to the incendiary prose of the rest of *Folklore*. Fortunately, he never entirely abandons the objective observer for the advocate, which both weakened and threatened the coherence of *Symbols*. But he still talked in generalities about "political dynamics" as a holistic science about society and offered familiar arguments about the conflict between the ideal and practical, social needs being met by sub-rosa organizations like political machines when the social needs are not perceived as legitimate, and how institutional doctrine is never a frank description of the actual practice.

This was familiar ground for Arnold's fans but of no interest to the unconverted. Arnold did not oppose principle but favored the practical over the ideal and judged every organization for how well it met the needs of the people, not how it adhered to logic or theory.[100]

Inexplicably, *Folklore* became a minor best seller,[101] going through seven printings between October 1937 and April 1938 and numerous additional printings after that. There is no remaining accounting of the royalties that Arnold received, but they must have been a welcome addition to his Depression-era professor's salary or his even more meager salary as a part-time New Deal brain truster.

Folklore of Capitalism was reviewed in not just the law reviews of the United States, Canada, and Great Britain but also in virtually every newspaper and glossy magazine including the *New Yorker,* and it made a number of the year end best book lists.[102] Perhaps most importantly, it also brought Arnold to the attention of the highest echelons of the New Deal.

Most critics viewed *Folklore* as a superior work to *Symbols*. Alfred Bingham even wrote that *Folklore* would rank with Darwin's *Origin of the Species* in the history of human thought. Others compared its impact to that of Marx, Veblen, Bentham, and Machiavelli. Even his critics admitted that the book was "very entertaining and very acute fun-poking at the pomposities and shams of our social order."[103]

Others were less favorable. One reviewer found Arnold's metaphysics so confusing that he basically did not know where Arnold stood in order to critique him. Harold Laski enjoyed the book but found it on a philosophical level "a real disappointment."[104]

Sidney Hook and Max Lerner were perhaps Arnold's most sympathetic, but perceptive, critics. Hook wrote that *Folklore* was "a little masterpiece of insight, expository skill and suggestiveness." Later though he honed in on Arnold's chief blind spot in both *Symbols* and *Folklore*:

> [There is] a revealing analogy which runs through this book as well as his *Symbols of Government*. The ideal politician is cast in the role of a trained psychiatrist. His function as head of the state organization is to make the patients (citizens) comfortable and "little of a nuisance" to themselves as possible. They can even be permitted their rantings (ideologies). The latter have only diagnostic value. They indicate the types of insanity by which patients are afflicted. No psychiatrist who knows his profession would dream of refuting them as part of his curative tech-

nique. The world may be regarded as one vast madhouse whose needs are ministered to by trained psychiatrists in the guise of patient politicians. This interesting analogy explains why Arnold is so indifferent to the kinds of ideologies which flourish in the political world and lumps them indiscriminately together. That is why he resents normative judgments as meddling intrusion by preachers and moralists who really constitute just another class of patients. That is why the methods of Hitler and Stalin seem to him unnecessarily crude.

For Hook, Arnold lacked a vision of the "good" that made his book brilliant diagnosis but naive as cure.[105]

Arnold responded in print in a more sober and scholarly tone than he had used in recent writings:

> If I were to describe the differences in our attitudes, I would say that Mr. Hook is an inspirational philosopher attempting to discover and analyze ethical formulas while I am an unphilosophical observer attempting to write what I have actually seen in my contact with governmental institutions. . . .
>
> However, I suspect him of thinking that more careful analysis of the concept of the good life in Germany would have prevented excesses of Hitler, and more thought on revolutionary principles on the part of the Russian people would have saved Trotsky. Certainly he thinks that my own observations of the conduct of political bodies would have been more accurate if I had first analyzed the good life. This is a necessary position for a philosopher to take. However, I think its chief utility is to give force and morale to good preaching, and that is not an accurate tool for describing moving social phenomena.[106]

Max Lerner praised Arnold for having written with a vividness that both made the book a hot topic of dinner table conversation of the intellectual elite and assured that no one tackling this topic in the future would ever write the same way. Lerner found Arnold to be a "brilliant amateur when it came to the psychology that animates much of Arnold's disdain for conceptualism and fierce commitment to pragmatism." But like Hook he focused on Arnold's inability to get away entirely from abstract ideals and his inconsistency as observer and the concluding chapters on how to govern. Unlike Hook, he ends with high praise:

Do what you will with Thurman Arnold, you cannot ignore him. He has placed himself squarely in the path of our attention, as few social thinkers have done in this decade; and his book is one of the best warrants of the vitality of our thought. There is in him a daring and irresponsibility that go with singular creativity. He takes intellectual risks that the more cautious and cloistered of us would consider dizzying. He is volatile, shifting, contradictory—but he is alive, and so is his book. Its confusion is a mirror and index of the confusion of our social system and our whole intellectual world; but its acid is the expression of a corrosive force in our culture which may yet dissolve those confusions and make social constructions possible.[107]

Despite the massive praise for *Folklore,* Arnold stuck to the view for the rest of his life that *Symbols* was his best work.[108] *Symbols* was certainly a much tighter and better organized work and had the benefit of building on previously published work during a period when Arnold was focused on scholarship and had few outside distractions. In contrast, Arnold wrote much of *Folklore* while also working in Washington for the Roosevelt administration, including key periods in 1936 and 1937 when Arnold was working night and day on briefs and arguments for the Supreme Court, other tasks for the New Deal, and the final drafting and editing of *Folklore* to meet his publisher's deadline.[109] *Folklore* is probably a more powerful and influential book than its predecessor, but large portions of it read as if they were dictated and supported by little other than Arnold's personal experience as a lawyer, professor, and governmental adviser. Indeed, Arnold admitted that this was precisely the point of *Folklore* in his reply to Sidney Hook in the *University of Chicago Law Review.*[110]

A large part of one's reactions to the relative merits of *Symbols* and *Folklore* depends on which book one read first. If one started with *Symbols,* then *Folklore* feels somewhat repetitive and even less tightly argued than *Symbols.* If the first introduction to Arnold was *Folklore,* that book seems more lively, more topical, and less abstractly intellectual than *Symbols,* which included numerous chapters taken nearly verbatim from prior law review articles, hardly a publishing form designed to appeal to the lay reader.

Folklore also struck a chord with the public that its predecessor did not largely because of timing. The years 1937 and 1938 were a critical period in the history of the New Deal, the Roosevelt administration, and the precarious economic condition of the country. *Folklore* had an impact even in a relatively crowded field of books that sought to explain the continuing depressed state of the economy and the roles of competition and planning in solving that crisis.[111] It was, in modern terms, what the "chattering class" read and discussed.

There is a lively cottage industry analyzing Arnold's scholarship and tracing its antecedents and descendants. A number of scholars point to Thorsten Veblen as an important antecedent for Arnold's work,[112] although Arnold himself denied reading Veblen's work or directly relying on it in either *Symbols* or *Folklore*.[113] Most of these attempts reveal more about the commentator than they do about Arnold. One commentator went so far as to link Arnold with the contemporary law and economics movement and its exclusive goal of wealth maximization.[114]

Nonetheless, a modern reader can find many of Arnold's ideas that resonate in modern legal and political thought. There is more than a nodding similarity between Arnold's cynicism toward the difference between doing law (or government) and theorizing about it and the later work of Stanley Fish.[115] Moreover, he displays an alarming lack of knowledge of (or even interest in) the methodologies of the natural science he purports to admire and recommend as a model for the social sciences. Much of Arnold's work looks like an amateur version of the semiotics that gripped the academy decades later with its analysis of signs, signifiers, and the signified.

However, to analyze too deeply the technical merits or defects of Arnold's writing is to miss the point of the entire joke. Arnold was brilliant but never an ivory tower academic as was the case of so many of his colleagues. He was a latecomer to the art of law review writing with the brashness and impatience of one who does not have the luxury of decades of grooming for the academy. He relied on bits and pieces of anthropology, sociology, and psychology without any technical mastery of those disciplines as they existed in the 1930s. What Arnold had, that many of his colleagues lacked, was the political, practice, administrative, and life experience that made his writing so memorable, while most of his contemporaries were so forgettable.

Arnold was a social critic in the tradition of H. L. Mencken, whom he befriended in the 1930s and who had read and commented on drafts of *The Folklore of Capitalism*.[116] He was an ironist in the tradition of

Thorsten Veblen. He was a comedian in the tradition of Groucho Marx. He was a cynic in the tradition of W. C. Fields. He was a radical, not so much because of the substance of his ideas but because he treated being right or wrong almost as not mattering. It is the ultimate irony and confirmation of his theories that Arnold entered the New Deal full time primarily because President Roosevelt needed to select a new head of the Antitrust Division to symbolize the administration's renewed commitment to antitrust enforcement but never bothered to familiarize himself with Arnold's actual views on the subject.

In March 1938, Arnold received word that President Roosevelt had nominated him to replace his former boss Robert Jackson as Assistant Attorney General in charge of the Antitrust Division. This time, leave from Yale was forthcoming, and Arnold would never again return to New Haven as a full-time professor or resident.

6

Trustbuster

No one will probably ever know exactly why Franklin Roosevelt hired Thurman Arnold as head of the Antitrust Division of the Justice Department. It may simply have been that the head of the Antitrust Division was the first important administration job available when Arnold's supporters and friends sought a full-time Washington position for him.[1]

Although part of the so-called FDR brain trust, Arnold had little previous contact with Roosevelt. In fact, he had only a half-hour meeting with the president while on loan from the Tax Division of the Justice Department to assist the Treasury Department with the preparation for hearings on tax evasion by the rich.[2] Roosevelt admitted he had not read *Folklore* when he nominated Arnold, and in general he had paid little attention to antitrust over the years. For example, in his 1933 book *Looking Forward*, President Roosevelt had devoted all of one brief historical paragraph to antitrust.[3]

The president's brain trust included such diverse personalities as Adolph Berle, Felix Frankfurter, Rexford Tugwell, Henry Wallace, Donald Richberg, Robert Jackson, Jerome Frank, Herman Oliphant, and Arnold, each of whom held contrasting views on the relative importance and effectiveness of competition enforcement versus planning in curing the country's ills. For most of the group, including Arnold prior to 1938, the value of antitrust and competition came in second.[4] No one in this group, or the rest of Roosevelt's inner circle, really knew if the president had a fundamental predisposition one way or another, but it was unlikely that he was a committed trustbuster.[5]

As Robert Jackson commented in his memoir of the New Deal,

> He [FDR] knew there were evils in the suppression of competition and that there were evils in competition itself, and where the greater evils were he never fully decided.[6]

Arnold himself noted that Roosevelt was not a man "who worked on any abstract theory of government" nor cared for "consistent theories."[7]

The entire history of the New Deal and competition was a contradiction. It had been preceded by the experience of war mobilization during World War I in which industry cooperated with government and colluded among itself under the direction of Bernard Baruch and his war board. Then followed the era of associationalism in the 1920s, during which the antitrust laws were sporadically enforced and key government officials, up to and including President Hoover, preferred industry cooperation to the robust competition mandated by the antitrust laws.[8]

Throughout the early New Deal period, the antitrust laws were at best one minor federal policy among many, and for some key New Dealers, an actual threat to prosperity to be replaced by some form of business-government cooperation and economic planning. For example, during the campaign of 1932, key Roosevelt advisors such as Rexford Tugwell and Adolph Berle believed that free market competition was impossible and a cause rather than a cure of the Depression.[9]

The first half of the New Deal focused on the National Industrial Recovery Act (NIRA), the Agricultural Adjustment Act (AAA), and the promulgation of industry codes and marketing orders that were the antithesis of the free market competition protected by antitrust laws.[10] Industry, with minimal government supervision, would draft codes of fair competition with only limited input from labor and consumers. The codes were intended to be legally enforceable against the entire industry, regardless of whether the individual business participated in the drafting or had agreed to be bound. Most codes directly or indirectly sought to control prices, prevent price discounting, legalize open-price systems, limit production, and standardize terms of sale to minimize non-price competition. There was frequent cheating in many industries, and competition would frequently break out despite the best intentions of the code planners.[11]

As the distinguished historian of the New Deal, Ellis Hawley concluded, "By and large . . . the codes reflected the desires of businessmen to create economic cartels that could check the forces of deflation."[12] The antitrust laws were repealed except for a vague and virtually unenforced provision prohibiting "monopolies or monopolistic practices."[13] Sales at less than the code price could be enjoined by the courts and violators subjected to significant penalties. Adlai Stevenson, who was briefly a lawyer with the AAA, noted, "In essence we're really creating gigantic trusts in all the food industries."[14] It was even the era where the popular board game Monopoly was first introduced.

The goal was to restrict production, raise prices, create profits, and restart business investment. Not surprisingly, to the extent prices increased, this further limited production, employment, and the purchasing power of consumers, leaving the country in even worse straits than at the beginning of the Great Depression. Over time, consumer interests, labor groups, smaller producers, antitrusters, and government purchasers became increasingly concerned with higher prices and began to oppose the NRA and its codes.[15]

Throughout this period, the Antitrust Division had been a backwater of the Justice Department. Formed as a separate division of the Justice Department in 1933, it perversely spent its early years enforcing the industry price-fixing codes of the NIRA and the AAA and representing a hodgepodge of federal agencies and departments in appellate matters.[16]

Those few true antitrust cases it brought often ended in disaster. In the landmark 1934 *Appalachian Coals* decision, the Supreme Court refused to outlaw a joint selling arrangement in the coal industry, despite past precedent that all price-fixing arrangements were per se illegal.[17]

After the Supreme Court declared the NRA unconstitutional in the 1935 *Schechter Poultry* case,[18] Roosevelt showed renewed interest in antitrust enforcement and competition over planning. Clearly some new policy initiatives were necessary. The recession of 1937 was a shock to the nation and a threat to the political health of the New Deal, already suffering from the defeat of the infamous court-packing plan and the proposed reorganization of the executive branch. Arnold attributed this change to Roosevelt's pragmatism in searching for new ways to end the depression regardless of philosophical consistency.[19]

References to the importance of antitrust began to appear in Roosevelt's public pronouncements. Key New Dealers such as Harold Ickes and Robert Jackson gave fiery speeches on the dangers of monopolies. Yet the President followed these initiatives with a message to Congress that included a renewed call for greater cooperation between government and business.[20]

The Antitrust Division did revive somewhat under the leadership of Robert Jackson from 1937 to 1938, bringing important cases in the auto, oil, and aluminum industries. But it simply had too much to do and too few resources. In addition to investigating hundreds of complaints of monopoly and restraint of trade, the Antitrust Division also defended or enforced the orders of administrative agencies including the Interstate Commerce Commission (ICC), Federal Trade Commission (FTC), and Federal Communication Commission (FCC). Even the defense of labor and agricultural regulations were normally referred to the, by now, badly misnamed and undermanned Antitrust Division.[21]

The Washington pundits viewed the Arnold nomination as part of the continuing struggle between the planners and the antimonopoly forces within the administration. In particular, Arnold's nomination to head the Antitrust Division was seen as a loss for Attorney General Homer Cummings, who, although friendly with Arnold, wanted a more conservative successor to Jackson, who was moving on to become the solicitor general. A column in the *Washington Star* described Arnold as the fourth choice in a contest over the direction of antitrust policy.[22]

Arnold's nomination also came at a time when the Senate was feeling buffaloed in a series of key controversial nominations by Roosevelt, including Hugo Black and Stanley Reed to the Supreme Court and Robert Jackson as solicitor general. Most also viewed the nomination as particularly auspicious for Arnold as following in the paths of Jackson and Stanley Reed toward eventual promotion to solicitor general, attorney general, and perhaps to the Supreme Court.

Arnold was attacked in the press as a radical and a professional smart aleck. Various papers weighed in by describing him as a "foe of capitalists," a "left-wing New Dealer" and a "capitalist critic." Most papers pointed out the irony in his selection, but the *Philadelphia Record* more accurately noted that although personally an opponent of Prohibition, Arnold had also produced the driest administration possible in Laramie as mayor. The *Baltimore Sun* wrote, "Now that he is going to be put in charge of this huge joke, it will be interesting to see whether he continues to laugh or whether he suddenly decides to take it seriously."

Arnold was quite uneasy about the upcoming hearings, although Senator Joseph O'Mahoney of Wyoming, a strong supporter and friend of Arnold, was the chair of the Senate subcommittee handling the nomination. Senators King of Utah and Burke of Nebraska, both conservative Democrats, promised to investigate Arnold's background closely because in their view too many men with a socialist taint were already in the administration.

Senator Borah, the great Republican populist of Idaho, was concerned for two reasons. Borah's public positions on the importance of antitrust were in conflict with the more cynical view of antitrust expressed in *Folklore*. Borah also was justifiably concerned about a completely gratuitous personal attack on him by name in *Folklore* for trust-busting crusades that were "entirely futile but enormously picturesque and which paid big dividends in terms of personal prestige."[23] All this produced a second surge in sales for *Folklore* as the press, the senators, their staff, and the public scrambled to see what Arnold had actually said.

Before the hearing, Arnold wrote to his parents:

> I go on before the Senate Judiciary sub-committee tomorrow, who have been taking sentences out of context of my book to throw at me—at least this is the rumor. I am caught between the conservatives who are afraid I am tougher than Jackson and the liberals who think my book is a satire on antitrust laws. The *New York Times* and *New York Sun* have urged that I be thoroughly investigated because I am a sarcastic joker not fit for solemn duties.[24]

Everyone predicted a lively and exciting hearing in the Senate.

On Friday March 11, 1938, in front of a full gallery, the subcommittee approved Arnold's nomination by a 4-0 vote after forty-five minutes of questioning almost entirely by Borah. The rest of the questions came from O'Mahoney who lobbed a few softball questions so that Arnold could affirm his belief in capitalism. When prompted, Arnold duly professed faith in capitalism, support for antitrust, and argued that antitrust was badly enforced and ought to be improved. Arnold claimed, in response to sharper questioning by Borah, that his book was merely a diagnosis and not a prescription for remedy.[25]

Max Lerner later wrote, "One who reads the account of the Arnold-Borah encounter in the committee room cannot but feel that the temper of Arnold's replies to Borah was not quite the temper of the book. There was more restraint in it, less joyfulness, less certitude, less of the sharp quality of the dissecting room."[26] Whether or not Arnold's testimony was entirely consistent with his personal beliefs or his writings, it was persuasive in the end.

When it came time for the subcommittee to vote, Borah on the left and King on the right withheld their votes, confirming Arnold's earlier concerns that he would be attacked from both sides. Borah claimed there were other matters about Arnold he wished to investigate before the matter came before the full Senate.

However, after Arnold's performance in the subcommittee, quick approval by the Judiciary Committee and full Senate was assured. The full Judiciary Committee recommended Arnold for the post on March 14 despite Senator King's statement that Arnold was "not qualified." There was no recorded vote, but three or four committee members were rumored to have opposed the nomination. Unlike the stormy debate and vote over Robert Jackson's nomination, the full Senate confirmed Arnold without a recorded vote on March 16 "amidst confusion preceding recess."[27]

He was sworn in on March 21. At his first press conference, he appeared ill at ease, sitting at Jackson's former desk, with his pipe clenched in teeth and his hands alternately hooked in his vest or folded across his ample stomach. He was said to resemble a slightly paunchy version of the actor Ronald Colman.[28]

Arnold began blandly enough with a prepared statement:

> All I can say at this time is that I intend to pursue a policy of enforcement of the Antitrust Laws which will be both fair and vigorous. I have just arrived in Washington and as yet I have not had the opportunity to acquaint myself with the various complicated matters now pending; therefore, in fairness to my colleagues and to my chief, I must restrict myself to this general statement. The only specific thing I can say now is that I am ready to go to work.[29]

Arnold had a profoundly difficult task ahead of him. Throughout the 1920s, the antitrust laws had been laxly enforced, if at all. Competition law had been all but abandoned during the NRA in favor of industry codes that made price competition an unfair practice to be stamped out by the government and the courts. Even after the formal demise of the NRA in the courts, many industries continued to adhere to informal codes of fair competition (illegal price fixing or cartels in another era) with the acquiescence, or even informal support, of key New Deal officials.[30]

Arnold was aware of the enormity of his task and of his reputation as a smart-alecky opponent of the value of antitrust itself. Arnold always viewed the latter as somewhat undeserved. In his autobiography, he noted that he supported price controls and production quotas in agriculture because competition had failed either to help the farmer or provide adequate food production for the nation. He said he had felt differently about the NRA, since business would bounce back and therefore did not need additional help through restricting production.[31]

In one important way, Arnold was helped immeasurably by the lax enforcement of the prior decade. Because of the lull in enforcement activity in the 1920s, the virtual repeal of antitrust during the NRA, and the continued support from the administration for industry coordination even after the formal end of the NRA, few in the business community felt the need to conceal their anticompetitive activities. There was much low-hanging fruit to be plucked by the Antitrust Division, but Arnold needed a way to ensure that the president and the public supported the renewed enforcement of the antitrust laws and that the remaining foes of antitrust within the New Deal were shunted to the sidelines of the debate and prevented from active interference.

Not surprisingly, Arnold saw his task in symbolic and institutional terms and not simply as the prosecution of individual antitrust cases. He wrote,

> I believed that my principal function was to convince American businessmen that the Sherman Act represented something more than a pious platitude; second, that its enforcement was an important economic policy.[32]

During this brief interlude, which historian Alan Brinkley has referred to as the "Anti-Monopoly Moment," Arnold seized on the image of antitrust as the nonpartisan traffic cop, the "cop on the beat," or the "referee" of the competitive process as the way to create a viable program of antitrust enforcement with broad public support.[33] This was a deliberate choice by Arnold, who had written so eloquently about the symbolism of such concepts as "law enforcement" and the distinction in the public mind between courts and bureaucracies as decision-makers.[34] As he explained in a letter to an acquaintance,

> My belief is that the only instrument which has a chance to preserve competition in America is antitrust enforcement through the courts. Tra-

ditionally we accept the courts as an institution which cannot be criticized without public protest in a way that was impossible for an administrative tribunal to function.[35]

Arnold went out of his way to distinguish antitrust enforcement from either "regulation" or the kind of emergency legislation experimented with in the NRA. Arnold praised the federal courts and a case-by-case method as the proper way to make antitrust policy, as opposed to the creation of new agencies or bureaucracies. He elevated public, rather than private, enforcement of the Sherman Act as the critical policy tool. He conceptualized both cartels and monopolies as "bottlenecks" on production and distribution that kept the industrial production of America from reaching the consumer and continued the now seemingly endless depression through artificial and private arrangements.[36] He wrote: "The four horsemen—fixed prices, low turnover, restricted production, and monopoly control—rode through our economy from factory to farm."[37]

He advocated that the proper mission of the Antitrust Division was that of a prosecutor using the courts, rather than agencies, to make law. The Antitrust Division would not be hostile to large business, only the abuse of power, and would operate as an expert body largely independent of politics. As a means of showing he was neither opposed to size alone nor anti-business per se, he cleverly praised Henry Ford as an innovative businessman beset by combinations of competitors, and later suppliers, intent on blocking Ford from producing cheaper and higher quality automobiles for consumers. He argued that vigorous antitrust enforcement was even good for a balanced budget, returning far more in fines than it cost to run the entire Antitrust Division.[38]

Always conscious of symbols, Arnold even bought himself a 1927 square-topped coupe of "ancient vintage" with high wooden spoked wheels for $45 at a time when he was making $9000. When the rear end of that car dropped off in 1942, he sold it for $5 and replaced it with an equally ancient 1930 LaSalle.[39]

Arnold discontinued the former occasional practice of using the threat of criminal prosecution solely to leverage defendants into negotiating a civil consent decree to avoid a trial and accept meaningless symbolic equitable relief. Consent decrees would be limited to those situations where defendants proposed industry-wide relief that fully restored competition beyond what could be achieved through a successful prosecution or civil action by the government and where the defendants permitted meaningful monitoring by the government, including opening their books and records to inspection.

Arnold did leave open the door to the exceptional circumstance where a consent decree was necessary to implement some innovative business arrangements without fear of government challenge, a situation he utilized on a number of occasions. Arnold's own use of consent decrees was attacked as making him the autocratic one-man regulator of the American economy.[40]

He also instituted a policy by which businesses interested in ascertaining the legality of future action could seek the opinion of the Antitrust Division as to its enforcement intentions toward the proposed conduct. In return, businesses could count on not being charged criminally, even if the government ultimately opposed the notified conduct.[41]

Arnold believed that the only thing that would make businessmen behave was the threat of indictment. When he brought a case, he would indict the individual defendants and have them fingerprinted like ordinary criminals. He shrewdly observed how even the mere bringing of an indictment usually brought prices down and an end to the alleged anticompetitive practices harming the public.[42]

Arnold was relentless in promoting himself, his vision for antitrust, the work of the Antitrust Division, and the need for ever greater resources, staffing, and budgets. He lobbied for competition policy and resources with Capitol Hill and the executive branch. He cultivated the press assiduously, spoke directly to the public, and continued to produce an astonishing stream of books, articles, and speeches, all while supervising and inspiring the Antitrust Division to new heights of activity. Significantly, one of Arnold's earliest initiatives came on April 16, 1938, when he began a new policy of extensive publicity to accompany each prosecution in order to educate the public and to provide guidance to the business community by setting forth the practices being challenged and why the government believed there was an antitrust violation.[43]

Arnold repeatedly used symbols and imagery to justify the mission of the Antitrust Division to Congress. He was spectacularly successful, vastly increasing the size and budget of the Antitrust Division. As Senator McCarran noted, on one occasion Arnold both defeated an attempt to cut his budget and emerged with an increase of $750,000: "He is the best salesman I ever listened to in all my life. He can come to the United States Senate to sell a red-hot stove and make you think it is a refrigerator." By the end of his tenure, commentators ranked Arnold and J. Edgar Hoover as both the most popular New Deal figures and its biggest prima donnas.[44]

From the moment Arnold entered office, he lobbied in speeches, broadcasts, articles, and books to increase the size and budget of the Antitrust Division, often citing the Securities Exchange Commission (SEC), which had over twelve hundred personnel and the Civil Aeronautics Board with a staff of over twenty-eight hundred. While he never achieved those lofty targets, he did more than anyone would have expected. From 1933 until Arnold left the Justice Department in 1943, the number of Antitrust Division employees grew from eighteen to nearly five hundred, and the budget more than quadrupled. The peak was reached in 1942 with a budget of $2,325,000 and a total staff of 583 persons. New cases jumped from eleven in 1938 to ninety-two in 1940, and investigations jumped from fifty-nine to 215 in the same period. By February, 1941, the Antitrust Division had ninety-three total criminal and civil cases pending involving 2909 defendants with twenty-four additional grand juries authorized or in progress.[45] Regional offices were established throughout the country to uncover, investigate, and prosecute antitrust violations with an eye and ear to what was going on both locally and nationally.

Arnold delegated to his chief deputy, Wendell Berge, the recruiting of a top staff and training them to create an effective organization with high prestige in the outside legal world and high morale inside the division.[46] Such luminaries as future Supreme Court Justice Tom Clark and future Attorney General and University of Chicago President Edward Levi served in the division under Arnold. With the help of a growing number of well-credentialed and ambitious young men, Arnold embarked on the most extensive program of civil and criminal enforcement in the history of antitrust. During his tenure as head of the Antitrust Division, Arnold brought nearly as many cases, including prosecutions against entire industries, as in the fifty prior years of federal antitrust law. He also created the first generation of true antitrust specialists the country had ever known, who would keep the Arnold flame for antitrust alive across the country for generations to come.

April 1938 brought the planning for Roosevelt's antimonopoly message to Congress. Arnold assisted in drafting the message along with Homer Cummings, Robert Jackson, Donald Richberg, the head of the NRA, and

Ben Cohen, the author of the Public Utility Holding Company Act. It was a stark illustration of the current balance of power between the planners and the advocates of competition, and it was apparent to all that Roosevelt finally intended to make a real attack on the problem of monopoly. Predictably, only Richberg dissented from the plan.

The message itself was symbolically important but rather mild in actual content. The president decried the "concentration of economic power" in the country and deplored the "concealed cartel system" and "the disappearance of price competition." The president thundered, "The liberty of a democracy is not safe if the people tolerate the growth of private power to a point where it becomes stronger than their democratic state itself."[47]

The recommendations were hardly stirring, however. Roosevelt asked for $200,000 in additional funds to expand the Antitrust Division, called for an investigation of the monopoly problem with a budget of $500,000, and proposed legislation to control bank holding companies (almost certainly the brainchild of Ben Cohen). No new specific antitrust legislation or initiative beyond the antimonopoly inquiry was sought.

Even this ambivalent message was the product of in-fighting between the Jackson and Richberg wings of the administration, each of which presented separate drafts to Roosevelt. Richberg's original draft revived the idea of self-regulation and industrial self-government as in the NRA. This was rejected by Roosevelt despite support from Cummings. Jackson then became the primary drafter of the final version sent to Capitol Hill.[48] Overall it was a slight victory for trustbusters in terms of specific proposals but a radical victory for Arnold and the other antitrusters in terms of the attitude toward the kind of wholesale cartelization previously endorsed by the NRA. To have the president talking about the "concentration of private power without equal in history" was sweet music to Arnold indeed.

The idea for the Temporary National Economic Committee (TNEC) had been floating around the Roosevelt administration since 1935.[49] Since then, it had been part of the continuing fight between the trustbusters, the planners, and others in the New Deal, who saw the TNEC as the vehicle to promote a variety of diverse ideas including new antitrust legislation, greater antitrust enforcement, concern over administered pricing, fear about underconsumption, attempts at greater economic regulation, and the national licensing of corporations.[50] Even Roosevelt was not set on the need for a TNEC until just weeks before his antimonopoly message, as he continued to dither between endorsing a renewed version of the NRA, promoting greater antitrust enforcement, or supporting federal incorporation of interstate businesses.[51]

The fight over the purpose and form of the TNEC continued on Capitol Hill. Senator O'Mahoney sponsored the Congressional resolution for the TNEC. Borah remained aloof to the idea of a committee, preferring to focus on the need for specific new antitrust legislation.[52]

The initial proposal for the committee called for two members of the Senate, two from the House, plus representatives of the attorney general, the Federal Trade Commission, and the Securities and Exchange Commission. The members would study the causes and effects of concentration on competition; pricing policies and effect on general level of trade and employment; and the effect of existing tax, patent, and other government policies on competition, price levels, employment, and consumption. A budget of $500,000 was to be appropriated for the work of the TNEC.

On June 7 a revised resolution passed the Judiciary Committee, calling for an expanded committee of six representatives of the Congress, plus representatives from the Commerce Department, Labor, the Treasury, Justice, the SEC, and FTC. The committee would have a direct budget of $100,000 and could hand out $400,000 to the agencies for staff who would do the heavy lifting for the committee. An additional $600,000 appropriation was eventually forthcoming.

Senator O'Mahoney and Arnold's former critics, Senators King and Borah, were named to the TNEC, with O'Mahoney as the chair. No prominent New Deal senators were included. The House nominees were Hatton W. Summers, a veteran Texas Democrat, B. Carroll Reece, an independent-minded Republican from Tennessee, and Edward C. Eicher, a liberal New Deal Democrat from Iowa. O'Mahoney became the driving force behind the TNEC, as King lost reelection and Borah died. The other Congressional appointees lacked influence, and frequent changes in the rest of the TNEC membership left O'Mahoney as virtually the sole enthusiastic member present from start to finish.[53]

The Commerce Department, as the voice of the business community, was widely viewed as sabotaging the mission of the TNEC. However, the other appointees were all tried and true New Dealers, including William Douglas from the SEC and Herman Oliphant, the general counsel of Treasury, who was a former antitrust scholar at Columbia Law School.[54]

The executive secretary of the TNEC was Leon Henderson, an economic adviser in the Commerce Department, who paradoxically supported both greater antitrust enforcement and greater governmental planning of the economy. The infighting over the mission and scope of the TNEC mirrored in many ways the fight over economic policy more generally in the New Deal.[55]

The TNEC met for the first time on July 1, 1938, and was immediately embroiled in battles over the scope of subpoenas, the site of its hearings, and which industries to study in what order. Finally it was agreed that it would work in teams of one legislator and one agency official with hearings to begin in September, later postponed until after the November elections. The investigation eventually meandered through the insurance, banking, steel, oil, liquor, investment banking, and automobile industries, while also examining in the process the impact of cartels, state fair-trade laws, patents, and various competitive practices.[56]

Arnold was assigned to head the inquiry into patents. To facilitate the hearings, Arnold agreed on behalf of the Justice Department that the TNEC's investigation would not be used to gather evidence for Antitrust Division prosecutions.[57]

Eventually the TNEC produced thirty-seven volumes of testimony and forty-three monographs. In all there were 20,000 pages of testimony, 552 business witnesses, and over 230,000 copies of the hearings and monographs sold by the Government Printing Office (GPO). The TNEC and the various agencies working with it spent virtually the entire budget allotted to them, returning a paltry $8000 out of more than a million, to the Treasury.[58]

The TNEC issued its final report on March 31, 1941. The report recommended repeal of the Miller-Tydings Act, which authorized state fair-trade laws, prohibiting horizontal mergers in excess of $5 million unless approved by the FTC, prohibiting basing point pricing, raising penalties for criminal antitrust violations to $50,000, creating federal regulation of trade associations, requiring mandatory licensing of patents at fair prices, and the national chartering of corporations.[59]

The TNEC produced detailed, thoughtful studies of the state of competition in various industries and the state of antitrust more generally, and made reasonable recommendations, but no new antitrust legislation emerged directly from the effort. Under Senator O'Mahoney's influence, the TNEC laid out the record in copious detail about the state of competition but left the drawing of conclusions to others. No one ever really did, and Arnold viewed the final work product of the TNEC with the same degree of enthusiasm that he viewed the earlier empirical work of the legal realists—as ignored and unread. After participating halfheartedly in the work of the TNEC at the beginning, Arnold soon left the work to his subordinates and concentrated his efforts on the nationwide enforcement of the antitrust laws.[60]

A few developments came out of the TNEC that made the exercise something more than the gigantic waste of time portrayed by Arnold. It was essentially "an antimonopoly document" with a nod toward Chairman O'Mahoney's long-standing interest in the national chartering of corporations.[61]

Although the final report of the TNEC was mild stuff calling for no dramatic changes in antitrust, it did trigger certain concrete results, particularly in the patent area. The hearings included a vivid demonstration of how the Hartford-Empire Company had monopolized the glass container market through the acquisition and misuse of patent rights and collusion with the competitors who held patent rights for related technologies. The Antitrust Division eventually charged Hartford-Empire in a separate monopolization case and ultimately required the company to license the vast array of patents it had accumulated and forego damages from past infringements.[62] The revelations also prompted Congress to amend the patent laws consistent with some of the TNEC's recommendations. Moreover the TNEC was the key impetus leading to the strengthening of the merger provisions of the Clayton Act in 1950 and a source of the eventual adoption of mandatory pre-merger notification.[63]

In addition, the TNEC stabilized antitrust policy and made it a fundamental part of the government's law enforcement and economic regulation policies. The decade that followed the TNEC produced a high point in both the reach of antitrust doctrine and antitrust enforcement, neither of which would have been possible without the dual efforts of Arnold as head of the Antitrust Division and the buttressing effect of the TNEC as state of the art economic research on the actual condition of the American economy.

Arnold's first large case involved the automobile industry. The big-three car companies had long coerced dealers to finance customer purchases through finance companies owned by the manufacturers and prohibited the use of independent finance companies as much as possible. The Antitrust Division had already investigated and challenged the practice in

Milwaukee, Wisconsin, but suffered a serious setback when the supervising judge threw out the case, offended that the Justice Department appeared to have used the threat of criminal indictment to seek a civil settlement.

Arnold was undeterred and sought a friendlier venue for round two of the litigation. He visited South Bend, Indiana, on a speaking trip and used the occasion to prepare to summon a new grand jury to investigate the same auto finance issues. The coercion of dealers and discrimination against independent finance companies was again the focus of the investigation. The grand jury investigation was expected to last six weeks, but indictments were issued in five days. Eighty-six firms and individuals were indicted including the biggest names in industry. Attorney General Cummings announced the indictments but also announced that he was willing to listen to voluntary offers for consent decrees.[64]

In the end, the Antitrust Division worked out a civil consent decree with Ford and Chrysler and obtained a conviction against General Motors. The settlement was a highly regulatory decree that imposed complex obligations on the car companies and a registration system on the entire automobile finance industry in order to assure fair and equal treatment by the manufacturers. It was as if the playbook for the Antitrust Division had come from Arnold's own writings. It was an ad hoc regulatory solution to address a pressing societal need dressed up in law enforcement terms in order to satisfy the folklore of the times.

Other early cases brought by Arnold were designed to appeal to consumer interests and to show how cartels and monopolies, in Arnold's terms "bottlenecks," were causing higher prices and artificial shortages. In Arnold's words, "To catch their imaginations you must talk in terms of concrete items in the family budget."[65]

In July 1938, Arnold brought a civil suit against the motion picture industry seeking to force the major studios to divest their ownership of movie theaters and change their licensing practices to independent exhibitors.[66] The suit made headlines both because Arnold announced that he would personally lead the case and because the complaint named all eight major studios and over 130 individuals, including the president's son James Roosevelt, and Charlie Chaplin, Douglas Fairbanks, Mary Pickford, and other prominent Hollywood celebrities who served on the boards of the studios.

In November 1938, the division brought indictments against the dairy industry, which Arnold claimed had raised the price of milk more than 40 percent. The case against the milk industry in Chicago supposedly produced $10,000,000 in consumer savings.[67]

Arnold claimed his antitrust campaign against the housing and construction industries saved consumers over $300,000,000. An internal Antitrust Division memo estimated that the "minimum" consumer savings from antitrust "pressure" in the tire, newsprint, steel ingot, potash, and sulphur industries at over $266,000,000. Even a case against local Washington, D.C., service stations produced estimated savings of $2,000,000.[68]

Each new case or grand jury investigation brought nationwide press coverage, often on the front page of the city where the case or investigation was brought. Arnold would tell anyone who would listen that this incredible flurry of activity was no crusade but simply "law enforcement."[69]

Almost simultaneously with this flurry of activity, trial resumed in the Alcoa monopolization case. The stakes were high. Alcoa was the most important case in a generation, rivaling those against Standard Oil and U.S. Steel in the past and the cases against AT&T and Microsoft in the far distant future. Andrew Mellon, the founder of Alcoa and former secretary of the Treasury throughout the Republican administrations of the 1920s, had been named as a defendant but died before trial began.

The case resumed on June 1, 1938, with Arnold at the counsel table. Alcoa was represented by Charles Evan Hughes Jr., the son of the former presidential candidate and Supreme Court justice.

The Antitrust Division promised to prove that Alcoa had "100 percent monopoly in virgin aluminum and bauxite industry throughout the Western Hemisphere" and controlled output throughout the "rest of world" through subsidiaries, affiliates, and a cartel with foreign producers. Alcoa originally had a lawful monopoly on the production of aluminum from bauxite ore through various patents that expired in the early part of the twentieth century. An earlier antitrust suit by the United States in 1912 had eliminated certain restrictive covenants and cartel arrangements with foreign producers, which had further buttressed Alcoa's monopoly of the American aluminum market. Nevertheless, Alcoa still sold more than 90 percent of the virgin aluminum ingot in the United States, although a growing amount of recycled ingot was also entering the market. Imports remained next to nothing due to Alcoa's continuing participation in international cartel arrangements. New domestic competition was almost impossible given Alcoa's aggressive expansion and its lock on sources of hydroelectric power, the single most important input for aluminum production after bauxite ore itself.

The trial lasted until August 14, 1940, after more than 40,000 pages of testimony had been taken and 10,000 pages of exhibits were entered into evidence. The *New Yorker* magazine claimed it was the longest trial in the history of the world and that the trial record was three times heavier than the *Encyclopedia Britannica* and thirty times longer than *Gone with the Wind*.[70]

The judge immediately issued a draft oral opinion dismissing all charges, which itself took nine days to deliver. When Arnold asked for permission to appeal before the judge finalized his opinion in writing, the exhausted district court judge replied, "If there is any legal way for me to get rid of this case, I'll do it so quick it'll make your head swim." Alas for the trial judge, the final judgment dismissing the case did not appear until July 23, 1942.[71]

The government appealed directly to the Supreme Court, but on June 12, 1944, the Supreme Court referred the case to the Second Circuit because it lacked a quorum of six justices to hear the case. The Court was down to only eight members because Roosevelt had not yet filled the seat formerly held by Justice Byrnes. Justices Jackson, Reed, and Murphy presumably were disqualified for their earlier work on the case for the Roosevelt Justice Department, with Chief Justice Stone similarly being disqualified because of his earlier involvement in prosecuting Alcoa while attorney general under Coolidge. Even if Roosevelt had filled the vacancy, there may not have been a quorum for this critical case given the president's penchant for choosing Justice Department and other New Deal insiders.

It was not until March 12, 1945, as Arnold was near the end of his own service as a federal appellate judge, that the Second Circuit upheld the government's case and created landmark precedent on what constitutes a monopoly: when a monopolist's actions in the market violate the antitrust law and when anticompetitive conduct outside the United States constitutes a violation of the Sherman Act.[72] Even then, the Court deferred the issue of remedy until after World War II.

All the while, Arnold and his staff worked at a furious pace and seemingly on dozens of matters at once. Far from shying away from investigating or attacking the sacred cows of the economy, Arnold seemed to delight in tormenting them. On August 1, 1938, Arnold announced a grand jury investigation of the American Medical Association's (AMA) opposition to group health plans. He focused on the District of Columbia,[73] where federal employees had formed the Group Health Association, Inc. (GHA) to provide a prepaid medical plan akin to a modern health maintenance organization (HMO). GHA had retained its own physicians who agreed to provide the members virtually complete medical care. The AMA, the D.C. Medical Society, and its officers and directors reacted by threatening to expel any member physicians who provided services to GHA or consulted with any GHA physicians, and further denied hospital privileges to any GHA physicians.

Arnold tied the medical industry's restrictions to the high cost of medical care, the failure to provide adequate medical care to lower income families, and even to preventable infant mortality.[74] Although commonplace today,[75] Arnold appears to have broken new ground in the AMA case by using FBI agents to assist in gathering evidence against the AMA.

The AMA case began a war of words. Arnold was attacked for everything from promoting socialized medicine to perverting the antitrust laws by attacking a voluntary professional association. Some critics wondered sarcastically if bar associations were next.[76] Arnold fired back by releasing a letter to counsel for the D.C. Medical Society expressing the expectation that his client would cease the "coercion of qualified people in the practice of their profession" and laying out his case in a nationwide radio broadcast on August 19.

Despite the controversy, Roosevelt personally was aware of and supported the AMA investigation, and Attorney General Cummings publicly backed Arnold as well.[77] Eugene Gressley recounts a marvelous scene in his collection of Arnold's letters:

> Cummings commented: "Thurman, this is the Goddamnedest thing I ever heard. You propose to indict a hospital, a local medical association, and all those doctors. Well, these doctors are leading citizens of their communities, and I play golf with some of them; you know if you do this there's going to be a lot of trouble and somebody's going to catch hell. Now who is it?" Thurman replied, "Well, you will!" Cummings just laughed and waved Thurman out, "All right, go ahead."[78]

It appeared at first that the case would not even make it to trial. The district court threw out the indictments on the grounds that the practice of medicine was not "trade" and thus not covered by the antitrust laws, only to be reversed on appeal.[79]

At trial, the defendants were convicted and fined $2500 for the AMA and $1500 for the D.C. Medical Society. The case ended in January 1943 with a total victory in the Supreme Court in a case that Arnold argued personally.[80] By a 6-0 vote the Court upheld the application of the antitrust laws against both the AMA and the D.C. Medical Society and held that they had engaged in an illegal boycott against the clinic.

No industry was safe if it demonstrated either signs of price-fixing or monopolization. Arnold obtained a landmark ruling that the insurance industry was engaged in interstate commerce, rendering it subject to the federal antitrust laws. This ruling was promptly overturned by statute in one of the few Congressional rebukes to Arnold's enforcement regime.[81] Other cases were brought or concluded against the retail, tire, fertilizer, tobacco, shoe, construction, dairy, and various agricultural industries. Nor did antitrust deal only with the blockbuster cases; Arnold brought indictments against local firms including the wooden ice-cream stick industry in New York. By the end of fiscal 1939, there were 1375 complaints pending in 213 cases involving forty industries with 185 continuing investigations.[82]

Perhaps no case was more important than the case against the oil industry. The oil industry had been plagued for years with falling prices and the problem of so-called hot oil produced in violation of state quota laws and dumped on the market, driving down the price, often below the cost of production. To counter falling oil prices, the major companies devised a plan where they would buy up excess oil at prevailing market prices. Each major oil company tracked the production of one or more of the smaller independent refiners and agreed to buy the oil of its "dancing partners" as it came on the market. Officials in the Roosevelt administration were aware of the plan and had given their unofficial acquiescence, if not outright approval, both during and after the NRA.

No one, of course, had sought or obtained the approval of the Antitrust Division, nor would it have been forthcoming. From the perspective of the Antitrust Division, it was plain and simple price-fixing. Nor were the nods and winks of the planning wing of the administration a defense. Although the case only concerned post-NRA activity, Arnold contended that the practices had been in effect since 1931, before the NRA began operation, were never covered by any NRA code, and continued after the NRA had been declared unconstitutional.[83] The indictment charged twenty-seven companies and fifty-six of their officers with criminal violation of Section One of the Sherman Act.

The case had a long and tortured history. The indictments had originally been brought in Madison, Wisconsin, in December 1936 while Jackson still headed the Antitrust Division. Following a number of guilty and nolo contendere pleas, twenty-six companies and forty-six individuals went to trial. The sheer scope of the case required over one hundred lawyers for the defendants, who leased an entire hotel for the trial.[84]

Just before jury deliberations, the judge dismissed the case against ten companies and sixteen individuals. The rest were found guilty by the jury. The judge granted new trials to some of the defendants and outright dismissals to others, leaving twelve corporations and five individuals guilty as charged. The corporations were fined $5000, and the individuals fined $1000. On appeal, all defendants were granted new trials on the grounds that the informal arrangement was not per se illegal, the trial judge had improperly excluded much of the defendants' proffered evidence, and the judge furthermore had given the jury improper instructions as to the law.[85]

To underscore the importance of the case, Arnold argued the appeal himself in the Supreme Court against William "Wild Bill" Donovan, later to become the head of the Office of Strategic Services (OSS) during World War II. Arnold told the justices that the agreement among the oil companies was "an attempt to set up the NRA again without control." According to press reports, Arnold got carried away and shouted that similar practices were so prevalent in the economy that "this case represents the most dangerous threat to the enforcement of the antitrust laws ever seriously presented to this court."[86]

Arnold again prevailed in the Supreme Court. On May 6, 1940, the Supreme Court affirmed the convictions of all defendants in a 5-2 decision written by William Douglas, Arnold's old friend from Yale.[87] Douglas had been on the Court barely one year, and the oil case was his first antitrust opinion. Douglas's opinion ran for nearly one hundred printed pages and did more than just vindicate the government's prosecution.

It established the key principles of modern antitrust law that remain intact today. First, it held that price-fixing was illegal per se regardless of why the defendants had conspired, whether the prices fixed were reasonable, or whether the defendants had raised, lowered, or merely stabilized prices. Moreover, avoiding ruinous competition was not a defense.[88]

Douglas wrote in a thundering style that would be typical of his years on the Court,

> Under the Sherman Act a combination formed for the purpose and with the effect of raising, depressing, fixing, pegging, or stabilizing the price of a commodity in interstate or foreign commerce is illegal per se. Where the machinery for price-fixing is an agreement on the prices to be charged or paid for the commodity in the interstate or foreign channels of trade, the power to fix prices exists if a combination has control of a substantial part of the commerce of that commodity.[89]

Then, in the most famous footnote in the history of antitrust, Douglas essentially held that, since the Sherman Act prohibited "conspiracies" in restraint of trade, the violation was complete with the agreement to accomplish the illegal objective even if the defendants lacked the power to carry out the plan or if the plan produced no actual effects in the markets.[90]

Although technically Douglas distinguished, rather than overruled, the earlier *Appalachian Coals* case, his rhetoric destroyed whatever was left in that earlier NRA-tinged decision, which had appeared to open the door to some price-fixing under some circumstances. Had *Appalachian Coals* remained the law of the land, criminal antitrust prosecution would have been virtually impossible. Each defendant would be able to raise any number of reasons why it might agree with competitors as to price or production, making proof beyond a reasonable doubt an impossible burden for the government.

The Court then rejected the defense that government knowledge, or even acquiescence, in the price stabilization scheme was a defense. According to Douglas, only Congress, not executive branch officials, could confer immunity from the antitrust laws.[91] Thus, *Socony-Vacuum* was also the final death knell for the planning wing of the New Deal and whatever informal versions of the NRA that existed after the *Schechter Poultry* ruling.

The one type of investigation that cut across industry lines was Arnold's crusade against the misuse of patents. Arnold railed every chance he could against the misuse of patents as a tool of price-fixing, division of markets among competitors, and monopolization. In a speech before the

American Business Congress broadcast nationwide over the Mutual Radio Network, Arnold said, "Since 1926 the most effective instrument of monopoly control and restrictions on production has been the abuse of the patent privilege." In a letter to one of Roosevelt's top aides he argued, "The real vice of the patent system does not lie in the law itself but in the various schemes which have perverted it into an instrument for monopoly control of corporations."[92]

He instituted numerous investigations and cases alleging that competitors had used patent and other intellectual property licenses as a disguise for traditional price-fixing and cartel arrangements in international markets.[93] He even vividly publicized how the control of a patent for a lowly screw fastener became a vital bottleneck, slowing down aircraft production and the war effort.[94]

As mentioned, Arnold brought a landmark case against the Hartford-Empire Company for monopolizing the glass container industry through its accumulation of patents and its licensing practice. He continued the earlier *Ethyl Gasoline* case and personally argued it in the Supreme Court, winning a ruling that patents could not be used to set prices for resale or to impose restrictions on matters outside the scope of the patent. Arnold also argued the *Univis Lens* case in the Supreme Court, in which the Court condemned the use of patent licenses as a device to control resale prices of the licensee to the public.[95]

Throughout this burst of activity, Arnold kept up a torrent of speaking engagements and writing projects. He wrote articles for such diverse publications as the *Yale Law Journal, American Bar Association Journal,* various state bar journals, *New York Times Magazine, Common Sense, Saturday Evening Post, American Mercury, Atlantic, Nation's Agriculture, New Republic,* and *Reader's Digest.*[96] Arnold continued to court the press, particularly Drew Pearson, whose daughter Elena eventually married Arnold's son George in 1946. Arnold appears to have never turned down an interview or an opportunity for coverage.

The press coverage of Thurman Arnold culminated in the August 1939 cover story in the *Saturday Evening Post* called "Trustbuster—The Folklore of Thurman Arnold."[97] The story was written by Joseph Alsop and Robert Kintner, who had covered Arnold extensively for their newspaper column "The Capital Parade." Arnold was no longer just a former law professor known to the relatively small circle of Washington insiders and sophisticated readers who bought nonfiction works such as *Folklore*. He was now an unlikely cover boy on a mainstream magazine that sold over three million issues coast-to-coast each week.

According to Alsop and Kintner, Arnold "looks like a small town store clerk and talks like a native Rabelais," and was the only New Dealer who was also a member of the Elks. The article introduced the nation to what Arnold's friends and associates already knew, that Arnold was so fast a thinker and talker, and so disheveled, that he often was mistaken for a madman precisely when formulating his most innovative legal strategies.

The article recounted Arnold's family history and his cross-country odyssey that began in Laramie, and it included numerous glossy photos of Arnold at home with his family and driving his 1927 Stearns Knight. Robert Jackson described Arnold as "a cross between Voltaire and a cowboy, with the cowboy predominating."

Alsop and Kintner then turned serious as to why Arnold was so intent on enforcing the very set of laws he had once derided as jokes. They reported that Arnold now believed that only vigorous antitrust enforcement could solve the dilemma of the Great Depression of want in the midst of plenty. They quoted Arnold more generally as saying, "Political democracy will not work unless it is founded on industrial democracy." They closed with Arnold opining that antitrust represented the "red lights of business traffic, and why shouldn't we seek criminal indictments if traffic violations are criminal offenses?"[98] Thus on August 12, 1939, was born the public face of Thurman Arnold, a role he would embrace and play for the rest of his life.

However, not all the press coverage was nearly so glowing. At different times, Arnold was denounced as a "Hitler" and a "dictator" in both editorials and in cartoons. *Collier's* magazine even attacked him as being against clean restrooms in gas stations as an alleged unfair method of competition.[99]

Ironically, the *Saturday Evening Post* profile came at the absolute low point of Arnold's tenure in the Antitrust Division. Earlier in 1939, Arnold had suffered humiliating defeats as trial courts dismissed indictments against the milk industry in Chicago and the AMA in the District of Columbia, and the Seventh Circuit in Chicago had reversed all the convictions in the oil case. Although each of these decisions would later be reversed by higher courts, most of the press viewed Arnold as washed up. They predicted he would be fired outright or would resign and return to

Yale in order to save face. Arnold persevered and, if anything, dug in his heels and developed his next great antitrust campaign against the building and construction industries. He vowed to stay until at least the spring of 1940, and may have in the process ultimately jeopardized his increasingly shaky series of leaves from Yale.

It was at this time that rumors of Arnold returning to Yale as dean of the law school began to surface. Following the appointment of Charles Clark to the Second Circuit, Arnold was briefly the candidate of the remaining hard-core realists to replace Clark as dean at the law school. However, the influence of the realists was waning both in numbers and prestige, and Arnold had burned too many bridges with the more conservative wing of the Yale faculty. At his strongest, Arnold only placed fifth in an informal faculty ballot. Eventually even his most ardent backers realized that Arnold could not rally the full support of the faculty and the Yale Corporation, the governing body of the university, and moved on to other less controversial candidates. Arnold knew this and thought there was little chance he would be chosen despite press accounts to the contrary.[100]

Shortly thereafter, Arnold's full-time affiliation with Yale came to an abrupt end. In 1938, the Yale Corporation had adopted a policy of limiting leaves to one year to protect its depleted faculty from further raiding by the New Deal. Despite pleas from Arnold and others, there would be no exception in his case. When Arnold made clear that he could not return for the fall 1939 term, Yale announced publicly that since he had not returned, his faculty appointment was over. Arnold learned of the decision from the press while visiting the new San Francisco field office of the Antitrust Division. While he put on a casual air at the time, Arnold was particularly upset both with the finality of the decision and the manner of its sending. He also faced the practical worries of no longer having life tenure at Yale to which he could return when his government service came to its inevitable end. Although Arnold eventually returned to Yale as a visiting professor in 1947 and to the law school many times for moot courts and law journal banquets, the end of his faculty status rankled him for the rest of his life.[101]

In 1940, the fiftieth anniversary of the Sherman Act, Arnold published *The Bottlenecks of Business*.[102] *Bottlenecks* did not even pretend to be a scholarly endeavor in the tradition of *Symbols of Government* or *Folklore of Capitalism*. It was an unabashed defense of the Arnold antitrust enforcement program. According to Arnold, *Bottlenecks* "irrefutably proved that in enforcing the antitrust laws there could be found the complete solution of all of the ills of the Great Depression."[103] If his previous books had a certain looseness in style, *Bottlenecks* simply rambled from start to finish. It best resembled a scrapbook, reprinting long quotes from books, internal Antitrust Division memoranda, newspaper columns and editorials, limericks, and cartoons both praising and denouncing Arnold's various efforts at the Antitrust Division.

Like all Arnold writings, it was nonetheless captivating. *Bottlenecks* made a direct play for public opinion in support of the cases and policies Arnold has been promoting. Arnold drew on his early work to characterize price-fixing and monopolization as a hidden tax on consumers that directly affected their standard of living. Arnold went further and claimed that antitrust could preserve democracy by preventing the private seizure of power in the marketplace.[104] Arnold linked the cartelization of the German economy and the rise of Hitler both to attack the remaining "economic planners" as incompatible with either free markets or political democracy and to inoculate, as best he could, antitrust enforcement against the demands of the coming war effort.

Like his earlier books, *Bottlenecks* was widely reviewed, praised by Arnold's friends and sympathizers, and criticized, often virulently, by his detractors. The combination of cases, writings, and press coverage led *Reader's Digest* in 1941 to call Arnold one of the ten most powerful men in Washington.[105]

The controversial suit against the Associated Press was filed in August 1942, shortly after Marshall Field tried to get AP service for the new *Chicago Sun* paper and was blocked by his rival Colonel Robert McCormick, the publisher of the *Tribune*.[106] Arnold had been aware for some time of the AP's restrictive bylaws that prevented AP members from sharing news with nonmembers and also gave current AP members a veto over AP membership for new entrants in their market. Earlier in 1940, he had unsuccessfully tried to get Eleanor "Cissy" Patterson, a family friend and publisher of the *Washington Times-Herald* and cousin of Colonel McCormick of the *Chicago Tribune,* to file a complaint when her paper had been blocked from AP membership by her competitor, the *Washington Post*. For family or personal reasons, she had refused to cooperate.

When Arnold later prosecuted her cousin and the rest of the industry, Patterson bitterly denounced Arnold and the case as an attack on freedom of the press.[107] At the height of the case, Colonel McCormick even called Arnold "an idiot in a powder mill," an epithet that Arnold treasured for the rest of his career.[108] Eventually, a majority of the Supreme Court saw the matter Arnold's way and required the restructuring of the AP bylaws to prevent newspapers from vetoing new AP members in their territories. The opinion by Justice Black stands as one of the few to link the goals of free competition under the antitrust laws to the free expression of ideas under the First Amendment.[109]

The main blemish on Arnold's record was his quixotic pursuit of a series of antitrust cases against labor unions. Part of Arnold's plan was to attack restraints involving entire industries affecting bottom-line consumer interests in their entirety, where attacking any single aspect would likely not remove the bottlenecks. In housing and construction, this meant attacking a web of interlocking restraints involving manufacturers, contractors, and labor unions that artificially inflated the cost of housing at a time when the national economy had not yet recovered from the crash of 1929.

Arnold conceived of the campaign against this deep-seated set of restraints on competition in manufacturing, distribution, and labor as an even-handed attack on misused economic power. Arnold wrote:

> Whenever a small group of individuals uncurbed by legal authority is permitted to dominate any important part of the production or distribution of the necessities of life, these results will inevitably follow:
>
> They seek to consolidate their power by destroying existing independent enterprise.
>
> They prevent new enterprise from entering the field.
>
> They restrict production and raise prices.
>
> They stop the introduction of more efficient methods of production in order to maintain obsolete ways in which they have a vested interest.
>
> They set up an arbitrary and despotic control over the industry and exploit members of their own group.
>
> They enter into politics, using money and economic coercion to maintain themselves in power.[110]

Although by no means antilabor, Arnold had a blind spot regarding the symbolism of attacking labor unions through the antitrust laws.[111] It was simply impossible to apply the antitrust laws equally to business and labor, even if Arnold was right on some theoretical level.[112] Under the common law and in the early days of the antitrust laws, labor unions had been attacked as unlawful conspiracies, their activities enjoined by the courts, and their leaders often imprisoned while manufacturers were free to conspire with virtual impunity. Congress had reacted by passing not one but two different provisions immunizing labor unions from the antitrust laws.[113]

What troubled Arnold was how labor, particularly in the construction industry, inflated costs, restricted production, blocked cost saving innovations, enlisted business in jurisdictional disputes with other unions, and generally contributed to the paradox of the depression of want in the midst of plenty. For example, Arnold wrote in his official capacity to a labor leader, "The union may not act as a private police force to perpetuate unnecessarily costly and economic practices in the housing industry."[114]

He also objected to the so-called secondary boycott, in which a union boycotted persons doing business with a firm involved in a labor dispute. Arnold objected to the coercive effect this tactic had on innocent and otherwise uninvolved parties and the way it greatly increased the power of some unions, like the Teamsters, over other unions, like the UAW, which were not in a position to engage in such behavior with the customers of the firms that employed their members.[115]

These views hardly endeared Arnold to most of his liberal, pro-labor friends and New Deal colleagues. Arnold had such conflicts with Attorney General Murphy over his labor cases that he contemplated resigning and joining a New York law firm.[116] Nonetheless, he held fast to his belief that labor restrictions were a hidden tariff, a private tax, a restraint on interstate commerce, and a huge contributor to increased prices to consumers from his earliest days as head of the Antitrust Division throughout the rest of his life. He reflected later in his memoirs:

> When a labor union utilized its collective power to destroy another union, or to prevent the introduction of modern labor-saving devices, or require the employer to pay for useless and unnecessary labor, I believe that the [antitrust exemption] has been exceeded and that the union was operating in violation of the Sherman Act.[117]

Arnold's first labor prosecution was an indictment of the carpenter's union and its president William Hutcheson for a jurisdictional strike against Anheuser Busch over which union had the right to install machinery in the company's plant. The Supreme Court held that the strike was legal and not an antitrust violation. Subsequent antitrust indictments against labor unions were struck down by the Supreme Court without comment other than citation to *Hutcheson*. The Court further stopped Arnold using the antiracketeering laws to the same effect.[118]

The normally savvy and politically astute Arnold was simply blind to the political danger in attacking a core element of the New Deal coalition. Some of his Congressional testimony on labor issues was so inflammatory that attorney general Biddle prohibited him from returning to Capitol Hill when subpoenaed to testify at a later hearing.[119] President Roosevelt's staff received and acknowledged dozens of letters protesting the labor cases and only a handful in support. At one point, the general counsel of the AFL called him "the greatest enemy of organized labor in America today."[120]

Even Arnold acknowledged that the labor cases were his "one conspicuous failure." What he couldn't understand was how he kept losing in the Supreme Court in increasingly brief and humiliating decisions or how these increasingly futile efforts were crippling his ability to continue an effective campaign of antitrust enforcement in other industries.[121]

The sheer length and size of most antitrust cases meant that older cases brought by his predecessor Jackson were finally coming to fruition, and some of Arnold's initiatives would not bear fruit until long after his tenure. Arnold had to wait until the mid-1940s, after he had left the Antitrust Division, for some of his most important victories. The final victory in the Second Circuit against Alcoa came in 1945.[122] The Supreme Court affirmed the decision against the AP in the same year and in 1946 affirmed the monopolization and price-fixing decision against the tobacco industry.[123]

The only area of antitrust Arnold left untouched was the law of mergers and acquisitions. Here there was simply nothing Arnold could do because of the state of the law. Although the original Clayton Act prohibited mergers and acquisitions that might substantially lessen competition, the law was limited to stock acquisitions involving direct competitors; and the Sherman Act proved to be an awkward statute to use to regulate the future competitive tendencies of most acquisitions.[124] Here the TNEC hearings and monographs were helpful in uncovering the trend of concentration in the American economy. The TNEC and subsequent FTC reports helped create the Congressional groundswell to pass comprehensive revisions to the Clayton Act in 1950[125] to create an anti-merger provision, which proved to be a true third leg to add to the Sherman Act's prohibitions against collusion and monopolization.

Perhaps the gravest challenge Arnold faced as head of the Antitrust Division was the wholesale repeal or practical nullification of antitrust in the face of the war planning and production leading up to the U.S. entry into World War II. The war effort threatened to derail antitrust enforcement as effectively as the NRA had done during his predecessors' tenure. As early as July 1940, Arnold saw the threat war preparedness meant for antitrust.[126]

Arnold fought back using antitrust to attack profiteering and impediments to preparedness during the early days of the war in Europe before Pearl Harbor, linking the attack on international cartels to the defense needs of the nations, showing the links between the international cartels and the Nazi war machine, and arguing against the return of a "cartelized" economy in the postwar era.[127] In *Bottlenecks*, Arnold eloquently described how anticompetitive agreements were injuring the national defense by

1. Throttling American capacity to produce essential war materials by foreign ownership and control of patents;
2. Cartelization of certain industries with price and production control in foreign hands;
3. Transmission to foreign companies of American military secrets;
4. Division of markets, fixing and restricting of price of materials essential to military preparation;
5. Collusive bidding on contracts for the Army and Navy.[128]

Once the war began, Arnold and the Antitrust Division helped the war effort in an even more tangible way. At the request of the Board of Economic Warfare, the Antitrust Division supplied extensive information relating to the availability of raw materials, the location of Axis factories, and the connections between Axis companies and domestic or South American companies. These efforts were headed by future president of the University of Chicago and future attorney general Edward Levi, then an attorney with the division on leave from teaching at the University of Chicago. Many of these reports were extremely detailed descriptions of factories, what the factories produced, and their locations and identifying landmarks so they could be targeted for bombing and verification of destruction. These reports were shared by the Board of Economic Warfare with both U.S. military intelligence and the British Ministry of Economic Warfare.[129]

Arnold also set out more generally to show how agreements between American and German firms had jeopardized war preparedness and how the very same firms had unsuccessfully tried to threaten the War Department with delays if the antitrust suit was not dropped.[130] In a nationwide radio address in 1942, Arnold cited a list of 162 cartel agreements between the thoroughly nazified I.G. Farben company of Germany and American firms.[131]

The *Standard Oil of New Jersey* case was the notable success of this effort. Standard Oil and I.G. Farben of Germany had agreed as early as 1929 to divide world markets, with I.G. Farben granted exclusive rights to artificial rubber and Standard Oil given the world market for petroleum products. The companies exchanged technology, Farben being the recipient of a great deal of Standard Oil work in the artificial rubber area while Standard Oil received little in return. One of the consequences of the deal was Standard Oil's inability to reenter the artificial rubber market without I.G. Farben's consent. This decision had profound consequences for war preparedness in the United States, particularly after the United States lost access to its natural rubber sources in Southeast Asia following that area's conquest by Japan in the early years of the war before Pearl Harbor.[132]

Arnold had the law and the facts on his side and was prepared to indict the companies and their executives through the grand jury process. If the United States had not already been at war, this probably would have happened. Instead, Standard Oil was able to exert its influence with the War Department, and Arnold was forced to accept a consent decree that freed up some key patents but only required the payment of a $50,000 fine.[133]

Even here, Arnold "leaked" the real story to the press and in Congressional hearings, which placed the record of the case before the public.[134] In a series of appearances before the Senate National Defense Committee, chaired by Harry Truman, and the Patent Committee, chaired by Homer Bone, Arnold laid out what he had been prepared to prove in court. Arnold relied so thoroughly on Edward Levi, the head of the Economic Warfare unit of the Antitrust Division, that he may have read the statement Levi prepared for the first time when he appeared before the Congressional Committee. At one point, he seemed so shocked by what he was reporting to the Committee that he turned to Levi and was heard to say, "Is this true?" This candid moment appeared to impress the Committee as much as the shocking news he was delivering.[135]

As if the original cartel arrangement wasn't bad enough, Standard Oil and Farben continued to try to keep their private deal together despite the war. Even after World War II began in Europe, there was evidence that Standard Oil had agreed with Farben to continue to suppress production of artificial rubber in the United States, even though the arrangement was increasingly one-sided in favor of I.G. Farben and the wishes of the Hitler regime. Arnold linked Standard Oil to attempts to keep its cartel going even during the war and to near espionage in giving German companies vital technological information. Standard Oil limited its own development of artificial rubber and blocked its commercial development by others, leaving the United States short of this vital commodity while production flourished in Germany thanks to Farben's uncontested control of artificial rubber. Although Arnold was always careful to attribute the cartel agreements to the desire to dominate world markets rather than lack of patriotism, Standard Oil's conduct was characterized by Senator Truman as approaching treason. Arnold demonstrated the existence of similar agreements between Farben and other American companies for magnesium and other products with similar effects, and he showed how the initial cartel agreements inevitably expanded to include other American and international firms until they encompassed all worldwide competitors in truly global cartels to the detriment of American's consumers and the war effort.[136]

Arnold himself was careful not to impugn directly the patriotism or loyalty of American companies as much as to attribute these actions to a regrettable, but understandable, attitude of greed that could only be cured through more antitrust enforcement both during and after the coming victory against the Axis. According to Arnold, "You cannot control prices unless you restrict production. You cannot restrict production without depriving a nation of wealth in peace, and of strength in war."[137]

Despite these revelations, Arnold was losing the antitrust battle to defense preparation and the war effort on a daily basis. The problem was that while the Standard Oils, DuPonts, GEs, and Alcoas were guilty of heinous conduct, these companies were also absolutely vital to the U.S. war effort, and many of their executives were now leaders in the war planning and production effort. Arnold was forced to agree publicly (if not entirely voluntarily) to defer to the War and Navy departments in the event they explicitly found that any particular antitrust violation was necessary for national defense. Perhaps it was inevitable that this would overwhelm his antitrust enforcement program, given the scope of the national emergency and the corporatist culture of the war planners themselves. Case after case was vetoed by the planning and defense authorities, including cases involving conduct predating the war. Arnold spent more and more of his time fighting with the war planners, including Hugh Johnson, who had been the first head of the NRA and still had little use for the antitrust laws. For the first time, Congress was cutting rather than increasing his budget and staff.[138]

The final straw appeared to be Arnold's attempt to criminally prosecute the railroads for price-fixing and to indict Averell Harriman, the chairman of the Union Pacific railroad, who would be appointed as United States ambassador to the Soviet Union later in the same year that Arnold would have indicted him.[139] The indictment was quashed in the name of national defense, and Arnold was effectively gone from the one job that he had truly loved.

Roosevelt offered Arnold a face-saving position on the federal appellate bench to take Wiley Rutledge's spot on the D.C. Circuit when Roosevelt appointed Rutledge to the Supreme Court. Arnold publicly pretended he wanted the judgeship, and Roosevelt pretended he was sorry to see him take it. Drew Pearson led a newspaper crusade to get Arnold to decline the appointment for the good of the country, but it is unlikely that Roosevelt would have kept him on in any event. Arnold himself quipped to a *Time* magazine interviewer that he was like the Marx Brothers, funny at first but something the public eventually grows tired of.

The conventional wisdom, even from friends (although philosophical opposites) like Rex Tugwell, was that Arnold's antitrust efforts, particularly in the defense area, were a short-term stir that had to be smothered in order to promote the consolidation, coordination, and centralized management of the war effort. Arnold disagreed: "Even during the war the symbol of the antitrust ideal was kept alive by the Department of Justice."[140] In any event, Arnold had the last laugh after the war as antitrust revived and included a vigorous prosecution of international cartels and sham patent and trademark licensing agreements designed to bolster those arrangements.[141] Moreover, the antitrust ideal spread to Germany (and to a lesser extent Japan) and led to the creation of a European Economic Community with an antitrust system eventually rivaling that of the United States.

When he left the Justice Department, Arnold was and still remains the longest serving head of the Antitrust Division in history. Even today, Arnold enjoys a special status among those who followed at the Justice Department, regardless of party politics or personal philosophies about antitrust. Former Attorney General Janet Reno reflected that during her childhood Arnold's name "was synonymous with what the New Deal meant." John Shenefield, head of the division under President Carter, notes that "his photograph looked down on us in the Front Office so it was as though he was sitting there at your elbow, evaluating your performance"; in making decisions the question was inevitably, "What would Thurman Arnold do?" James Rill, head of the Antitrust Division under the first President Bush, describes Arnold as one of the two AAGs "head and shoulders" above the rest. Anne Bingaman, President Clinton's first head of the Antitrust Division, described Arnold as having "created the modern Antitrust Division. His vigorous enforcement of the antitrust laws and his constant proselytizing of the benefits of competition raised the profile of the division and convinced the American public of the benefits of our nation's antitrust laws. The debt of the American public to Thurman Arnold cannot be overstated."[142]

Bingaman is correct. Without Thurman Arnold, there would be no modern antitrust law or government antitrust enforcement. Just as the Supreme Court destroyed the legal underpinning for the corporate collectivism underlying the NRA codes, Arnold destroyed the moral and economic basis for the culture of cartels in America and abroad. He upped the criminal and civil consequences for such business behavior, forced price-fixing underground, delegitimized it by making it both anticonsumer and un-American, created a stable mandate for antitrust as part of an expanded role of the federal government in policing a healthy national economy, and made it impossible for antitrust to be repealed in the future or completely undermined by changes in the prevailing political winds. But after five frenetic years of practicing what he had decidedly not preached as an academic, Arnold's next brief stop was the relative quiet and solitude of the appellate bench.

7

The Short Unhappy Judgeship of Thurman Arnold

By 1943 the antimonopoly movement as the symbol of the later New Deal was over, and Thurman Arnold had completed burning all his bridges. Despite his many successes (or perhaps because of them), his enforcement decisions had enraged both the industries he attacked and their political supporters within the Roosevelt administration. The combination of the agricultural, automobile, metals, container, medical, rubber, motion picture, newspaper, energy, construction, and railroad industries, as well as the labor movement, covers most of the American economy. Throw in the demands of the war effort, and Arnold's tenure was unsustainable.

Nor was there anyone on the inside to save Arnold. Strong Arnold supporters like Frank Murphy, Robert Jackson, and William Douglas were by now all on the Supreme Court and no longer as influential within the Roosevelt administration. The older advocates of planning within the administration under the early New Deal and the NRA had never favored Arnold's approach and were certainly not inclined to intervene to save him. Nor were the businessman now involved in the war effort who were frequently past or present targets of the Antitrust Division. Arnold never had much direct contact with President Roosevelt, who was at best ambivalent about Arnold's crusade. The hundreds of letters of support from the public, and even a few of the business leaders he had challenged, were sweet but had no impact on the decision to remove him.

In his autobiography, Arnold describes the offer of a judgeship as a bolt out of the blue and one he was delighted to accept.[1] Roosevelt, however, knew how uneasy Arnold was about leaving the Antitrust Division, which was his one true professional love. In January 1943, the president wrote to Arnold:

I know you leave your post in the Department of Justice with mingled feelings. You, of course, have keen regret at leaving the body of men in the Antitrust Division among whom you have built such an excellent esprit de corps. I know also that you can leave them with the assurance that the same vigorous enforcement of the antitrust laws will continue.

I hate to see you go but I know that you want to and I, therefore, bid you Godspeed and great success in your new career. The same qualities of intellect and of heart which you brought to the Department of Justice will serve you well in your new career on the bench.[2]

Arnold's later memory of excitement in a judicial appointment is suspect, and Roosevelt's profession of loss in Arnold assuming the bench amounts to something between a face-saving gesture and a white lie. Nonetheless, Arnold accepted the judicial appointment, probably seeing the handwriting on the wall.

Arnold was given an adulatory going-away party attended by eight hundred friends and coworkers. Wyoming Senator O'Mahoney was toastmaster, and fulsome tributes were given by the attorney general, the Majority Leader of the Senate, the Speaker of the House, Senator Robert La Follette, the president of Kaiser Aluminum (a beneficiary of increased competition in the aluminum industry), Justice William Douglas, and a host of others. Arnold topped off the evening by delivering a farewell address broadcast nationwide on the Mutual Broadcasting Network radio network, in which he linked the freedom to produce and the rights of consumers under the Sherman Act with the goals of World War II in seeking a politically and economically free postwar order.[3] As he left the Antitrust Division, Arnold was hailed as one of the ten most powerful men in Washington. In contrast, in modern times it is virtually inconceivable that a subcabinet appointee would even be known by the public, let alone that his farewell speech would be deemed worthy of live national network media coverage.

Unlike his earlier appointment to head the Antitrust Division, Thurman Arnold's judgeship was confirmed without controversy by a voice vote in the Senate on March 9, 1943.[4] He thus became Associate Justice Thurman Arnold of the U.S. Court of Appeals for the District of Columbia, replacing Wiley Rutledge, whom Roosevelt elevated to the U.S. Supreme Court. While today the D.C. Circuit enjoys the reputation as the most important court in the country after the Supreme Court and a true stepping-stone to that prized appointment, this was not the case in 1943. That honor went to the U.S. Court of Appeals for the Second Circuit, which covered appeals from the federal district courts in New York, Connecticut, and Vermont. The Second Circuit included such luminaries as Learned Hand, his cousin Augustus Hand, Arnold's former Yale colleague and boss at the Agricultural Adjustment Agency Jerome Frank, and Arnold's former mentor and Yale law dean Charles Clark. The Second Circuit, as the appellate court for Wall Street, decided some of the most famous and important cases in the country, including the final decision in the monopolization case against Alcoa in 1945, which Arnold had supervised at the Antitrust Division.[5]

Had Arnold been appointed to the Second Circuit with his many friends and a prestigious docket, the Supreme Court with such friends as Douglas, Frankfurter, Murphy, and Jackson, or even the Tenth Circuit covering his native Wyoming, Arnold's judicial career might have been a lengthy and fulfilling capstone to an already remarkable career. Instead, Arnold rationalized his selection for the D.C. Circuit on the basis of senatorial prerogative.[6] The senators from each state traditionally nominate the judges for the federal district and appellate courts within their jurisdiction. In contrast, the D.C. Circuit was the only circuit court that was viewed as presidential patronage, since the District of Columbia had no senator.

While this is true, it is only part of the story. The Supreme Court is another court for which there is no tradition of senatorial prerogative, and there was in fact a contemporaneous opening. Despite many rumors in the press that Arnold was in line for various slots on the Supreme Court from the time of the Louis Brandeis vacancy on, there is simply no evidence that Roosevelt ever considered Arnold, who was a subcabinet level appointee (despite being a famous one), for this lofty post. In comparison, prior to joining the Supreme Court, William Douglas had been chair of the Securities Exchange Commission, Frank Murphy had been attorney general, Robert Jackson had served as both solicitor general and attorney general, and Hugo Black had been a U.S. senator. The administration received numerous unsolicited letters urging Arnold's appointment for attorney general, solicitor general, and the Supreme Court. These were never treated as anything other than routine correspondence to be politely acknowledged and not otherwise considered.[7]

Even taking senatorial prerogative into account, Arnold had always been friendly with Joseph O'Mahoney, the longtime Democratic senator from Wyoming, who presumably would not have been opposed to a nomination to the Tenth Circuit for Arnold had a timely vacancy been available. This would have, of course, required Arnold to move back to Wyoming or to one of the other states within the Tenth Circuit, a decision he ultimately was never willing to make. All the evidence points to the conclusion that the judge-pickers in the Roosevelt administration, with the president's concurrence, viewed the D.C. Circuit as the appropriate judicial reward for Arnold's meritorious, but divisive, service as head of the Antitrust Division.

In 1943, the D.C. Circuit was a mixed blessing for any appointee, let alone the mercurial Arnold. There was no superior court or appellate court for the District of Columbia to hear the myriad local criminal and civil matters. This modern local court system for the District was not created until 1970.[8] As a result, the U.S. District Court for the District of Columbia heard all but the most lowly cases in the District, and the D.C. Circuit heard *all* appeals from these cases. In contrast, the other federal appellate courts heard only a smaller number of more significant cases involving federal statutes, the Constitution, and treaties as well as so-called diversity cases between citizens of different states where a substantial amount of money was at stake.[9]

Besides joining the court, 1943 was a busy and important year for Arnold and Frances. They moved from McLean, Virginia, and purchased the 200-year-old Summerhill estate in Arlington, Virginia. Frances then undertook the extensive renovation, furnishing, and upgrading of the interior and gardens of this elegant home. They also still owned the New Haven house, which fortunately had been rented for slightly more than the mortgage payments.

After completing the spring term of the court, the Arnold family, with loyal secretary Marguerite O'Brien in tow, decamped to Laramie for the summer. Arnold and O'Brien worked out of an office at the Wyoming Law School drafting his assigned opinions. While in Laramie, he gave the commencement address at the university as well.

He bought a ranch property in order to formally reestablish his Laramie residency to keep his future residency and political plans open, and he appeared in person to argue before the Lands Commission for permission to build certain improvements on his ranch. Although Arnold had always retained Wyoming residency and re-registered to vote in Wyoming starting in 1943, he never lived in Wyoming, apart from short trips and summer vacations, following his move to West Virginia in 1927. While Arnold flirted with running for the Wyoming senate seat in 1948, he never took the plunge.

Both sons were now in the service. George was a Marine in the Pacific who eventually participated in the invasion of Guam. Thurman Jr. ("Turno"), was a Navy junior lieutenant also in the Pacific, who was later sent to England on a secret mission perhaps connected with D-Day. Arnold smoothed the way socially for Turno through letters of introduction to academics like Harold Laski and notables including the head of Imperial Chemicals, with whom Arnold was on friendly terms despite that firm's leading role in a number of international cartels under investigation at the Justice Department.

Sadly, the Arnolds had to return to Laramie in the fall of 1943 following the death of his father. C. P. Arnold died peacefully in his sleep at the age of eighty-three, maintaining his health and his vigor until the very end of his life. C. P. left an estate valued at more than $50,000, consisting mostly of land and improvements. His will had originally designated Thurman's mother and younger brother Carl as co-executor, but Thurman was added as co-executor after Carl's sudden and unexpected death in 1941.

Throughout his time on the bench, the D.C. Circuit never had its full complement of assigned judges and had as few as three in the spring of 1944, increasing the workload on Arnold and the two other members of the court. In a little more than two years, Arnold heard 168 cases in total and wrote sixty-five opinions, most of them during his first year on the bench. As was the custom of the times, he concurred separately or dissented in only a handful of additional cases.[10]

Arnold heard no antitrust cases and would have had to recuse himself in any event on government antitrust matters he had supervised during the preceding five years. Almost none of the cases raised the kind of earthshaking matters that Arnold had critiqued as a scholar, assisted as a part-time New Dealer, or directed at the Antitrust Division. Instead, the opinions consisted of an enormous number of per curiam or brief signed affirmances of criminal convictions and denials of petitions for habeas corpus from prisoners and inmates at government mental institutions. There were an equal number of minor contract, tort, insurance, procedure, tax, estate and trust, matrimonial, custody, and child support cases. Even the appeal of government agency decisions, a major source of the modern D.C. Circuit docket, were mostly routine affirmances that the agency decision in question was supported by substantial evidence.

The opinions were mostly stiff, formal, and boring affairs. Arnold did not cite his own academic work, or that of his fellow realists, as William Douglas and Jerome Frank routinely did in their opinions. It was for the most part straight, by-the-books appellate judging constrained by the law and the facts, propositions that Arnold and his fellow realists had long contested was the case.

Only rarely did Arnold's well-honed sense of humor shine through. In *James Heddon's Sons v. Coe*,[11] Arnold opined on the ability to trademark a herringbone design for fishing lures. He summarized the issue and his decision by stating,

> Appellant contends that the mark serves no useful function, and that there is no evidence of an increase in sales. It therefore argues that the above findings are without support. To prove lack of utility, experts were called who testified that within certain broad limits it makes no difference to a fish how an artificial lure is shaped or marked. It is the flash of color and the movement of the object which attracts the fish. Fish, according to these experts, are incapable of distinguishing variations of color or design.
>
> We would be reluctant indeed to undermine the folklore of fishing by making such a revolutionary finding of fact. It would constitute such a serious reflection on the intelligence and discrimination of fish that no angler with a spark of loyalty could fail to resent it.[12]

A more typical case was *Bailey v. Zlotnick,* in which the issue was the "extent to which landlord is liable to a tenant for the negligence of an independent contractor who repairs the premises at the direction of the landlord."[13] The fact that such cases were important to the parties did not make them either important or interesting to Arnold as a judge.

Arnold was able to make his mark in three principal areas. Because of the location of the Patent Office in Washington, D.C., most of the significant appeals of the denials of patents came before the D.C. Circuit. This is one of the few areas in which it was more advantageous to be a judge on the D.C. Circuit in the 1940s than today. Since 1980, by statute, all patent appeals are heard by the newly created U.S. Court of Appeals for the Federal Circuit.[14]

In key cases, Justice Arnold construed patent rights narrowly in order to protect competition. In *Monsanto Chemical Co. v. Coe*, Arnold analyzed the scope of a series of patent claims related to the chemistry for softening water. He expressed the concern that "what multiple claims actually do in the ordinary case is to state a single invention in as many different ways as possible in order to give the resulting patent as much scope as possible." He tied this concern to the very purpose of the patent clause of the Constitution to promote, rather than retard, science and invention. He affirmed the patent commissioner's decision to limit the number of claims granted patent protection for essentially the same invention. He also sounded a familiar theme in stating, "In many industries the careless extension of a patent on a formula or a way of doing things has already turned patents into instruments to suppress new inventive ability, new experimentation and new initiative. Industrial empires have been given power to suppress production and to organize domestic and international cartels through patents of carelessly defined scope which created a prima facie monopoly right over technical information."[15]

In *Special Equipment Co. v. Coe*, Arnold affirmed the rejection of a patent for a machine that was merely a portion of a previously patented pear-cutting device. Arnold viewed the request for a second patent on a partial subcombination of the first machine, which had no independent use in the real world, as an improper and unlawful attempt to extend the patent monopoly to the production or use of unpatented goods. He concluded, "It seems, therefore, a safe, practical test to limit the number of distinct patents rights in a single machine to those which the inventor expects to exploit separately, and not to suppress. Distinct patent rights should not be granted for the sole purpose of handicapping future inventors whose discoveries would not otherwise infringe the complete patent."[16]

These holdings, while not technically antitrust cases, were clear extensions of the principles from the cases that Assistant Attorney General Arnold had brought to prevent the cartelization or monopolization of key industries through the restrictive licensing of patents and other intellectual property rights.[17] Interestingly, *Monsanto Chemical* and *Special Equipment* both relied heavily on antitrust precedents. In both cases, the antitrust rhetoric was correct in the sense of being a cautionary tale about the importance of clearly (and narrowly) defining patent rights lest innovation and competition be destroyed. At another level, they were clearly extraneous to the actual cases, with neither defendant having been charged with, or suspected of, the specific parade of horribles being dragged out by Arnold. Perhaps as a result of the somewhat gratuitous use of antitrust rhetoric, both cases had separate concurrences, relatively rare in those days. Regardless, Arnold proudly wrote to his old congressional ally, Senator Homer Bone, of his hopes that his opinions would create "a little new patent law."[18]

Arnold also wrote significant opinions in criminal law, particularly in the area of the insanity defense.[19] In *De Marcos v. Overholser*,[20] Arnold, on behalf of a unanimous court, denied the habeas corpus petition by an inmate seeking release from the Saint Elizabeth Mental Hospital in which he was confined following the determination that he was "of unsound mind and that his release would be dangerous." Arnold used the opinion to explore the uneasy relationship between law and psychiatry in dealing with the insanity defense.[21] The case must have been a relief, since it represented a rare opportunity to delve back into issues that had fascinated him since his earliest days on the Yale faculty.

It was, however, an uneasy vehicle to explore these issues. The petitioner had filed an unsuccessful habeas petition in 1940, and the only new issue was whether the court was required on its own motion to obtain a report and recommendation from the Commission on Mental Health. Arnold wrote that

> Habeas corpus is a proper remedy to challenge the continued confinement of persons who claim to be restored to mental health. Yet the right to bring habeas corpus would be of little value to an indigent person unless expert testimony were available to him to rebut the opinion evidence of the staff of the institution who believed he should be continued in custody.[22]

Given a judge's reluctance to release an allegedly insane criminal against the wishes of the experts who cared on a daily basis for the petitioner, Arnold correctly observed that it was probably more important to provide an indigent habeas petitioner with an independent psychiatric examination than to give him independent counsel. Arnold thundered that such an examination by the commission should be granted whenever requested or whenever the court believed it appropriate on its initiative, but with the greatest reluctance he concluded that the petitioner had affirmatively waived his rights to any such hearing.[23]

The case also represents a precursor to Arnold's subsequent 1958 pro bono representation of the Nobel laureate poet Ezra Pound. He secured Pound's release from the very same facility using an expert report from the very same Dr. Overholser, the director of the facility, who had been the defendant in all the Saint Elizabeth cases that came before Arnold on the bench.[24]

Arnold's immense but underused judicial talents are best represented in two civil liberties decisions at the end of his career on the bench. In *Walker v. Popenoe*,[25] Arnold heard the appeal of the U.S. Post Office's decision denying mailing privileges because of the sexual content of a pamphlet entitled "Preparing for Marriage." The court restored the mailing privileges because of the failure to provide a hearing, but Arnold concurred separately to discuss the broader censorship issues. In his concurrence, he stated,

> The statute under which the Postmaster General acted in this case makes the mailing of obscene matter a serious crime. It also provides that obscene material shall not be conveyed in the mails. The Postmaster General construed this statute as giving him power to exclude from the mails, without a hearing, any publication which in his judgment was obscene. The court below correctly decided that the order barring appellees' pamphlet from the mails without a hearing was a violation of due process.[26]

Arnold concluded, "Appellees have been prevented for a long period of time from mailing a publication which we now find contains nothing offensive to current standards of public decency. A full hearing is the minimum protection required by due process to prevent that kind of injury."[27]

The *Popenoe* case was merely a dress rehearsal for Arnold's most famous opinion. Just one week after the issuance of the *Popenoe* decision, Arnold wrote his masterpiece on government censorship, *Esquire v. Walker*. Here, the postmaster general had revoked *Esquire* magazine's second-class mailing privileges. This decision cost the magazine an additional $100,000 per year to mail first class and jeopardized *Esquire*'s status as a general circulation magazine. The postmaster had not found *Esquire* to be obscene, but rather held that its content was "morally improper" and not for the "public welfare and good."[28]

The vast majority of witnesses opposed the government position at trial. One particularly poignant example was H. L. Mencken, who testified about his past experiences when the *American Mercury* magazine was effectively shut down without judicial review by the denial of similar mailing privileges. Among the government witnesses were literally a rabbi, a priest, and a minister, which must have conjured up any number of bad jokes in Arnold's fertile imagination.

Arnold's opinion for the court restoring *Esquire*'s mailing privileges was both devastating and dismissive to the entire premise of the government's case:

> It does not follow that an administrative official may be delegated the power first to determine what is good for the public to read and then force compliance with his ideas by putting editors who do not follow them at a competitive disadvantage. It is inconceivable that Congress intended to delegate such power to an administrative official or that the exercise of such a power, if delegated, could be held constitutional.[29]

Arnold cited the famous test from Oliver Wendell Holmes's dissent in *Abrams v. United States*,[30] later adopted by the Supreme Court in *Brandenburg v. Ohio*,[31] that it is the marketplace of ideas and not government censorship that should determine the competitiveness of unpopular ideologies and points of view. Arnold continued,

> Since we hope that this is the last time that a government agency will attempt to compel the acceptance of its literary or moral standards relating to material admittedly not obscene, the voluminous record may serve as a useful reminder of the kind of mental confusion which always accompanies such censorship.[32]

Arnold's next weapons were sarcasm and wit:

> The first source of that confusion is, of course, the age old question when a scantily clad lady is art, and when she is highly improper. Some refined persons are hopeful that an answer to this vexing riddle may be found. Others are pessimistic.

He illustrated this point with the absurd testimony of one government witness about an *Esquire* photo of a woman in a bathing suit at the beach, which the witness said was improper for depiction in a magazine photograph but proper for the beach itself.[33]

Arnold continued with an additional line of attack: "A second source of confusion in determining what kind of literature furthers public welfare is the dividing line between refined humor and low comedy."[34] The essential point was an inability to find a meaningful dividing line between the occasional vulgar lapse and a vulgar dominant purpose and the equally important question of who is allowed to decide such questions. Arnold's opinion was hailed as a triumph of free speech in the press, and Arnold himself was lauded widely as a champion of civil liberties from people as diverse as H. L. Mencken and former attorney general Francis Biddle.[35]

In contrast, Arnold's final opinion for the D.C. Circuit was a return to the mundane. In *Reeves v. Bowles*,[36] Arnold wrote a brief opinion upholding the Office of Price Administration's regulation of the maximum rates for the rental of taxicabs in the District of Columbia.

Arnold's judicial duties, if unfulfilling, were hardly onerous. His appointment diary for the court years shows a steady stream of visits with the movers and shakers of the day. Abe Fortas and Arnold's former colleagues from the Antitrust Division were the most frequent visitors. After the issuance of the *Esquire* opinion, he lunched with H. L. Mencken at Mencken's invitation as a tribute to that opinion. Arnold frequently engaged in correspondence and idle chitchat with old Wyoming friends about returning home to either reenter private practice or perhaps to run for the U.S. Senate. As his days on the bench drew to a close, Arnold met frequently with Arne Wiprud, a former head of the Transportation Section of the Antitrust Division, who would become his partner in private practice once he left the bench.

Throughout this period, Arnold had remarkably little to do with antitrust issues. He passed on none as a judge, and out of friendship and respect to his former colleagues did not publicly comment on what his successors in the government were doing. He did however publish several versions of the same article defending his rather solitary views about how the antitrust laws should apply with equal force to labor unions, earning himself fees in excess of $1600 for an article commissioned by *Cosmopolitan*, reprinted in *Reader's Digest*, and eventually translated into French.[37]

Immediately prior to resigning, Arnold swore in his former colleague, successor as head of the Antitrust Division, and eventual Supreme Court

Justice Tom Clark as attorney general. Then on July 3, 1945, he met with President Harry Truman at the White House, presumably to inform the president of his resignation. On July 9, he left the court.

In Arnold's own carefully chosen words some twenty years after his resignation, he stated the reasons for his decision to leave the bench:

> I think it was my preference for partisan argument, rather than for impartial decision, that made me dissatisfied with a career on the appellate court. Furthermore, I was beginning to doubt whether a person of my temperament could ever be an ornament to the bench. I was impatient with legal precedents that seemed to me to reach an unjust result. I felt restricted by the fact that a judge has no business writing or speaking on controversial subjects. A judge can talk about human liberties, the rule of law above men, and similar abstractions. All of them seemed to me dull subjects. To sum it up, a person who is temperamentally an advocate, as I am, is not apt to make a good judge.[38]

Much closer to the actual event, he wrote to a cousin in Germany:

> I resigned from the United States Court of Appeals in Washington, D.C., about two years ago because I found the work of a judge much duller than that of an advocate. I think I might have liked the trial court but on the appellate court we sat in groups of three and all we did was to listen to argument and write opinions. I felt that a more active life was more to my taste, and so after much indecision I finally resigned and went into practice."[39]

Around the same time, he also noted in a letter that the bench "was too leisurely a job to be a satisfactory career."[40]

His Yale colleague and friend William Douglas wrote years after Arnold left the bench,

> Thurman served with distinction as a judge on the Court of Appeals. But he seemed in those days to be caged. His mind was far too active, his interests too wide to find satisfaction in the miscellany of cases coming before a federal court.[41]

Abe Fortas noted the same thing in his tribute to Arnold's life in the *Yale Law Journal*:

> He did not like the absolutes of pronouncing judgment, nor did he enjoy the process. An appellate judge deals with issues that are largely prefabricated, pre-processed by others. For Arnold, the four corners of a record-on-appeal, the limits set by the mind and ingenuity of others, were the walls of a prison. His genius was too rambunctious, his mind was too fertile—too eager to soar and dive—to be content within these limits.[42]

To the columnist Drew Pearson, his friend and in-law, it was clear that Arnold simply was "bored stiff with the court." Arnold himself captured the same flavor more directly in agreeing with a colleague's assessment that he preferred to "make my living talking to a bunch of damned fools than listening to a bunch of damn fools."[43]

While both the long and short versions of Arnold's explanation of why he left the bench are both correct and amusing, they also represent a missed opportunity for a committed legal realist to reflect on the role of judging. Unlike his mentor Jerome Frank, Arnold did not use his judging for inward reflection on the binding role of either facts or rules or the place for realist skepticism on the bench.[44] Nor did he use his opinions, or his limited extrajudicial writings, to explore the role of power underlying seemingly neutral legal rules or the role of social science, rather than conceptual thinking, in developing legal rules as he had done as a professor.

In part, Arnold appeared constrained by the very rules he had so aptly critiqued at Yale. In part, Arnold the realist was merely bored and wanted to move on to the next chapter in his colorful and successful life.

Despite disliking having been a judge, Arnold played off it quite successfully later in life. He continued to receive an enormous amount of press that invariably discussed both his antitrust and judicial background. Strangers and new acquaintances often referred to, or corresponded with, him as Judge Arnold, which he certainly did not correct. Most of the younger associates in his subsequent private practice only referred to him as Judge Arnold. In fact, even his own grandchildren called him "Judgie."[45] It was in the end a valuable asset that helped Arnold precisely because he left the bench after so brief a time.

8

A Firm Beginning

Arnold began his fourth try at private practice with Arne Wiprud, a former colleague from the Antitrust Division, who was an expert in transportation issues as well as the author of a book called *Justice in Transportation* for which Arnold had written the introduction.[1] The firm consisted of the two partners, a single associate, Reed Miller, who had worked with both partners in the Antitrust Division, and Marguerite O'Brien who served as Arnold's secretary from his days in the government until his death.[2] Arnold also maintained an affiliation with an old friend, Joe O'Sullivan, in Laramie.

The partnership, however, was brief and unsuccessful. The principal case they handled was the *Pullman* litigation, a private follow-on suit to a government monopolization case against the Pullman Corporation that Arnold had brought as head of the Antitrust Division. As a result of the government case, Pullman had to choose to keep either manufacturing of sleeping cars or the service end of the business. Pullman chose to divest the manufacturing side of the business, seeing little future in new sleeping cars in the face of the newly emerging commercial air travel business. The newly formed law firm of Arnold & Wiprud represented a group of investors, led by Cyrus Eaton, who were seeking to acquire the Pullman assets. Eaton's company, Otis & Co., announced a bid of $75 million to acquire the sleeping car division of Pullman and committed to a $500 million renovation of the sleeping car business. Eaton was opposed by a consortium of railroads who sought the assets for their own use.

The case was high profile, and Arnold was once again in the public spotlight. Only this time the newspapers were divided as to whether Arnold was helping preserve competition or simply treading on past government connections. Arnold viewed his role as fighting for the same principles which I stood for in public life, namely competition in industry including the transportation industry. . . . I am continuing the same effort which I made at the Department [of Justice], to carry out the purposes and policies of the decree [against Pullman]. Unless an independent group, competitively minded, enters this picture, all the public benefits which can be derived from the decree will be dissipated in inaction. This means that control will again drift back to the same old crowd which has monopolized the sleeping car business in the past.[3]

While it was not Arnold & Wiprud's only case, it was by far their most important. Arnold in fact also handled a number of small matters for Coca-Cola, represented a minor movie actress in a dispute with Warner Brothers, and defended a new entrant in the pen market being sued for patent infringement.[4] But Pullman was the only case that mattered for the future of the firm.

Arnold and Wiprud fought the case up to the Supreme Court. The Supreme Court ultimately split 4-4, thus affirming without opinion the trial court's approval of the sale of the business to the railroads.[5]

In the wake of this defeat, Arnold dissolved the partnership[6] and turned to his former student, faculty colleague, and fellow New Dealer Abe Fortas. With Reed Miller and Marguerite O'Brien in tow, they opened the firm Arnold & Fortas in an office at 821 15th Street in the District, along with a new associate, Milton Freeman, who had been a former assistant solicitor at the SEC. Also along for the ride were Norman Diamond, a former government lawyer just out of the military,[7] and Walton Hamilton, Arnold's former colleague from Yale and the Department of Justice, now ready to practice law at the age of sixty-five. Hamilton was in particular a most intriguing choice. He was an economist by training who taught at Yale Law School but never attended law school. Hamilton was admitted to the bar of Georgia only by virtue of a special proclamation of the state legislature. As Fortas drolly would describe the new partnership and its interesting collection of lawyers and staff, "The purpose of the firm was to provide a means for its two partners to make a living."[8]

Arnold had known Abe Fortas since he had been a law student at Yale in the early thirties. Brilliant, yet viewed by many as abrasive, Fortas racked up an impressive academic career, capped by graduating second in his class and serving as editor-in-chief of the *Yale Law Journal*. Although hired by Yale as a research fellow at the urging of Arnold and others in the realist camp, Fortas spent little time in New Haven after graduation. Instead, he made his mark in Washington in the Roosevelt administration, first as part of the legal staff under Jerome Frank in the Agricultural Adjustment Administration. Here he continued his relationship with Arnold, who moonlighted with Fortas on the defense of the constitutionality of the AAA's peach production restrictions.[9] Fortas then turned to his other Yale mentor and booster William Douglas, joining Douglas at the SEC to conduct the great hearings on corporate reorganization.

When Douglas left the SEC to take his seat on the Supreme Court, Fortas found a new mentor within the New Deal in Harold Ickes, the Secretary of the Interior. Fortas first joined the Interior Department as general counsel of the Public Works Administration, later headed the Division of Electric Power, and at the tender age of thirty-one became the under secretary of the Interior in 1942. He was the youngest under secretary in the Roosevelt administration, and perhaps in history. In all these positions, Fortas was meticulous, hardworking beyond imagination, and a careful coalition-builder, quite at odds with the earlier rap of a cold, manipulative, abrasive sort. He was quickly justifying his reputation as the most brilliant conventional lawyer of his time.

Like many New Dealers, his official titles and portfolios seriously understated the scope of his influence and power. Over the span of about a decade, Fortas played a key role in the law and regulation of the agricultural sector under Jerome Frank; the securities industry under William Douglas; and the management of federal lands, mineral resources, electric power, and the administration of the commonwealth of Puerto Rico under Harold Ickes.

Arnold and Fortas shared certain similar backgrounds as outsiders. Arnold was the lifelong Westerner and Fortas the Southern Jew having grown up in Memphis. Both originally had felt wildly out of place in East Coast Ivy League schools, Arnold having been an awkward cowboy from Laramie and Fortas being one of the few Jews in Yale Law School in the 1930s.

The final piece of the puzzle was Paul Porter, who joined the firm one year after its founding in 1947. Porter was from Kentucky, a graduate of the state university and law school who had worked his way through law school as a reporter, columnist, and later city editor for the *Lexington Herald*, a solidly liberal Democratic paper. After law school, he practiced for a time in his home town of Winchester, Kentucky, and then became the managing editor of newspapers in Oklahoma and Georgia. He wrote articles on the plight of the sharecropper that attracted the attention of Henry Wallace, who invited him to Washington. His first position in Washington, D.C., was as press director of the AAA, the only place where he, Fortas, and Arnold (albeit on a part-time basis) worked together before founding the firm. Later on, he served in more high-profile positions, including chairman of the Federal Communications Commission, head of the Office of Price Administration, and as special ambassador to Greece, all of which spawned valuable connections for Porter and the firm.[10]

Despite their common origins as outsiders, the "founding fathers" of Arnold, Fortas & Porter could not have been more dissimilar personally, professionally, or socially. Physically, Arnold was medium height with a tendency toward paunchiness, laconic and droll, and utterly without the ability to self-censor. Fortas was small, lithe, and highly reserved. Only a handful of lawyers ever felt they saw Fortas relax despite working with him for decades. While Fortas had a decent sense of humor, he could not compare with Arnold's wit, although he frequently tried. Porter was a large man, about six feet four inches tall, a tremendous storyteller, a terrific rainmaker, and the very definition of the hale fellow well met.[11]

Arnold and Fortas also differed greatly about the value of competition. While Arnold had made his mark reviving antitrust enforcement, Fortas had done virtually the opposite. He had spent the majority of his time in the AAA, the hotbed of economic planning under the likes of Henry Wallace, Rexford Tugwell, and Jerome Frank, and later in the bituminous coal division of the Department of the Interior, probably the only truly successfully cartelized industry under the NRA.[12]

Socially, the partners rarely mixed except at firm functions.[13] Arnold, who was considerably older than either of his partners, enjoyed frequent dinner parties and mingling primarily with his long-standing New Deal friends, particularly Justices Douglas and Black and their wives, columnist Drew Pearson who was now his in-law, iconoclasts who appealed to him such as Alf Landon, and socialites Cissy Patterson and Evalyn Walsh McLean. Even better was a night at home with Douglas, Black, and various other liberal politicians and judges, drinking, playing cards, and arguing about politics. Fortas's circle was more intellectual and oriented around music, a lifelong love as both listener and player in string quartets. Porter's social life revolved more around the country club scene.

As lawyers, their styles were similarly disparate. Most describe Fortas as "a superb lawyer," "the most brilliant all around conventional lawyer," the "best advocate," or "the most extraordinarily able lawyer" they ever met and one who was "uncanny in his ability to derive the heart of a matter." In contrast, Arnold was "unbelievably creative," "a national treasure," "an authentic genius," "an immense mind with a puckish sense of humor," and "a fourth-dimensional mind" who saw connections between ideas that no one else could perceive. It is the term "genius" or its equivalent that unites virtually everyone's recollection of Arnold, whether they knew him at Yale or the Justice Department or practiced with him.[14]

Fortas used a story from the canned peach case he and Arnold had tried for the AAA to illustrate the point. Arnold got frustrated with the junior staff's inability to find a case in the Justice Department library to support their position that the court could issue an injunction to stop a violation of the marketing agreements for the peach industry. Thurman said, "That's nonsense. There's a case on every point," and went to the shelves and came back with a case precisely on point. When asked by Fortas how he did it, Arnold replied, "It was very simple. This involved canned peaches, can, can, can reminded me of sardines. I looked under sardines in Words and Phrases and I found the case." To Fortas, that was genius.[15]

Arnold conducted frequent bull sessions with the younger lawyers in his office, never made any of the associates feel bad about their work, and was lavish in his praise. As a result, he inspired affection, love, and even worship from a large group of lawyers at the firm, many of whom viewed him as their mentor. This was fortunate since Arnold needed diligent assistants. He was not the kind of lawyer to fill in the blanks himself, and he relied heavily on others to provide the details for a brief or argument. He was the big picture conceptualist providing unconventional solutions for the most intractable problems. Arnold described the difference between the three partners' styles in commenting on a case he was handling involving the banana industry: "I'd try that case carload by carload, Paul would probably try it bunch by bunch; but only Abe would try it banana by banana."[16]

Fortas was the stern taskmaster, "cold, aloof" and "rough on the young people," intolerant of any deviation from total excellence. While charming to clients, he was respected but not loved by most of the young lawyers, who typically received a tongue lashing when their work product failed to meet Fortas's exacting standards. Porter was somewhere in the middle but was also "very gregarious," and "a great storyteller"; he "had the ability to make you feel at home" and was the "ultimate politician." Somehow it was a "magic combination," a "tremendous harmony" that made all three partners fit together remarkably well, and they complemented one another's strengths and covered for each other's relatively few weaknesses.[17] One client remembered a saying in Washington at the time that if Arnold, Fortas & Porter took a case that would get a lot of publicity "Thurman would ask 'How do we stand on the law?' Abe would ask 'We're all right on the law, but how do we present it to the public?' And Paul would add, 'Whom do we know?'"[18]

Arnold and Fortas had a special bond. They would defer to each other in a way they would rarely do to anyone else. In introducing Arnold at a firm dinner in 1965, Fortas, who had just left the firm for the Supreme Court, would say,

> I love him very, very much, and I'm sure you all love him. There is no man that I have ever known that I admire as much as I do Thurman, or from whom I have learned as much as I have from him. I've learned so much about what life is and what the obligations of a man are, and what it is to be a man, and what it is to cope with fear, and what it is to fulfill a man's destiny, from Thurman Arnold.[19]

They also had Yale, where their intellectual lives had been formed as teacher and student and later colleagues in the heady days of the realists in the 1930s. As they began their new practice, they returned to New Haven for one final time as faculty, co-teaching a weekly afternoon seminar on corporate and antitrust problems and using a single case as the basis of the semester's study. For Arnold it was a bittersweet return to New Haven, now that most of the full-time faculty he knew were either long gone or retired.

Splitting a once a week seminar on top of a growing practice was hardly the same as being a full-time faculty member, and it matched up better with Fortas's skills for meticulous preparation than Arnold's more free-form bloviations. Former Attorney General Katzenbach, a student in that seminar and a devoted fan of Arnold from reading his books as a POW in Germany during the war, recalled, "Abe was a much better teacher than Thurman, because Abe had done his homework and Thurman hadn't always. Thurman was a fun teacher and you learned from him, but he was bombast(ic) and funny." For example, on the first day of the seminar Arnold was up to his classroom tricks. He asked the class, "What was the purpose of a football game?" looking for the word "competition." When the students tentatively offered "to win," Arnold challenged them with "then why don't the two teams just cooperate?" To Katzenbach's disappointment, shared by others in the class, this was fun, but it didn't compare with Fortas's quiet brilliance.[20]

Soon, events would keep all three partners fighting for their own, as well as their clients' professional lives back in Washington on a full-time basis. The firm faced its greatest challenge and achieved its early prominence in representing literally hundreds of persons accused of Communist sympathies during the McCarthy era. The persecutions began as early as 1938 with the formation of the House Committee on Un-American Activities, which was later renamed as the infamous House Un-American Activities Committee, or HUAC.[21] From the late 1940s on, the challenge intensified as Senator Joseph McCarthy of Wisconsin and others portrayed whole segments of the U.S. government and civil society as rife with homosexuals, Communist agents, sympathizers, fellow travelers, and unwitting dupes of a global conspiracy by the Soviet Union for world domination. The State Department was the original target of the campaign, but all parts of the federal government, academia, and Hollywood quickly fell under suspicion.

President Truman, while not particularly sympathetic to this crusade, was hardly in a position to aggressively counter the attacks, which fairly reflected the national mood in the early days of the cold war. Russia now had the atomic bomb. Countries in eastern Europe appeared to be falling almost daily to Communist rule and Soviet hegemony. Events were going badly in China where the Communist rebels of Mao Tse-Tung were gaining territory and the support of the population at the expense of the Nationalist government. Even Greece was embroiled in a civil war, and a Communist government was a distinct possibility.

Truman also was president virtually by default. Selected by Roosevelt in 1944 in place of Henry Wallace, Truman had barely even met with Roosevelt during his brief vice-presidency. Unaware of Roosevelt's dire physical condition, Truman was shocked when he received word on April 12, 1945, that the beloved four-term president had passed away. Less than two years later, the glow of the end of the war already faded, Truman looked like a weak accidental president destined for defeat in the 1948 presidential elections, if he even dared to run.

Desperate for a show of strength, Truman announced to a Joint Session of Congress on March 12, 1947, what would be known as the Truman Doctrine—that the United States would support those countries fighting Communist insurgents. As part of the Truman Doctrine, he would back the noncommunist factions in Greece and Turkey.

Nine days later, he would announce the domestic counterpart of his plan, an executive order calling for a loyalty program for all employees of the executive branch.[22] Truman's biographer David McCullough contends that Truman only grudgingly approved the executive order and did so primarily to rally support for foreign aid for Greece and Turkey and to head off more draconian legislation from Congress.[23] Regardless of the degree of Truman's enthusiasm, his actions had devastating effects.

Although not the first effort to investigate and review the loyalty of federal government employees,[24] the Truman plan was the most comprehensive. Executive Order 9835 called for a loyalty investigation of every person entering the civilian employment of any department or agency of the executive branch. The investigation would include information from the files of the FBI, any intelligence agency, the House Committee on Un-American Activities, local law enforcement agencies, schools, employers, and "any other appropriate source." For current employees, each department and agency in the executive branch was charged with devising its own procedures "for an effective program to assure that disloyal civilian officers or employees (were) not retained in employment." The steps outlined in the executive order were considered the "minimum requirements" for the required loyalty program.

A person accused of being disloyal was entitled to written notice in sufficient detail to enable him or her to prepare a defense and adequate time to do so. The charges were to be stated as specifically and completely as the head of the department or agency believed in his discretion were consistent with security considerations. The accused also had to be informed of the right to reply to the charges in writing, the right to the administrative hearing, the right to appear personally with an attorney or other representative, and to present evidence through witnesses or by affidavit.[25]

Each department or agency was required to have a loyalty board of at least three representatives who would conduct administrative hearings for anyone charged with "being disloyal." The decision of the loyalty board was appealable to the head of the department or agency and then to the Civil Service Commission's Loyalty Review Board.

The legal standard for refusing employment or removal was "reasonable grounds" for "belief that the person involved is disloyal to the Government of the United States." In making this determination, the various boards could consider the commission or advocacy of actual crimes such as espionage or treason, but also more chillingly for serving "the interests of another government in preference to the interests of the United States" and for membership in any organization, association or movement designated by the attorney general as "totalitarian, fascist, communist, or subversive."[26]

In speaking about the loyalty program that fall, President Truman said,

> I believe I speak for all the people of the United States when I say that disloyal and subversive elements must be removed from the employ of the Government. We must not, however, permit employees of the Federal Government to be labeled as disloyal or potentially disloyal to their Government when no valid basis exists for arriving at such a conclusion. The overwhelming majority of Federal employees are loyal citizens who are giving conscientiously of their energy and skills to the United States. I do not want them to fear they are the objects of any "witch hunt." They are not being spied upon; they are not being restricted in their activities. They have nothing to fear from the loyalty program, since every effort has been made to guarantee full protection to those who are suspected of disloyalty. Rumor, gossip, or suspicion will not be sufficient to lead to the dismissal of an employee for disloyalty.[27]

According to the president, the newly established loyalty boards were "definitely not 'kangaroo courts.'" Appeals further protected the accused, and the Loyalty Review Board of the Civil Service Commission, comprised of citizens with "no ax to grind," "not concerned with personalities," whose judgment "will be as detached as is humanly possible," was the final check.[28]

While many liberals of the day praised the program, thinking Truman had stolen the ball from the Republicans and defused and deferred a sensitive issue, Arnold thought it was the worst mistake the president had made. Arnold presciently observed to his partners that when you ask for an $11 million appropriation to hunt witches "you've got to find witches."[29]

The firm's involvement in loyalty cases arose quite by accident when in 1946, Milton Freeman, a new associate at the firm, brought in the case of an acquaintance who had been fired from the War Manpower Commission for alleged Communist sympathies. The firm lost the case but soon acquired the reputation of one of the few establishment-type firms willing to take on such cases.[30]

The volume of the cases grew until virtually everyone in the firm had some involvement. At its peak, between one-quarter and one-half of the firm's workload consisted of pro bono loyalty cases.[31] The system was that an associate would handle the preparation of the initial responses to the Loyalty Board. The associate would interview the government employee and assist the employee in denying the accusation of Communist party membership or in any of the organizations identified on the attorney general's so-called Red list. It required careful thought and drafting, since in many cases the task was proving the negative—that the employee was not guilty of vague charges by unknown accusers. The associate then helped the employee obtain the greatest number of character references from fellow employees, supervisors, friends, professors, and public figures whenever possible attesting to their loyalty, opposition to the Communist party, and the impossibility of the charges against them.

If there was a hearing, the associate would attend and assist the employee in responding to the board's questioning, lead the employee through a carefully rehearsed direct examination, and present whatever character testimony could be arranged. There were no witnesses on the other side to confront because the board would not reveal the sources of its information or produce any accusers for cross-examination.

The firm lost most of the cases that were litigated but won many small, quiet victories when an agency accepted the employee's affidavit and no further action was taken. What the firm needed more than anything was a test case that could challenge the constitutionality of the entire loyalty program before the lawyers drowned in the paperwork of handling each case as it came. Thurman Arnold thought he had that test case in Dorothy Bailey.

Dorothy Bailey was an $8,000 a year training supervisor in the U.S. Employment Service (USES). The USES trained staff for state and local employment offices around the country. Neither the USES nor Bailey had any connection to national security whatsoever.

Dorothy Bailey did, however, have a background that made her a target of the loyalty machine. She was an executive board member of the Public Workers Union and a former president of her local union chapter, which had the reputation of being a left-wing union with many Communist members. While it is almost certain that the accusations against Bailey of being a Communist or a Communist sympathizer originated with someone connected with the union, the identity of the accusers has never been known. Bailey and Arnold speculated that it could have been either conservative opponents within the union who wished to discredit her or, even more nefariously, actual Communists who would benefit strategically from her removal.[32]

Following receipt of an accusation of disloyalty, Bailey went to see Milton Freeman at Arnold, Fortas & Porter (AF&P) through the recommendation of mutual friends. The familiar system swung into action with Bailey meticulously filling out the necessary affidavits, interrogatories, and denials of membership in the Communist party or knowing membership in any organization under its control. The most damning piece of information she had to confront was having attended an open meeting of the Communist party on one occasion as part of a required assignment for a seminar at Bryn Mawr College. Freeman then gathered glowing character references for Bailey from over fifty friends, coworkers, and professional acquaintances from across the country, ranging from housewives in Connecticut, employment service officials from numerous states, and the dean of the medical school at Howard University.

In September 1948 the Loyalty Board convened its hearing. The board grilled Bailey, with Freeman and Paul Porter by her side, about every detail of her affidavit and the anonymous accusations it had received about her loyalty. For an entire morning, Bailey denied ever knowingly being a member or attending meetings of a parade of organization the board contended were Communist fronts, including the "League of Women Shoppers." She denied following Communist direction in her union duties or supporting anyone she knew was a Communist. She described and documented numerous public positions she had taken as an individual and a union member that contradicted or opposed that of the Soviet Union or the known position of the Communist party. She admitted visiting the Soviet Union on one occasion but denied "speaking glowingly" about its system. Pursuant to the rules in place, the board denied all requests to reveal the identity of the accusers or to permit Bailey to confront the witnesses against her.

In November 1948 the board ruled against Bailey and in December denied her administrative appeal. On February 18, 1949, the Loyalty Board sent its notice removing Dorothy Bailey from federal employment, stating "that reasonable grounds exist for the belief that Miss Bailey is disloyal to the Government of the United States." The board ultimately based its decision on information from anonymous FBI informants. The board quite candidly admitted that it did not know who had made the accusations against Bailey, or their credibility, other than that the FBI vouched for the anonymous informants.

The next step was federal court with Porter and Arnold taking the lead at this stage. The complaint charged that the firing of Dorothy Bailey not only violated the Civil Service statutes and the internal regulations of her agency and the Loyalty Board, but it was also an unconstitutional deprivation of her right to confront her accusers and her rights to due process.

The district court could not have been less sympathetic. The court first denied a request for an injunction blocking Bailey's separation from the government, chiding the plaintiff and her attorneys for being premature. It then threw out the case on the merits, holding that the president's loyalty program was valid and constitutional, that Bailey was not entitled to permanent Civil Service protection, and that it was not unconstitutional to fire Bailey on the basis of a "partial hearing" even where the adverse information was secret and hearsay.

In the D.C. Circuit, Arnold handled the briefing and argument before the court where he had recently sat as an associate justice. Arnold focused on the constitutional issues: the failure of the board to even know the source of the accusations against Bailey, let alone allow her to confront her accusers. Arnold's brief pounded on the fact that the informants against Bailey were not identified and were unknown to the board or to the accused. The FBI official who received the reports was not identified and did not appear at the hearing. The reports were certified as reliable by other officials who, in turn, were neither identified nor present before the board. Arnold analogized the loyalty program to the courts of Nazi Germany and the nineteenth-century French Dreyfus case and wrote, "It is unthinkable that the President of the United States in this un-American manner puts federal employees at the mercy of the secret police."[33] At oral argument, he called the loyalty program a "travesty of justice" unprecedented in the history of Anglo-Saxon law.[34]

In March 1950, the D.C. Circuit affirmed the lower court by a 2-1 vote, with Arnold's former colleague Justice Edgerton writing the dissent.[35] The majority, Justices Prettyman and Proctor, conceded that Bailey did not have a trial in any sense of the word and that her situation appealed "powerfully to our sense of the fair and the just," but then proceeded to defend Bailey's dismissal in technical fashion. The majority held that Bailey was not entitled to any civil service protections given her recent conditional reinstatement following a brief layoff. More important, the majority upheld the executive order that created the loyalty program and its application to Bailey. In essence, the court revived the old distinction that government employment was a privilege and not a right and could therefore be curtailed or removed for any reason or no reason at all. The majority thus sustained the lower court's dismissal of Bailey's case in all meaningful aspects.

The Edgerton dissent was as dramatic and as no-holds-barred as Arnold's brief and argument. Edgerton began his opinion by stating,

> Without trial by jury, without evidence, and without even being allowed to confront her accusers or to know their identity, a citizen of the United States has been found disloyal to the government of the United States.[36]

Edgerton ridiculed the majority's holding that Bailey had been removed on the basis of any "evidence," let alone "all the evidence" required by Truman's executive order:

> However respectable her anonymous accusers may have been, if her dismissal is sustained the livelihood and reputation of any civil servant today and perhaps of any American tomorrow are at the mercy not only of an innocently mistaken informer but also of a malicious or demented one.[37]

He concluded:

> On this record we have no sufficient reason to doubt Miss Bailey's patriotism, or that her ability and experience were valuable to the government. We have no reason to suppose that an unpatriotic person in her job could do substantial harm of any kind. Whatever her actual thoughts may have been, to oust her as disloyal without trial is to pay too much for protection against any harm that could possibly be done in such a job. The cost is too great in morale and efficiency of government workers, in appeal of government employment to independent and inquiring minds, and in public confidence in democracy. But even if such dismissal strengthened the government instead of weakening it, they would still cost too much in constitutional rights. We cannot preserve our liberties by sacrificing them.[38]

Edgerton's moving dissent was the only published opinion that would ever support Bailey's position in her case.

Arnold felt that the Supreme Court was certain to side with him, but first he had to convince the court to take the case. The Supreme Court has virtually unlimited discretion as to which cases to take, with four votes needed to hear a case. Despite the opposition of the solicitor general, on June 5, 1950, the Supreme Court gave Dorothy Bailey her four votes and agreed to hear the case.[39]

The opening brief for Bailey in the Supreme Court began simply and straightforwardly: "The fundamental question is whether the President's Executive Order 9835 requires a fair hearing. Plainly no fair hearing was given petitioner. She asserts that such a hearing is required."[40] The government's brief argued that the term "evidence" in the executive order did not mean "evidence" as that term was used in a court of law, that no due process was owed to a government employee losing a job, and that the loyalty program was necessary in the fight against Communism.

By the time Arnold filed his reply brief for Bailey, the language was pure Arnold:

> The Government's brief in effect admits that the procedure in Dorothy Bailey's case is indefensible. By its silence on the point, the Government confesses that, as applied in the Bailey case, the elaborate hearing procedures set forth in the President's Loyalty Order are meaningless trappings; an empty gesture to the fundamental principles of our democracy, devoid of substance. . . . She was convicted by nameless investigators who certified to her nominal judges that her nameless accusers were reliable.[41]

At oral argument, Paul Porter handled the main argument, taking more than an hour split over two days. Arnold handled the rebuttal, following the argument of Philip Perlman, the solicitor general. Porter reported to a friend that the argument had gone "very well I think from our point of view" and that veteran court observers told him that they had "never seen a Solicitor General take the pummeling which Perlman got from Felix [Frankfurter], Jackson, and Black." Porter was certain that they could count on votes from Frankfurter, Douglas, Black, and Jackson. Porter thought Reed was the key to a fifth vote and victory. Arnold was similarly encouraged by what he heard at oral argument.[42]

But it was not to be. On April 30, 1951, the Supreme Court split 4-4 on the Bailey case. Justice Clark, Arnold's former protégé at the Antitrust Division who had supervised the loyalty program as Truman's attorney general, did not participate.⁴³ Thus, the decision of the lower court was automatically affirmed without opinion or precedent.

Arnold never knew how close he came to total victory. At the initial conference of the justices after oral argument, there was a 5-3 vote in favor of Bailey. The tentative fifth vote came from Sherman Minton, not Stanley Reed as they had expected. But over the next few months, Minton changed his mind and produced the unexplained 4-4 affirmance without opinion that was the public face of the Court.⁴⁴

Following the Supreme Court decision, Bailey was fired from American University where she had worked since her termination from the U.S. Employment Service. In true Arnold, Fortas & Porter fashion, the firm decided to hire Dorothy Bailey as the office manager for the growing firm, and she worked there quite happily for years until her husband's work ultimately posted them to Africa.

Even a later victory in the Supreme Court did not result in the dismantling of the loyalty program. The later case involved John Peters, a physician and a distinguished professor at the Yale Medical School with an international reputation. Besides his teaching and scholarship, he had done research for the military and served as a special consultant to the U.S. Surgeon General. His loyalty case was, if anything, even more surreal than the ordeal endured by Dorothy Bailey.

On January 7, 1949, Peters received a letter informing him that information relating to his loyalty had been received; enclosed was an interrogatory requesting information regarding membership in various organizations and support for various causes suspected of Communist leanings. Peters answered the interrogatories within ten days with the help of counsel and in February received a letter stating that the Loyalty Board of the Federal Security Agency determined that no reasonable grounds existed for believing that Peters was disloyal.

Then in December 1951 Peters received another letter from the board containing sixteen charges of activity supposedly showing disloyalty, most of which were covered in the earlier letters. Peters again responded, denying membership in the Communist party or any organization linked to it. In April 1952 a hearing of the Loyalty Board took place. In May of that year, the board again concluded that there was no reasonable doubt as to Peters' loyalty to the United States.

The next spring, the Loyalty Review Board on its own initiative decided to review the prior hearing and reach its own conclusions. In May 1953 another hearing took place in which the Review Board, in all but one instance, considered accusations against Peters from unknown persons. Even in the one instance where the Review Board knew the identity of the accusers, it refused to divulge that information to Peters. For the rest of the accusers, the board could not have divulged the identity of the accuser even if it had wanted to, since it did not know their names or the circumstances surrounding the accusations.

Peters testified at the hearing, again denying membership in the Communist party, or any sympathy with the Soviet Union, the Communist party, or any front group. Several prominent character witnesses testified on his behalf that there could be no reasonable doubt as to his loyalty, including Charles Seymour, the former president of Yale; Hugh Long, the dean of the Yale Medical School; and Charles E. Clark, the former dean of the Yale Law School and then judge on the U.S. Court of Appeals for the Second Circuit.

This time, however, the Review Board concluded that "on all the evidence, there is a reasonable doubt as to Dr. Peter's loyalty to the Government of the United States" and ordered his separation from his part-time affiliation with the Surgeon General's office. All further appeals were unsuccessful, including Arnold's request to discuss the case with then Assistant Secretary of Health Education and Welfare Nelson Rockefeller.

The next step was federal court, Thurman Arnold taking the lead with the assistance of Milton Freeman and Yale Law School Professors Fowler Harper and Vern Countryman. Once again, the strategy was to get to the Supreme Court as fast as possible and take on the constitutionality of the executive order and the Kafkaesque procedures of the Loyalty Boards. Peters lost in the trial court and on appeal, with Arnold virtually begging the D.C. Circuit to turn down his appeal so he could get to the Supreme Court, conceding that the issues raised had been decided against him in the *Bailey* case.[45]

In the Supreme Court, there was partial victory for Peters, but an undiminished loyalty program was left standing. Arnold argued the case against future Chief Justice Warren Burger, who was at the time assistant attorney general of the Justice Department. Arnold's strategy was to concede all procedural issues and concentrate on the constitutional issues of due process and lack of confrontation of Peters's secret accusers.

To Arnold's ill-contained mounting frustration, Justices Frankfurter and Harlan ignored his approach and instead focused on technical procedural violations by the Loyalty Board and the Review Board rather than the core constitutional issues. Only Arnold's sense of decorum, and his duty of loyalty to his client, prevented him from forgoing a potential narrow victory for his client in favor of an all-out victory or defeat on the constitutionality of the loyalty program as a whole. After argument, the parties were instructed to file supplemental briefs on the technical issue of the Review Board's power to reopen a favorable decision of a Loyalty Board. This incensed Arnold, particularly because both he and the government agreed on the need for a constitutional ruling.[46]

The final Peters decision was a victory of sorts for the client but a defeat for Arnold's litigation strategy of striking a mortal blow against the entire loyalty program.[47] The decision confirmed Arnold's worst fears that the Court would duck the constitutionality of the loyalty program. In an opinion by Chief Justice Warren, which received six votes, the Court reversed Peters's dismissal on the grounds that the Loyalty Review Board exceeded its authority in reopening the favorable report of the Loyalty Board. According to the Court, the Review Board could only act as an administrative appeal board for an employee who received an unfavorable initial determination and not as a roving commission reopening those proceedings with which the Review Board independently disagreed.

For Peters, there was vindication but no reinstatement. Since his appointment had expired in the interim, the Court declined to order him reinstated.

Only Douglas and Black discussed the constitutional issues and wrote that the executive order establishing the loyalty program and the procedures used were constitutionally suspect. Justices Reed and Burton dissented and would have upheld the determination against Peters without reaching the constitutional issues. The Court obviously understood the magnitude of the issues it was ducking, but this was as far as it was prepared to go in 1955 on this politically and socially explosive issue.[48]

The *Bailey* and *Peters* cases look almost reasonable in comparison to that of the Fort Monmouth ten. These research scientists were dismissed for disloyalty following an accusation by Senator McCarthy of mass Communist infiltration of the entire facility. The typical Loyalty Board, relying on secret evidence not disclosed or subject to cross-examination, found reasonable grounds to question their loyalty. The dismissals were then affirmed by a review board *where the very identity of the review board itself was unknown to the defendants*. Only after seven years of litigation did the defendants prevail in the court of appeals and receive back pay for their unlawful discharge.[49]

For Arnold, the entire loyalty process violated all the tenets of the American ideal of a fair trial:

> The first is, that the accused be confronted and have an opportunity to cross-examine the witnesses against him. The second is that he be tried for something he actually has done and not something which he has thought or has a tendency to do because of his character. . . . And the third element is that the tribunal or court which tries him must be in a position to make an independent judgment.[50]

All three of the founding partners worked on the Lattimore case through an endless series of congressional hearings and perjury indictments.[51] Owen Lattimore was a professor at Johns Hopkins University and an internationally renowned expert on Asia, and particularly China, where he had served as the political adviser to General Chiang Kai-shek. Lattimore was affiliated with the Institute of Pacific Relations (IPR), a Honolulu organization under the auspices of the YMCA, and served as the editor of its quarterly journal *Pacific Affairs*. The IPR had been targeted by the anticommunist right in 1946 and particularly after the fall of China to Communist forces in 1949.[52] While the IPR had a number of Communists on its staff, Lattimore was not one of them.

While Lattimore was traveling in Afghanistan on United Nations business in March 1950, Senator McCarthy denounced him on the Senate floor as the top Soviet spy in the United States. Once he learned what had happened in faraway Washington, D.C., Lattimore rushed home and through his wife retained Fortas. Meanwhile, his wife, students, and colleagues at Johns Hopkins scrambled to assemble his many writings and prepare his defense. All three partners met with Lattimore when he returned, and once they were assured that he would fight the charges all the way, they agreed to represent him pro bono. Judge Patricia Wald, then an associate with the firm, recalls that the entire firm met to discuss whether or not to take the Lattimore case and everyone voted to take the case with only one negative vote.[53]

While McCarthy eventually withdrew the specific charge of espionage, neither Lattimore nor his attorneys had any idea of the nature of the ordeal ahead. In April, Lattimore, with Fortas and Porter by his side, presented a fiery forty-two-page prepared statement to a Senate subcommittee denouncing Senator McCarthy by name and refuting point-by-point the accusations the Senator had made against him and then answered the committee's questions. Lattimore, in his memoir, *Ordeal by Slander,* gave a sense of the nature of the circus for which he was the inadvertent star attraction:

> There was some pushing around before we could get seated. Photographers wanted pictures of Eleanor and me. The klieg lights went on for the newsreel and television cameras. They were mostly right in my face, and greatly increased the eye strain in reading my statement. A little knot of cameramen squatted on the floor, in front of me and to the left. Most of them wanted to get pictures of me during the hearing, showing animation or emotion or an arresting gesture. All day, their flash bulbs kept going off at unpredictable intervals, adding to the strain.[54]

The subcommittee, under the leadership of Senator Tydings, ultimately found the charges against Lattimore baseless. That exoneration cost Senator Tydings dearly; he was defeated for reelection shortly thereafter and failed to save Lattimore from further abuse.

Eighteen months later, Lattimore was called before a different Senate subcommittee in executive session, under the direction of the far less forgiving Senator McCarran. Much of the questioning dealt with Lattimore's affiliation with the Institute of Pacific Relations. Seven months of public hearings followed, attacking Lattimore's loyalty with great publicity. Only at the end did the committee grant Lattimore's request to be heard in open session. The committee questioned Lattimore for twelve straight days, according to Arnold, the "longest congressional interrogation of one man in congressional history."[55]

Following intense congressional pressure, Lattimore was indicted by the Justice Department for perjury toward the end of 1952. Lattimore was charged with falsely testifying before Congress that he had never been a "sympathizer" or "promoter" of Communism or Communist interests and that he had been unaware of the Communist affiliations of certain coworkers. At this point, Arnold took over the case assisted by former Wyoming Senator O'Mahoney, who had remained in private practice in Washington, D.C., after leaving the Senate. As Arnold told a friend, "When a man is tried for his sympathies, it having been charged that he is sympathetic to Communism, and he has to go back though his entire life and writings to show he isn't, as against excerpts torn out of context, none of us is safe." Later, Arnold was even more blunt: "If the First Amendment does not protect a man who gives an economic or political opinion from indictment on the grounds that he was insincere, the right of free speech is clearly in danger."[56]

At least now Lattimore's case would be heard in federal court with greater procedural safeguards. The case was assigned to Judge Luther Youngdahl, a former Republican governor of Minnesota, but a man whom Arnold respected as having an innate sense of fairness and a strong aversion to political pressure. Youngdahl dismissed the first count as so utterly vague that it failed to inform the defendant of the nature of his alleged crime. The dismissal was sustained on appeal.[57]

The government brought a new indictment in the summer of 1954 that reiterated the same basic charge, this time in somewhat more detail. The gist was the same. Lattimore had lied before Congress when he denied being a "follower of the Communist line" or a "promoter of Communist interests" during the period from 1935 to 1950. The indictment and any defense involved a minute examination of Lattimore's thoughts, deeds, and extensive writings throughout his professional career during turbulent times when the United States had been both friend and foe of the Soviet Union on different occasions.

Through large periods of his travail, Lattimore virtually lived at Arnold, Fortas & Porter preparing for hearings or court appearances. His wife was frequently with him, assisting in the compilation of facts about Lattimore's life and checking passages in his voluminous writings to rebut specific accusations of disloyalty or perjury. Pat Wald recalled many occasions where Lattimore was hustled out the back door of the AF&P office on 19th Street to avoid the press and curious onlookers.[58]

Judge Youngdahl eventually rejected a controversial government attempt to disqualify him on the grounds of bias and again dismissed the main counts against Lattimore as "formless" and a violation of the Sixth Amendment.[59] The Court of Appeals split 4-4, affirming the dismissal without opinion.[60] This razor-slim margin was all that saved Lattimore from further prosecution. The government declined to appeal to the Supreme Court and eventually dismissed the remaining minor charges, thus ending with a whimper its five-year effort against Lattimore.

All but one of these many loyalty cases were handled pro bono. The Lattimore case alone amounted to $2.5 million in foregone billings. Arnold even returned the occasional unsolicited donation of fees and costs from friends and supporters of clients in the loyalty cases.[61]

The only fee the firm ever accepted for its work on loyalty cases was a $5000 payment from the actor Jose Ferrer. In 1951, Ferrer was identified by HUAC as affiliated with a plethora of Communist front groups, along with the actress Judy Holliday, only one week after he won the Oscar for his role as *Cyrano de Bergerac* and Holliday won hers for *Born Yesterday*. But before taking on Ferrer as a client, the actor had to acknowledge in writing that the firm would have total control of the matter and further state that he was not a Communist and would make full disclosure to the committee.[62]

Fortas represented Ferrer at his congressional hearing and coordinated a delicate strategy of telling his story to both assuage the entertainment community and not injure Ferrer's reputation with the public at what would otherwise be the height of his career. The firm sent a press release the day before the hearing to *Variety,* the *Washington Post,* the *Star, Times-Herald, Daily News,* and the National Press Club telling Ferrer's side of the story. Trying to get Ferrer's message out ahead of the upcoming attacks in the hearings, the firm argued that Ferrer was deeply democratic and anticommunist and had merely lent his name to thousands of civil rights causes principally involving the black and Puerto Rican communities.

Fortas followed standard procedure from the less high profile cases and obtained a combination of letters and affidavits from old friends and powerful individuals, including one from Cary Grant attesting to Ferrer's character and loyalty. Ferrer's affidavit and testimony painted a picture of fringe involvement with a vast number of organizations. This required a laborious search of records and recollections by both Fortas and Ferrer to document what if anything Ferrer had done with various groups seven to ten years before. Many of the groups and activities were related to the 1944 reelection of President Roosevelt. Under Fortas's direction, Ferrer documented his many appearances for the armed forces, the Red Cross, the American Jewish Committee, and other organizations beyond reproach.

At the hearing itself, Ferrer admitted that he had endorsed a successful Democratic candidate for the New York City Council who was later convicted as a Communist party chief, but (like most of the voters) never knew that he was a Communist. He further admitted "plain stupid carelessness" in allowing his name to be used by groups that turned out to be

Communist fronts. The committee excused Ferrer after a day of hearings so as not to interrupt his appearance on Broadway in the *Twentieth Century* with Gloria Swanson, but he endured a second day of hostile questioning later in 1951. The committee ultimately took no further action and Ferrer's career continued without lasting damage.

Fortas advocated a different strategy in informally advising Lillian Hellman in connection with her appearance before HUAC in 1952. Here, Fortas recommended that Hellman answer all questions pertaining to her beliefs and activities and simply refuse to answer any question in connection with any other individual. This strategy, which Thurman Arnold opposed as throwing their client to the wolves, was extremely risky to Hellman and without constitutional protection. Somehow it all worked out without further legal action against Hellman, who ultimately was represented at the hearing by liberal stalwart Joseph Rauh.[63]

Despite the high profile of several of the AF&P loyalty cases, the clients were rarely famous or important and more typically included a social science analyst for the National Institutes of Health, an information officer at the State Department who took movie film of his 1935 European trip, a clerk at the American embassy in Russia in 1939, a census consultant, a meteorologist in the Commerce Department, an engineer at the FCC, a clerk in the Library of Congress, and so on. Each victim had his or her own tale of woe from the stress of accusation, denial to classified material, suspension from work, and problems with getting new or equal employment in the private sector. The burden of each case was significant, since it normally required rebutting outright fabrications, reconstructing events as far back as twenty years, and documenting the innocent nature of events now being characterized in a far more sinister light. It was almost hopeless if the person actually had a sensitive job, worked in the military, was connected with actual defense work, traveled extensively or worked abroad, or was not a citizen and thus subject to immigration pressures.

Once word got out about AF&P's work on these cases, referrals came pouring in from the ACLU, other attorneys, sympathetic senators, coworkers, and relatives. The firm was frequently contacted by total strangers who had read about previous cases in the press. At one point, clients were actually being referred by the less hostile members of the House Un-American Activities Committee itself. Firms from around the country also contacted AF&P lawyers for advice on their own cases.

The number of loyalty cases rose from about thirty-five in 1948 to over two hundred by 1951.[64] Everyone at the firm did at least some work on these cases, while handling more than their share of work for paying clients. When the work became overwhelming, the firm declined a number of new cases and frequently turned to a young solo practitioner, Murdaugh Madden, the son of a U.S. Court of Claims judge, who took on many of these cases for a modest fee.

Arnold best summed up the madness of this era in a short, but brilliantly acerbic, article in *Harper's Magazine* in 1948 entitled "How Not to Get Investigated: Ten Commandments for Government Employees."[65] Claiming that each "commandment" was taken from actual cases, he advised only semifacetiously:

> 1. Do not attend any social gathering, no matter how large, at which a "subversive" may also be present. This includes dances.
> 2. Never talk, even to your neighbors or at social gatherings, about controversial issues. If your views offend someone, they may show up in report in a distorted fashion and you will never even know who gave the information.
> 3. Do not subscribe to the *New Republic* or the *Nation,* or any other liberal publication. Maybe it's communist and you don't even know it. Don't read any books about Russia even out of curiosity, because you can never prove it was only curiosity. You will be safer if you can honestly swear that you do not know where Russia is or what it is like.
> 4. If anyone sends you as a gift a publication of the sort described in the foregoing Commandment, cancel it at once, with an indignant letter. Otherwise it may be taken to mean you have communist friends.
> 5. Do not ever attend the large annual reception at the Russian Embassy. How can you prove that you merely wanted to see what the Russians look like and to eat caviar? I recently advised a friend of mine not to attend a party at the Polish consulate in New York City.
> 6. Do not contribute any money for the legal defense of some old acquaintance or college classmate charged with disloyalty, for even if he is found innocent, you may be charged because of your contribution.
> 7. Do not marry anyone who, however many years before, had radical associations in college. Avoid, if you can, marriage with anyone who has ever visited Russia, read Karl Marx, or contributed to war relief drives for the Spanish Loyalists.

8. Be particularly careful never to ride in an automobile in which a "subversive" may be another rider. The car pool is a favorite object of suspicion.
9. Do not yourself be unduly critical of Fascists or Nazis, and carefully avoid the company of those who have been outspoken on these subjects.
10. If any relative of yours, no matter how distant and no matter how much you disagree with him, has ever been a "radical," do not take a government position at all. The salary can't possibly be worth the effort it may take to defend yourself.[66]

Arnold was only being half-facetious in an era where the Army was circulating bulletins that advised that Communists could be identified by their use of such words as "vanguard," "reactionary," "chauvinism," or "hootenany."[67] Turning deadly serious, Arnold went on to conclude:

This attack on government employees is a poor way of fighting a cold war against Russia, and as counterespionage it is sheer nonsense. Secret investigations of private lives, opinions, and associations can never strengthen a democracy. Instead, they bleed it white of those corpuscles of independent thought which are essential to the character of democratic government. In independence of thought and action is the safety of our country. It is not difficult to drive such independence out of government.[68]

By the early 1950s, the press of the firm's existing pro bono cases and the growth of its business practice led the partners to decline most new loyalty cases except where there was a personal connection. Even though the firm had never won the total victory it had sought, it had won important skirmishes that restrained the worst excess of the cold war era and helped turn the tide until the hysteria subsided and the courts regained the courage to protect the innocent, and even admitted Communists, from arbitrary discharge from their jobs.

Why then did Arnold, Fortas & Porter risk so much to take these unpopular and unremunerative cases at such a critical and fragile time in the firm's existence? A classic story involving Paul Porter illustrates the courage and humor the partners used in confronting this crisis. Porter encountered an in-house lawyer for one of the firm's corporate clients at the bar of their country club. The lawyer rather hostilely inquired, "Paul, I understand your firm is engaged in defending homosexuals and Communists." Without batting an eye, Porter replied, "That's right. What can we do for you?"[69]

All three of the founding partners were lawyers who had spent the majority of their careers in the federal government and could easily imagine themselves the targets of investigation and forced resignation or worse. Indeed, given the political leanings and past memberships of the partners, such investigation would have been inevitable. Fortas and Porter were closely aligned with liberal causes. At the Department of the Interior, Fortas had tried to protect several subordinates from red-baiting accusations, and in 1940 he was briefly under investigation as to certain organizations he had allegedly joined. Fortas at one point had even argued that the United States should share information about nuclear weapons with the Soviet Union.[70]

Arnold himself was a Yale intellectual, a liberal New Dealer, former National Law Guild member, a supporter of the Spanish Loyalists, and a proud advisory board member to the *Nation* magazine. He rarely turned down the opportunity to donate money or lend his name to liberal groups and causes, many of which were beginning to turn up on "red" or "pink" lists. In fact in 1953, unknown to Arnold, the FBI initiated the gathering of at least routine background information on Arnold because of his role in opposing the loyalty program.[71]

As early as 1940, Arnold had publicly written about the pendulum swinging against the spirit of reform of the New Deal and manifesting itself in both reactionary legislation and "in red hunts against dissenting groups which still have faith in sweeping government change."[72] Still, some of Arnold's admirers were unsure where Arnold would take his stand. I. F. Stone writing in 1943 observed that Arnold was

> distinctly a populistic middle-class radical who might even end up on the far right. I should like to emphasis "might" because it would be unwise to draw too logical conclusions from some of Arnold's weirder ideas. It is just as possible to imagine him a fervent anti-fascist in a period of crisis. For he is courageous, generous, and warm-hearted, equally removed from the poles of bigotry and milk-and-water liberalism.[73]

There was one kind of case that the firm would not take. Despite some criticism from the very community that AF&P was defending, the founding partners made a decision not to represent any clients who were admitted Communists or who intended to assert their rights under the Fifth Amendment in refusing to answer whether they were Communists. Abe Fortas explained in declining to represent a certain witness before HUAC in 1949: "[W]e don't think we can ever afford to represent anybody that has ever been a Communist." On at least one occasion, the firm met with an admitted Communist union leader but declined to represent him after it became clear that the client would not cede control of the strategy and conduct of the case to the firm.[74]

Many of the surviving AF&P lawyers speculate that the founding partners were simply highly patriotic anticommunist liberals not willing to go the final step and defend admitted Communists. There had always been an important liberal faction to the anticommunist coalition, with key left liberal groups like the National Lawyers Guild and the ACLU eventually seeking to expel Communist members as damaging to the core values of the group.[75] Arnold's personal views were certainly consistent with this view, having resigned from the National Lawyers Guild when he perceived growing Communist influence. More generally, he viewed the Communist party in the United States as an "unmitigated nuisance" in its attempts to influence mainstream liberalism.[76]

The question of control of the case appears to be of greater significance. In a 1950 letter to the editor of the *Washington Post* responding to an editorial denouncing the failure of the entire bar to represent admitted Communists, the three partners cited a lack of control of the case for their own refusal to handle such cases. While chiding the organized bar generally for failing to stand up for the rights of the accused in the loyalty oath period, the three partners nonetheless argued:

> [L]awyers are justified in refusing to represent clients if they feel that they do not know what the facts are and unless they have freedom to decide on the arguments to be made and how they should be presented.... [S]ome of the refusals to represent the Communist leaders may have been due to a reasonable belief on the part of the lawyers approached that the Communists would not permit them to discharge the obligations of their profession in a creditable manner, but would insist themselves upon controlling the defense to be made.[77]

Regardless of the reasons behind this choice, others had to do the heavy lifting in defending the myriad of criminal, labor, and immigration cases brought against admitted Communists well into the 1950s. In addition, many vulnerable individuals targeted for prosecution or scrutiny by the congressional investigating committees, particularly in the private sector, were forced to rely on smaller firms and individuals associated with the National Lawyers Guild or other segments of the American left, which were themselves subject to harassment and often also targets of the McCarthy movement.[78]

Perversely, this decision not to represent admitted Communists, though controversial within the firm and the civil liberties movement, may have helped the clients AF&P chose to take, since they benefitted from the firm's reputation as a hard-charging firm ready to defend vigorously only those who denied membership in the Communist party or its front organizations. It was also certainly easier, although not pleasant, for the firm's business clients to swallow.

The best illustration of the tightrope the firm walked in the loyalty cases was its limited involvement in representing the Screen Writers Guild in countering the studio blacklist of any writer who refused to testify in congressional hearings. The firm did not represent any of the writers who had invoked the Fifth Amendment and were now essentially unemployable. Instead, it represented the union in devising the best strategy to counter the collective boycott by the studios. This case is ironic at so many levels. It is the only known case that combined Arnold's interest and expertise in antitrust, the motion picture industry, and loyalty matters and was on behalf of a labor union, which had more normally been the target of Arnold's antitrust cases while he was in the government.[79]

Time and time again, the younger lawyers who worked on these cases marveled at the partners' willingness to risk the firm because they thought defending the loyalty cases was the right thing to do.[80] Yet the costs proved to be remarkably manageable. The firm kept most of its corporate clients and added many new ones until the proportion of paying work to the declining number of pro bono cases toward the end of the McCarthy era approached that of AF&P's competitors in the D.C. bar. In the process the firm also earned a reputation for toughness that proved invaluable in its development as a Washington institution.

9

Building a Washington Law Firm

When Arnold reentered private practice in 1945, he was a 54-year-old ex-judge with no clients but one important promise of a retainer. While on the bench, he began a friendship with Robert Woodruff, the chairman of Coca-Cola, who would become Arnold's first and lifelong client. As head of the Antitrust Division, Arnold was criticized for being opposed to all forms of big business. While this was far from the truth, Arnold struggled to find an example of a large firm that he regarded as fully complying with both the letter and spirit of the antitrust laws. Coca-Cola became that example.[1]

Coke's business model was simply different from that of most large national corporations. Its system of locally owned bottlers created a network of substantial, independently owned businesses that was the complete opposite of the corporate colonization of the West and small-town America Arnold had detested since his days as a Laramie lawyer. Coke sold syrup to local bottlers who then resold the syrup and bottled soft drinks. This system also poured money and jobs into outlying communities, rather than Coke being an absentee owner sucking money and decision-making authority out of the markets in which it operated. In Arnold's view, Coke did not seek to control prices or drive out its competitors. It appeared to be an efficient national business distributed thorough a highly competitive system of bottlers and vending machines not dominated by any one firm.[2]

Arnold never took enforcement action against Coca-Cola while at the Justice Department and began to pepper his speeches and testimony with references to Coke as a model corporate citizen. His intent appeared not to cozy up to Coke as much as to insulate himself from the charge that he was anti–big business.

Woodruff and others at Coke began to notice the favorable references to their company. Once Arnold was on the bench, Woodruff made contact but corresponded only sporadically until Arnold began to seriously contemplate returning to practice. Conversations intensified, and Judge Arnold made a trip to Atlanta to discuss possibilities at the end of 1944, which included a formal dinner and visit with liberal Georgia governor Ellis Arnell.

Once Arnold decided to reject overtures from a large New York firm, he began to focus on entering practice on his own so long as there was some reasonable prospect of financial security. The negotiations with Woodruff produced an agreement that Coca-Cola would guarantee Arnold $25,000 a year for at least five years. At the same time, Arnold obtained promises of two additional retainers adding up to an additional $25,000 a year from the Chesapeake & Ohio Railroad and Otis & Company (the investment banking firm not the elevator company). Arnold was now set financially for the foreseeable future at a salary of four times his judicial pay, with the freedom to take the kind of cases he enjoyed on behalf of clients who generally benefitted from the expansion rather than the restriction of competition.[3]

He wrote former Texas Congressman Maury Maverick on his decision to leave the bench, without naming Coke or his other retainers by name:

> It was a hard decision to make, but some clients showed up who were interested in my economic ideas and willing to pay me substantially for pushing them if I got off the Bench. So I really believe that I can not only make a living, but also do something for independent business in this country. . . . I am going to try to avoid cases which involve defending people for violation of the antitrust laws. It was the necessity of handling that type of case which led me to turn down a New York firm when I went on the Bench. Now I will be independent and I think sufficiently prosperous and I will not have to take that kind of business.[4]

While Arnold never appeared to represent antitrust defendants, the rest of the firm certainly did. This was the era when Fortas was the supreme rainmaker attracting clients such as Lever Brothers, the Commonwealth of Puerto Rico, Pan Am, and Federated Department Stores. By the early 1950s, Porter began to build a lucrative radio and eventually television practice before the FCC. Over time, younger partners like Norman Diamond added institutional corporate clients like Krogers to the firm's roster of blue-chip corporate clients.

. . .

In addition, Abe Fortas knew Lyndon Johnson, who became the firm's most important unofficial client. They had met in 1941 when Johnson was a new congressman and a privileged but junior insider in the New Deal circles revolving around Tommy Corcoran.[5] As Robert Caro has discussed in his masterful biography, Johnson had reached the end of the line politically in 1948. President Roosevelt had favored Johnson as one of the few New Deal supporters in the South and a prodigious fund-raiser for the Democratic party. However, Truman had cut Johnson out of any real influence in his administration. Johnson also had lost a senatorial primary in 1941 and seemed doomed to a middling career in the House of Representatives or a quick exit from politics altogether.

Johnson opted to run in the 1948 senate primary against former Texas governor Coke Stevenson, one of the most popular public figures in the history of the state and someone who had never lost an election. In a crowded field, Johnson was able to force a runoff against Stevenson but was trailing badly in the head-to-head contest for the Democratic nomination. During the runoff, Johnson outspent his rival, blanketed the state with print and broadcast media, toured the state relentlessly in a helicopter to reach the far-flung hamlets of Texas, distorted his own record, and flat-out lied about Stevenson's. Johnson also bought votes at both the wholesale and retail levels, but the best he could do was an apparent loss by 115 votes out of a state-wide count of nearly 1 million. Days after the polls had closed but before the results were certified, one precinct in a rural country controlled by a boss loyal to Johnson reported an additional 201 votes for Johnson, with only 2 additional votes for Stevenson, resulting in an 87-vote "landslide" for Johnson.[6]

The additional names that were belatedly forwarded were written on the voting list in one ink color different from all the varieties used by the earlier voters on the poll list and were listed in alphabetical order! Stevenson supporters briefly viewed the highly dubious list but were never permitted to take the list with them. Of the eleven people listed that the Stevenson forces were able to contact, none had actually voted. Some had been sick and others had even been out of town on the day of the election. What remains unknown is what similar frauds were perpetrated by the Stevenson forces elsewhere in the state.[7]

Stevenson's supporters unsuccessfully sought relief through Texas election law. However, they found greater luck in federal court. The Stevenson contingent sought out a conservative anti–New Deal judge who was a friend of their candidate, even though it meant an all-night drive to find the judge at his home on the Louisiana border. They argued that the electoral fraud had deprived Stevenson of equal protection of the law and due process under the federal Constitution. They convinced the federal district court judge to order a temporary injunction against printing the ballots for the general election with Johnson's name until an investigation could be completed.

Johnson's supporters were frantic for two reasons. Further investigation could well uncover the fraud that Stevenson had alleged and demonstrate that vote counts had simply been changed once Johnson's team knew exactly how many votes were needed. Johnson also faced a practical deadline regardless of whether Stevenson was ever successful in proving the alleged fraud. Texas state law had a firm deadline for printing ballots. If Johnson's name was not on the ballot, he would almost certainly become the first Democrat to lose in a state-wide race since the Civil War.

Time was running out on an appeal that, even if successful, might extend past the deadline for the ballot printing. According to Caro, Johnson's legal team was baffled, and the candidate himself stepped in, saying "Where's Abe?"[8]

Fortas was in Dallas taking depositions on a matter for Neiman-Marcus, and he quickly joined the Johnson team. Once briefed on the problem, he came up with a strategy that bet everything on the decision of a single man, Justice Hugo Black, the Supreme Court justice who supervised the U.S. Court of Appeals for the Fifth Circuit where Texas was located. Black was himself a former senator, staunch New Dealer, and social friend of Fortas, Johnson, and Arnold. But in between the district court and the Supreme Court was the Fifth Circuit Court of Appeals. Fortas essentially proposed deliberately losing the appeal as fast as possible so as to get in front of Black before the ballot deadline. If Fortas was wrong, Johnson's political life was over.

Johnson listened and approved the gamble. Fortas drafted a brief laying out the issues. He then deliberately sought out the single circuit court judge *least* likely to grant a stay against the district court's injunction. The point was to lose fast and get to the Supreme Court. The Friday hearing lasted four hours, and the judge deliberated for another five hours and then announced that he did not have the authority to stay the district court's injunction.[9]

The next day an all-star legal team met in the AF&P offices to draft the petition to Justice Black. Porter, Fortas, and Arnold were joined by stalwart New Dealers Ben Cohen, Tommy Corcoran, Hugh Cox (Arnold's former deputy at the Antitrust Division), former attorney general Francis Biddle, and Joe Rauh. Thurman Arnold and Paul Porter served the document personally to Black's chambers.[10]

Fortas arranged for a hearing in Justice Black's chamber for the next available day. Fortas, along with Thurman Arnold and Paul Porter, appeared before Black, with the lawyer for Stevenson present as well. Fortas argued that the federal court had no jurisdiction over a matter of state election law. As Black rocked in his swivel chair, dressed in sports clothes and considering the arguments, hearings continued in Texas as special masters with federal powers questioned witnesses and examined election records in the disputed county. If the fraud was substantiated, Johnson's career was over regardless of what Black ruled. Even if Black accepted Fortas's argument, Johnson's political career was still over if the ballots were printed without his name as the Democratic candidate.[11]

Black recessed for lunch and to work on an expedited decision. After lunch, Fortas's "one shot" had come through. Black sided with Johnson and held that the federal court had no jurisdiction to hear Stevenson's challenge to the certification of Johnson as the winner. The federal injunction that prevented listing Johnson as the Democratic candidate for the Senate was dissolved, all further hearings stopped in Texas, and the ballots went to press.[12] From that moment on, Abe Fortas was Johnson's lawyer and Arnold, Fortas & Porter was his firm. From then on, the firm would gain much and eventually suffer bitterly from the Johnson-Fortas connection.

However, for the next twenty years, both Johnson and Fortas prospered. As Johnson became the most powerful senator of the twentieth century, vice-president, and then president following the assassination of John Kennedy, Fortas remained his lawyer and close adviser. Being the president's lawyer, and being known as such, gave Fortas a unique advantage in the Washington, D.C., legal market. This special relationship with Johnson, combined with his superb skills, allowed Fortas to generate as much as three-quarters of the firm's clients by the 1960s.[13]

Arnold's clients were always quite a bit different from the clients of the rest of the firm's partners. Although he had a lucrative and growing practice from the mid-1940s through the mid-1960s, Arnold rarely had the institutional corporate clients that were Fortas's speciality and the bread and butter of any business law firm. There were, however, exceptions like Coca-Cola, the vital mainstay of the firm's practice in its early years, Otis

& Company, the investment firm of Cyrus Eaton who had sought to acquire the sleeping car business of Pullman, and smaller family-owned businesses like the famed Kiplinger financial newsletter.

Arnold's more typical clientele involved one-time projects. These ranged from congressional testimony on behalf of firms seeking greater market competition[14] to individual pieces of litigation, often on behalf of plaintiffs challenging the same corporations and conduct that Arnold had fought in government on behalf of the Antitrust Division. His door always remained open for associates and partners to discuss their own cases and to help cut the Gordian knots that stymied the rest of the firm. Even if his solutions initially appeared not to make sense, they invariably did after a few days reflection.

For most of his own cases, he traveled the country like a knight errant, trying cases when they could not be won by motions or settled. His cases ranged from lengthy antitrust trials, to criminal cases in Kentucky, to pretrial matters from coast to coast, and even corporate cases in Venezuela.[15] He visited the great and small cities across America, often remaining on the road for weeks at a time. He also maintained a heavy speaking schedule, now aided by a speakers bureau, which generated paid bookings for him at trade associations, universities, and charitable organizations.

The practice then as now was to engage local counsel to assist the lead trial lawyers appearing in local courts where they were not known and where they did not know the local jury pools, lawyers, judges, and courtroom customs. Mostly by luck, Arnold worked with an astonishing array of local talent including Irving Goldberg, who went on to serve as chief judge of the U.S. Court of Appeals for the Fifth Circuit in Texas. But even the renowned Goldberg could not save Arnold from being harangued by a federal judge in Texas for filing certain briefs not permitted by local custom, a story Goldberg frequently told friends and law clerks.[16]

Another case brought Arnold the services of future Supreme Court Justice Byron White as his local counsel in a Denver antitrust case. White assisted Arnold in a civil antitrust case in one of the handful of court appearances White ever made in his career before entering government service and later being selected for the Supreme Court by President Kennedy.[17]

Arnold represented the plaintiff, Cinema Amusements, which owned the Broadway Theater, a downtown Denver movie palace. The Broadway was an independent movie house, not owned by one of the major movie studios. It competed primarily with the theaters owned by the studios and, as a result, had difficulty booking the best films. The previous operators lost their lease, and Cinema Amusements leased the theater in November of 1944. The major studios continued to put the squeeze on the Broadway and sought to buy it out and eliminate the competition. Instead, Cinema Amusements retained Arnold, and he went to war against the major studios just as he had done as head of the Antitrust Division during the previous decade. Only this time, he enjoyed a tremendous advantage since the defendants had already been found guilty in the government case of violating the antitrust laws.

At trial, Arnold skillfully laid out the discrimination and harassment that the theater operator suffered at the hands of the studios and the damages it suffered as a result. He delivered one of the most lucid and moving opening arguments in what would otherwise be a rather ordinary business dispute, explaining the purpose of the antitrust laws to a jury of ordinary citizens who probably had never heard of antitrust law before. After a brief general introduction, he gave as good a description of the antitrust laws as one will find:

> Now, this is a case for damages under the anti-trust laws of the United States, and unless you have been engaged in interstate commerce business you are not apt to know very much about those laws, and it would not be proper for me to begin to explain the impact of those laws upon this case, because that is the function of the Court; but I do think that you cannot follow the evidence very well unless you know the general function and purposes of these laws which have been passed and enforced for 60 years, and which in their various amendments are very detailed.
>
> I'm not going into any single statutory provision of the law, but simply to give you a broad enough outline to know how the case fits into the general aim of that legislation.
>
> The anti-trust laws are distinctly an American institution. America believes in freedom of competitive opportunity, that the freedom of competitive opportunity should be protected and those who prevented competitive opportunity of individual business men should be penalized.
>
> Now, many people think that the anti-trust laws are aimed to prevent American business from growing big. That is not the purpose of the anti-trust laws. The great nationwide concerns, of which the defendants are examples, have been one of America's principal contributions to the efficiency of our economy and to our economic leadership.

Properly utilized, without combinations against individual businesses, these great concerns give not only to the consumers, but to individual businessmen goods and services which the individual businessmen need, at a cheaper cost.

And so we are not going to introduce any evidence complaining about the size of these corporate defendants.

What the anti-trust laws are principally aimed at is preventing, ladies and gentlemen of the jury, combinations among great nationwide concerns which deprive the local individual business man of a fair chance to get the products they sell at terms which they can profitably compete at. It is the combination of these businesses which will be the subject matter of the case, and which we will attempt to show you, that they did, by their concerted action, not by the action of any single one of them, deprive the Broadway Theater of any chance of a fair competitive market.

He then summarized the evidence, related it to the law, and made it come alive and make sense in a way that was moving and persuasive. The jury bought every word and, despite inconsistent testimony by a key witness for the plaintiff and a perfectly competent defense by opposing counsel, awarded the plaintiff $100,000 in damages, which were automatically tripled under the antitrust laws, in addition to granting the plaintiff its full attorneys' fees and costs. The verdict was sustained on appeal and Arnold was able to continue to do well by doing good.[18]

At first glance, Arnold's reputation as a judge on censorship issues and his reputation as a civil libertarian appeared to have won him the controversial assignment to defend *Playboy* in its early years against an attempt by the postmaster general to bar it from the mails on obscenity charges. However, the client came through less lofty avenues, having been recommended by a friend of Arnold's from his Chicago days. Nonetheless, Arnold won a critical victory on behalf of *Playboy* in front of Judge Luther Youngdahl, the same judge who would so courageously dismiss the Lattimore cases, winning a temporary restraining order allowing the continued mailing of *Playboy*.

Arnold also defended *Playboy* when the Attorney General of Vermont indicted a newsdealer for selling the magazine. Arnold's brief was easily the equal of his judicial opinion in the *Esquire* case, surveying the history of obscenity as applied to art, literature, religion, librarianship, and popular culture from the time of Plato to the present. Arnold topped off his tour de force with a footnote characterizing the state's position as: "No nudes is good news."[19] Although Arnold actually lost the argument before the Vermont Supreme Court on technical procedure grounds, he won in the end when Vermont eventually dismissed the case on the eve of trial.

Besides his substantive expertise in antitrust and civil liberties cases, Arnold also developed a speciality of representing clients in Supreme Court appeals. He was frequently asked to draft the petition for certiorari, the request for the Court to hear the case. If successful, he typically briefed and argued the case. In terms of the sheer number of cases, Arnold ranks toward the top of the small but prestigious Supreme Court bar of his era.

Arnold had a unique written and oral style before the Supreme Court. He was one of the few successful lawyers who could write a simple declarative sentence. One of his partners described it this way: "He wrote like Hemingway while most lawyers wrote like Proust."[20]

At oral argument, he was a sight to behold giving less deference to the Court than almost any other advocate of his day. He was informal and frequently sarcastic, even combative, depending on the issue and the case. His style was "thrilling," "loose and folksy," more like "a conversation between learned men" than a traditional formal argument.[21] In the *Peters* case, Arnold used this example from his younger days in discussing the unfairness of the McCarthy era loyalty boards:

> It reminds me of my early practice in Wyoming, when the people were stealing homesteaders' cabins. The defendant was indicted for stealing a cabin. He was convicted on practically no evidence. The attorney for the defendant protested. He said, "Didn't you know the man was innocent?" The foreman of the jury said, "Yes, but we have to have an example so we can stop this kind of thing."

In his argument in the *Pullman* antitrust case, "Arnold simply made no mention of legal issues. Instead he spoke of the unexploited educational and romantic appeal of train travel—opening the glories of the western landscapes to sightseers from all parts of the U.S.A. and foreign nations."[22] It was effective as well. In a case such as *Pullman*, where no one expected Arnold to get any of the justices to side with him, he in fact lost only by a 4-4 vote.

It was not that unusual how Arnold approached these cases, given his normal style and the fact that most of the justices were friends or past professional colleagues. One justice, Tom Clark, had even started off as

Arnold's assistant in the Justice Department and had a widely published photograph showing him lighting Arnold's pipe while Arnold floated on his back in a swimming pool.

Like the rest of AF&P, Arnold opposed the growing power of the government when asked by a client, although he appears not to have represented any clients against the Antitrust Division of the Justice Department. He did represent Rodale Press, a health and fitness publisher, in a fourteen-year battle with the Federal Trade Commission. As part of a broader FTC campaign against quack nutrition, the commission charged that the publishing company had misrepresented health claims about the value of diet and exercise in combating heart disease. Arnold viewed the case in broader constitutional and censorship terms. The FTC played into his hand by critiquing the claims in the book line-for-line. Eventually Arnold just wore out the commission. He survived losses in front of an administrative law judge and the full commission, only to gain victory in the court of appeals, which found that the FTC impermissibly kept switching theories as to whether the actual contents of the book or merely the advertising for the book were false and misleading.[23]

Arnold also had an admiration for postwar Germany and represented several German clients. He still had German relatives and was acutely aware of the suffering and deprivations of ordinary Germans during the economic and political reconstruction of the country after the defeat of the Nazis. He admired the way Germany (and later the European Economic Community) embraced economic competition and antitrust law as part of its denazification and rebuilding. In contrast, Fortas, as was the case with many American Jews in the postwar era, would have nothing to do with German businesses or products because of their links to the Nazis and the Holocaust.[24]

Arnold still found time to continue as the merry prankster. The firm's phone number was one digit off from the number for reserving a Pullman sleeping car for rail travel. It was a coincidental but delicious irony given Arnold's unsuccessful representation of Cyrus Eaton in attempting to purchase Pullman. Arnold frequently worked at the firm on Saturday mornings (or at home with the firm's phones forwarded) and grew increasingly irritated with the continuing stream of wrong numbers. After a number of polite explanations that the callers had reached a wrong number, Arnold began simply to take reservations for non-existent sleeper cars. Sometimes he announced that particular trains were completely sold out, special fares were available if the caller reserved immediately, and on occasion offered instant upgrades and other food and beverage specials, all causing consternation and irritation to both customer and the company when the traveler arrived at Union Station to find that no such specials or even reservations existed. When Arnold grew too busy to continue playing these games himself, he convinced Lewis Dabney, the son of family friends, to answer the phones and take the reservations on behalf of the Pullman company.[25]

Arnold's last serious foray into legal scholarship came as a reply to Henry Hart's foreword to the *Harvard Law Review*'s 1959 Supreme Court Review, probably the most coveted single spot in an American law review. Each year, the students of the *Harvard Law Review* devote an entire issue to an analysis of the past term of the Supreme Court. All the work is student written except the foreword, which is a single invited article from a law professor selected by the students.

Professor Hart of the Harvard Law School was the leading proponent of the legal process school of jurisprudence, which had replaced legal realism as the principal philosophy for American law.[26] In stark contrast to the legacy of legal realism, the legal process school was centered at Harvard and argued for a vision of law stripped of politics or ideology. According to this view, a decision was only legitimate if it was the product of reasoned elaboration and careful legal reasoning, separate from the result of the court or agency decision.

In his foreword, Hart first analyzed the demands on the justices' time. Making a series of complicated assumptions about the average work year for a justice and the amount of time a justice spent on each task (such as deciding which cases to hear, listening to oral argument, court conferences, reading briefs, writing opinions, etc.), Hart estimated that the justices had only 372 hours each year for collective deliberation about how to decide cases and craft the resulting opinions.[27]

He then criticized the substantive work product of the Supreme Court as sloppy, poorly reasoned, bad technical lawyering, and political rather than judicial in nature. Hart suggested that the work product of the Court could be improved through the reduction of the caseload and increased time for collective deliberation. Only Justice Frankfurter, Hart's mentor and former Harvard faculty colleague earned a passing grade.[28]

For example, Hart criticized the craftsmanship of the recent opinions of the Court:

They lack the underpinning of principle which is necessary to illumine large areas of the law and thus to discharge the function which has to be discharged by the highest judicial tribunal of a nation dedicated to exemplifying the rule of law not only to itself but to the whole world. Only opinions of this kind can be worked with by other men who have to take a judgment rendered on one set of facts and decide how it should be applied to a cognate but still different set of facts. Only opinions of this kind can carry the weight which has to be carried by the opinions of a tribunal which, after all, does not in the end have the power either in theory or in practice to ram its own personal preferences down other people's throats.

Hart continued:

But few of the Court's opinions, far too few, genuinely illumine the area of the law with which they deal. Other opinions fail even by much more elementary standards. . . . It needs to be said with all possible gravity, because it is a grave thing to say, that these failures are threatening to undermine the professional respect of first-rate lawyers for the incumbent Justices of the Court, and this at the very time when the Court as an institution and the Justices who sit on it are especially in need of the bar's confidence and support.[29]

Most, including Arnold, understand this as a thinly veiled attack on *Brown v. Board of Education* and its end of school desegregation and the Warren Court's expansion of civil liberties and constitutional protections for criminal defendants.

Hart's thesis was in every way an anathema to Arnold. It was highly critical and insulting to Arnold's friends and former New Deal colleagues on the court. Hart's ideology in pressing for technical competence above the substance of the results also smacked of the formalism and abstract conceptualism that Arnold had attacked so relentlessly since his early days a law professor at Yale.

There is also an unexplored personal side to the Hart-Arnold feud. One of Hart's earliest works as a law professor in the 1930s was an anonymous "hatchet job" at the behest of Felix Frankfurter attacking the study of the Connecticut courts that Arnold had undertaken with Charles Clark. Clark knew the authorship of the memo that Frankfurter had distributed, and there is no reason to think he would not have shared this with his colleague and friend Arnold.[30]

Arnold turned to several of his associates, including Charles Reich, to assist him in his reply to Hart. Reich, a recent Yale graduate, had clerked for Justice Hugo Black. During his clerkship, Reich and the other clerks actually lived at Black's home while Black was between marriages. There he had met and befriended Arnold. Reich had an invitation to join the Yale faculty after graduation from the law school. Instead he sought to gain practice experience before teaching at Yale, where he later became one of the most prominent law professors of the 1960s and the author of *The Greening of America* and *The New Property*, work as influential as Arnold's. Reich worked closely with Arnold for nearly five years at AF&P before returning to teach at Yale. During this time, he was frequently used more like a law clerk and a sounding board than a traditional associate at a law firm. On the reply to Hart, Arnold used his traditional drafting method of summoning his trusted secretary, Marguerite O'Brien and dictating directly to her in Reich's presence as she typed Arnold's words. Reich then added the legal research, and Arnold and Reich revised the drafts before repeating the exercise several more times.[31]

The result was devastating. Arnold's reply, entitled *Professor Hart's Theology*, characterized Hart's effort to discredit the Court's more liberal ruling as "pompous generalizations dropped on the Court from the heights of Olympus." Arnold makes clear that he objects most to Hart's "sweeping generalizations which indirectly discredit other opinions, never mentioned, of the members of the Court who have shown the most courage in defending civil liberties in a time of national hysteria."[32]

For Arnold, Hart's critique was the musing of a detached academic who would prefer that Supreme Court opinions be pretty, rather than helpful in the real world. Arnold began with Hart's recommendation that the Court abandon taking cases with primarily factual issues in dispute, such as the liability of employers of federal workers for negligence. Arnold first noted that such cases represent a tiny minority of the cases that the Court took and that such cases were in fact critically important to real people in the real world rather than ivory tower academics.[33] It is a rare law review article that includes language as blunt and righteously indignant as:

Without the precedents furnished by the Supreme Court in its infrequent decisions involving jury verdicts, untold thousands of plaintiffs would be deprived of an argumentative weapon essential to their protection against the kind of reversal that was so frequent when I was a mere negligence lawyer without hope of ever becoming one of Professor Hart's first-rate lawyers. Only a person who has never tried a negligence case could fall into Professor Hart's error of saying that such cases are not of utmost importance as precedents in similar cases. To say that it is a waste of the Court's time to provide such precedents is to show a callous disregard of the rights of injured persons.[34]

Arnold continued:

Professor Hart is saying here that Justices who disagree with him about the importance of enforcing proper standards for jury verdicts (a function which Congress has given them) are guilty of a misuse of power. The fact that in [these] cases the Court is setting standards which directly or indirectly affect the lives of millions is of no consequence to Professor Hart.[35]

Arnold similarly dissects Hart's critique of a case in which the Supreme Court allowed the review of state court decisions that use state law as a pretext to bar review in federal court of the constitutional rights of convicted defendants. Arnold's response to Hart's twenty-page critique of the technical failings of the Court's opinion in *Irvin v. Dowd* boiled down to the proposition that "every man, however lowly, is entitled to a trial by an impartial jury" and when a state court adds a trivial state law reason to block federal review of its decision, the federal court should still proceed to hear the case.[36]

Arnold then turned to Hart's basic proposal that the Supreme Court should allow for "the maturing of collective thought" by taking fewer cases and producing better reasoned opinions that would produce greater acceptance by the bar and lower courts. Hart hoped a more reflective Court would produce "impersonal and durable principles of constitutional law."[37] While Arnold acknowledges that "these are the clothes which the Court must wear in order to retain its authority and public appearance," no Court in the real world could possibly operate that way. Arnold, the former judge, pointed out the importance of compromise to create and hold together a majority of justices to actually decide a case. Moreover, for Arnold the entire process of "maturing of collective thought" simply does not exist:

> There is no possibility that I could pool my wisdom with Professor Hart's so that the wisdom of both of us, "successfully pooled," would "transcend the wisdom of" either of us. The reason is that I do not think his wisdom is real wisdom, and I am sure that he has the same opinion of mine. To lock the two of us in a room until I came to agree with the theology of Professor Hart by the process of the "maturing" of our "collective thought" would be to impose a life sentence on both of us without due process of law.[38]

Arnold concludes:

> The only kind of court that could successfully follow Professor Hart's prescription would be a court composed of men without deep-seated convictions about current national problems, a court whose members have not had enough previous experience with the controversial ideas which the Court must eventually express as law to have ever taken sides in the struggle; such a court might be found in a Trappist monastery. The reason for the proliferation of concurring opinions and dissents in the present Court is that the Court is made up of men of deep-seated convictions in times of revolutionary change when an old order is giving place to a new. It is just that simple.[39]

For Arnold, Hart cared nothing for the substance of a case, but only the failure of the Supreme Court to follow certain tenets of "procedural theology" in crafting an opinion that pleased legal academics. Furthermore, Hart concealed a conservative philosophy under the guise of neutral principles and an affinity for legal reasoning. This remains an extremely important issue of the philosophy of law that has been fought in every generation of American law and continues to attract combatants even today. Arnold remains, for all generations, one of the most eloquent defenders of his world view.

Moreover, time has proved Arnold right as to the specific controversy with Hart. The Supreme Court has in recent years dramatically reduced its case load and oral argument to less than half the time it once was.

There is simply no indication that the quantity of collective deliberation has increased or that the quality of the resulting opinions has improved along the lines advocated by Hart.

Arnold invested less and less time personally in pro bono matters as his practice and his travel schedule grew, yet there were still moments reminiscent of his work on the loyalty cases. Besides the loyalty cases, Arnold is probably best known for securing the release of Ezra Pound, the Nobel laureate, from Saint Elizabeth's Hospital, the Washington, D.C., hospital for the mentally ill, ironically the subject of several of Arnold's opinions as an appellate judge.

When Ezra Pound was in Italy during World War II, he made a series of propaganda broadcasts on the radio to American soldiers, which ultimately led to his arrest on charges of treason. Although much of his broadcasts was unintelligible anti-Semitic gibberish that mostly betrayed his precarious mental condition, he urged that "Hitler and Mussolini are your leaders" and that President Roosevelt was "insane, a criminal, or both." After the war, he was captured and imprisoned in Pisa by the Army and then eventually arraigned for treason in Washington, D.C., in 1946. Pound was found to be suffering from paranoia to such an extent that he was unable to advise counsel or assist in his own defense. Since he could not be tried, he was committed to Saint Elizabeth's Hospital in late 1946.[40]

For the next twelve years, key people in the arts and even officials in the Justice Department voiced their dissatisfaction with Pound's continuing commitment. Among the louder voices in dissent were T. S. Eliot, Ernest Hemingway, Carl Sandburg, Robert Frost, Archibald MacLeish, e.e. cummings, and even U.N. Secretary General Dag Hammarskjöld. Pound's continued confinement became a greater and greater embarrassment to the federal government, especially after he received a distinguished prize from the Library of Congress for a new volume of poetry written while at Saint Elizabeth's.

The higher-ups in the Department of Justice remained unmoved during the tenure of Attorney General Herbert Brownell. Brownell eventually resigned in 1957, and shortly thereafter Robert Frost wrote the new Attorney General William Rogers, asking what his mood was about the release of Pound. The response from Rogers was a good sign of what was to come for Pound: "My mood is your mood."[41]

Rogers and others in the Justice Department gave Frost Thurman Arnold's name. Frost met with Arnold on April 11, 1958, and Arnold agreed to take the case. Frost immediately mentioned to the press upon leaving his hotel later that day that Arnold had been brought on to secure the release of Pound, unfortunately before Arnold had been able to contact Pound's wife Dorothy, who was still Pound's legal guardian. Despite hearing about Arnold's involvement through the newspapers the following morning, Dorothy gave Arnold permission to proceed.[42]

The problem was that were no legal grounds to dismiss the indictment. The indictment was not defective in any way. If the government could prove the charges in it beyond a reasonable doubt, Pound's actions indeed constituted treason. The only real defense was Pound's insanity, which Pound refused to assert as a defense in any event. A petition for habeas corpus for his release had already been unsuccessful. All Arnold had to go on was "the general principle that the situation had become ridiculous."[43]

Arnold entered into a quick, but delicate, negotiation with the Justice Department. While the department, even under Rogers, would not dismiss the indictment on its own accord, Arnold hoped that it would not oppose his motion to do so, even though the motion lacked any shred of legal support. The department, fearing a publicity backlash, refused to tell Arnold what its position would be. Despite fearing embarrassment and futility, Arnold inferred much into the department's silence and proceeded.

Arnold moved to dismiss the charges of treason against Pound on April 14, 1958. On Friday, April 18, Arnold stood in front of Judge Bolitha J. Laws and presented his motion for the dismissal of the indictment of treason. A collection of statements was appended to the motion in support of Pound from the likes of Frost, W. H. Auden, Carl Sandburg, T. S. Eliot, and Ernest Hemingway. Frost also made suggestions for Arnold's brief, making it the only time that Arnold could remember his own work being edited by a nonlawyer, let alone a Nobel Prize winning poet.[44]

Arnold had wanted Frost to be present to read his statement in open court. However, Frost was unavailable on the actual court date and demanded that Arnold postpone the hearing. Arnold, afraid the Justice Department would change its mind, refused. The poet reluctantly agreed to let Arnold read the statement on his behalf. Arnold, standing in for Frost, declaimed in part: "Mr. Thurman Arnold admirably put this problem of a sick man being held too long in prison to see if he won't get well enough to be tried for a prison offense."[45]

The medical evidence Arnold used at the hearing was provided by the affidavit of Dr. Winfred Overholser, the superintendent of Saint Elizabeth's, the same superintendent whose actions Arnold had reviewed on several occasions as a federal judge. The statement by Dr. Overholser was essentially the same thing that he had been saying for the last twelve years of Pound's committal, but Arnold made sure that there were a few crucial differences. Along with the usual conclusions that Pound was insane and unfit for trial, Arnold made sure that part of the affidavit also included an unconditional recommendation for unsupervised release. As Frost put it, Overholser was in essence opining that "Ezra Pound is not too dangerous to go free in his wife's care, and too insane ever to be tried—a very nice discrimination."[46]

With the consent of the government, Judge Laws threw out the twelve-year-old indictment against Pound. The one paragraph ruling consenting to the fiction of Arnold's motion and the delicate dance of the government was based on two grounds: First, that Pound would never be mentally competent to stand trial, and second, that the allegedly traitorous broadcasts made from Italy may have been the result of insanity. Pound was hugged by his wife and left the courtroom convinced that he was being released because he was a great poet. The entire court proceeding took ten minutes. Pound spent the next three weeks gathering up his belongings from Saint Elizabeth's. He then returned to Italy to live with his daughter, presumably happily, if insanely, ever after.[47]

The case was a wonderful illustration of the absurdity but importance of symbols in the law that Arnold had been writing about since the 1930s. Here was a case that the government was unable to prosecute but was also unwilling to dismiss because the defendant stood accused of treason in a recently concluded war. Although the government was unwilling to dismiss the case, it was prepared to agree to do so if the defendant just asked. Despite having no real grounds to do so, Arnold observed the proper forms and went through the required dance. The government was magnanimous in its consent and with the imprimatur of the court, justice was done.

Nothing else could have brought about this most appropriate resolution. A dismissal by the government would have condoned treason and signaled weakness in the continuing cold war. A motion to dismiss the indictment opposed by the government was also doomed to fail. Any deal between the government and the defense without the court's blessing looked like special pleading for a famous defendant and would have been viewed as illegitimate in the eyes of the public. The elegant solution arrived at by Arnold with the participation of the other players simply was the living embodiment of the arguments in *The Symbols of Government*.

Arnold had tremendous entree into Washington society through his friendship with two of the most unique and different grandes dames of the District, Cissy Patterson and Evalyn Walsh McLean. Cissy Patterson was an eccentric social and business leader in Washington and was both friend and in-law to Thurman Arnold. Cissy was the grandmother of Ellen (Elena) Pearson who married Thurman's son George, although Cissy famously had refused to attend the wedding because of her feud at the time with Elena's father Drew Pearson.

Cissy was also heir to the Patterson and Medill newspaper fortune, which had begun with the *Chicago Tribune* in the nineteenth century and expanded to include the *New York Illustrated Daily News, Long Island Newsday,* and the *Washington Times-Herald,* which Cissy had purchased from the Hearst chain, a bitter family rival. She was cousin to Colonel Robert McCormick, the isolationist Republican publisher of the *Chicago Tribune,* and sister to Joseph Patterson, the publisher of the *New York Illustrated Daily News,* who was similarly isolationist, but otherwise more supportive of Roosevelt's New Deal.

She was a person of great extremes. As a young girl, she had been presented at the courts of the Russian Czar and the Austrian Emperor. She married a ne'er-do-well Polish count and eventually fled his Polish estate with her infant daughter, following physical abuse at his hands. Along with her ability to live in the lap of luxury based on family wealth, in 1920 she built a hunting lodge in the wilds of Wyoming outside of Jackson Hole with no electricity or indoor plumbing and went hunting wild goats and sheep with the ranch boss.

Cissy was the author of two novels and then became an editor and writer for the rival Hearst chain mostly to amuse herself and annoy her family. At different times she was either great friends with, or mortal enemies of, the other great hostesses of Washington society including Alice Roosevelt Longworth and Evalyn Walsh McLean. On many occasions, the Arnolds dined at the Patterson mansion on DuPont Circle and met an eclectic crowd, including former Kansas governor and 1936 Republican presidential candidate Alf Landon, with whom Arnold remained friends despite their very different views about the world.[48]

The Arnolds' friendship with Cissy, as with most of her relationships, ran both hot and cold. The friendship survived a feud over Arnold's antitrust suit against the Associated Press in which he sided with the *Chicago Sun,* the principal rival to her cousin's *Chicago Tribune.* Cissy sided with her cousin, even though Cissy's paper itself had been refused membership to the AP because of the very bylaws that Arnold successfully challenged. Moreover, Arnold and Patterson remained close until Cissy's death, despite at least one angry argument between Cissy and Frances, culminating (according to Arnold family lore) in Frances slapping Cissy in the face at a dinner party.[49]

Arnold was also one of the last of a dying breed of counselors-at-law, generalists who provided legal advice to sophisticated individual clients who looked to their personal attorneys for help beyond just a narrow area of expertise. In that capacity, Arnold helped Evalyn Walsh McLean, said to be the wealthiest woman in Washington. Her husband had been the owner of the *Washington Post* and the *Cincinnati Enquirer,* and Evalyn was considered the leading hostess of old-line society in Washington. She was also the owner of the Hope diamond, and the more impressive, but less infamous, 92 1/2 carat Star of the East, as well as many other valuable gems and pieces of jewelry. Mrs. McLean even had a special hook put on the Hope diamond so that she could attach the Star of the East to it and wear both gems together. It was said that Evalyn Walsh McLean collected diamonds the way other women collected hats.[50]

Arnold was a frequent guest at Friendship, the McLean estate in northwest Washington. There he and Frances dined frequently with the cream of Washington society and a diverse group of political and influential national leaders, including Harry Truman, Helen Keller, and Monsignor Fulton Sheen.

Arnold, Sheen, and Supreme Court Justice Frank Murphy were also executors of McLean's will, which Arnold had prepared. Arnold, his wife Frances, Justice Murphy, Monsignor Sheen, Cissy Patterson, Frank Waldrop, who was Patterson's editor-in-chief at the *Times-Herald,* and McLean's family priest were with her when she died on a Saturday in the spring of 1947. The first order of business was to collect and safely store Mrs. McLean's massive jewelry collection until it could be formally inventoried and appraised through the probate process on Monday when the courts reopened. McLean had left most of her $1 million collection of jewelry in a wooden box with some pieces simply lying around the house. According to Arnold's partner, Edgar Brenner, "The bracelet, brooches, necklaces, and other pieces were scattered around the house in numerous locations, some of them even underneath sofas and chair cushions, in vases and toes of slippers. The Hope Diamond itself was hidden in the back of a table top radio."[51] Arnold made a quick, rough inventory and stored everything in a cigar box so full of diamonds that it could hardly shut.

He then turned to the practical question of what was to be done with this treasure trove until Monday morning. Arnold was afraid to simply leave the box in his home or office. Arnold and McLean's maid visited local banks in McLean's chauffeur-driven Cadillac with the jewels on the front seat, only to learn that all the area bank vaults were on time locks which could not be opened until Monday. No jewelry store would take the McLean diamonds because it was above the value of the insurance they carried.

Desperate, Arnold finally managed to reach J. Edgar Hoover who agreed to seal and store the world's most valuable cigar box in the FBI safe with a posted guard until Arnold came on Monday and took them to the bank for storage. The estate was opened without incident, although FBI memoranda strongly suggest that the only reason that Hoover and his staff agreed to take the McLean jewels was that they were under the impression that Mrs. McLean was "critically ill" rather than deceased, in which case Arnold would have lacked authority to act on her behalf without court appointment as her executor (which of course could not be done at least until Monday). How much Arnold actively deceived the bureau, merely acquiesced in their confusion, or benefitted from the FBI turning a blind eye to the actual time of death is unknown.[52]

Both the Star of the East and the Hope diamonds continued to attract much public attention after leaving the McLean household. The famed New York jeweler Harry Winston eventually bought the Hope diamond and the rest of the McLean estate jewelry in 1949 for $611,500. Later a relative surfaced claiming that she had lent McLean one of the pieces of jewelry which was to be sold to Winston. The item was returned to her, but the inventory was never adjusted. When the mistake was discovered, an abashed Arnold, as executor, offered Winston a check for $30,000 for the piece at a time that he had nowhere near that amount in his personal checking account. Winston graciously declined, proclaiming: "Don't worry about it. I bought by the lot."[53]

Winston then sold the Star of the East to King Farouk of Egypt, but he was never paid as the King was deposed shortly thereafter. It took years of negotiations and litigation before Winston eventually was able to retrieve the Star from a safety deposit box in Switzerland.

Winston had similar bad luck with the Hope diamond, further contributing to the so-called Hope diamond curse. Unable to sell the unique necklace, Winston eventually donated the Hope diamond to the Smithsonian in 1958 where it remains on public display today.[54]

The death of the other grande dame of Washington, Cissy Patterson, produced an irony in terms of Arnold's commitment to competitive markets. When estate taxes prevented the editors inheriting the paper from continuing to operate it, it was purchased by Cissy's cousin Colonel McCormick. As the losses mounted, Colonel McCormick eventually sold the *Times-Herald* to the *Washington Post*, originally owned by the husband of Cissy's friend and social rival Evalyn Walsh McLean. The two papers were then promptly merged, leaving Washington with only a single morning newspaper.[55] Arnold, representing neither party to the deal, could only watch from the sidelines and content himself with receiving his morning news from a monopolist, despite having known both families who had been such vigorous competitors for years.

Arnold, Fortas & Porter continued to grow despite the demise of the New Deal, the burden of the loyalty cases, the Republican White House victory in 1952, and the end to whatever influence and friendship AF&P had within the executive branch. While the feared downturn in legal business from Eisenhower's triumph never came, the night of Stevenson's defeat at Arnold's house was like a wake for the New Deal as Arnold watched with Black, Douglas, and his close friends the Dabneys on a portable TV.[56]

In 1950 AF&P had only nine attorneys. In 1952, the firm hired its first woman associate, Pat Wald, who stayed at the firm less than a year due to family reasons but who would later join the D.C. Circuit and serve as its chief judge. By 1960, the firm had eighteen lawyers, and five years later there were a total of thirty-five lawyers at AF&P. The firm's growth was bolstered in 1960 by the acquisition of the tax group from the Paul Weiss law firm and with it Carolyn Agger, the wife of Abe Fortas and a formidable tax lawyer in her own right.

Until the mid-1950s the firm was a partnership in name only. Only the founding partners shared in profits, although Abe Fortas insisted on sharing equally with Arnold and Porter, despite having the lion's share of the business and control of the firm. The rest of the lawyers with the title of partner enjoyed only a salary and bonus with little or no managerial control over the running of the firm.[57] By the mid-1950s, a revolt by the younger lawyers brought a measure of true profit-sharing, but the vast majority of shares remained within the hands of the founding partners.

From 1960 on, the firm had to contend with the double-edged sword of Fortas's unofficial role as counselor to the vice president and later president, which required more and more of his time and energy. By 1965, Fortas was on the Supreme Court, and the firm faced a bright but unknown future without one of its founding partners, its largest business getter, and only managing partner since its inception.

Throughout this period of massive growth Arnold was invaluable in attracting the younger lawyers who joined the firm. Many were in the mold of the Arnold and Fortas, outsiders but with elite educational credentials. Abe Krash was a former newspaperman like Porter and a native of Wyoming like Arnold. Bud Vieth was from Iowa and had been editor-in-chief of the law review at the University of Iowa. Reed Miller had been on the law review at West Virginia where Arnold had been dean.

The firm was well known and admired at the Ivy League schools for its work on the loyalty cases, and it had a reputation of having interesting people, liberal causes, and excellent clients. Influential judges such as Charles Clark, William Douglas, and Hugo Black would recommend the firm to their clerks. A later associate, Gerald Stern, heard Arnold address a dinner for the Legal Aid Society at Harvard Law School where Arnold had worked as a law student. Stern later joined the firm after working in the Justice Department and flatly says: "I wouldn't have gone to the firm except for Arnold."[58]

The firm physically grew to accommodate the growing number of clients and attorneys. In 1948, Arnold Fortas & Porter relocated to the Ring Building at 18th and M streets, then an undesirable and commercially deserted part of town. In 1952, the firm moved to a townhouse on the corner of 19th and N, which had once belonged to Teddy Roosevelt and the archconservative former Supreme Court Justice Pierce Butler. Over time, the firm grew by acquiring adjacent townhouses purchased by different partnerships of the senior lawyers. This hodgepodge of townhouses created a rabbit warren of connected and adjoining offices and buildings.[59]

Arnold's office was on the first floor of the main building just past the entrance, in a former solarium that overlooked the garden in the back. He had a large ornate hand-carved desk with twenty-two drawers, and he lined the walls with the obligatory signed photos of the public figures who were his friends and confidants. On the desk, "an assortment of papers, briefs and mail [was] usually piled one foot high" in "no discernable organization."[60] Down the hall, there was a room with free Coke, courtesy of Arnold's representation of Coca-Cola. Fortas's office was at the opposite end of the first floor, and Porter's office was directly above Fortas on the second floor.

There were weekly luncheons for partners and associates and summer barbeques at the Arnold home. Every day at five, the firm, led by Arnold and Porter, would gather for drinks in the garden room on the ground floor to rehash the events of the day, talk through difficult issues and cases, and generally swap stories of the past and present. Only Fortas and Norman Diamond were not regulars at this daily event. The garden room gatherings, the circulation of the yellow sheets (copies of every letter written by every lawyer in the firm), and the unusual listing of both partners and associates on letterhead and legal directories created an atmosphere of shared mission and a camaraderie that united a small but growing firm and created lasting memories.

The growing group of AF&P lawyers and staff also gathered every Christmas for a party where the principal entertainment was Arnold as toastmaster with supporting roles from the other founding partners. Even after he joined the Supreme Court, Fortas typically returned and took his turn at the microphone.[61] Fortas and Arnold would trade quips and stories with Arnold usually getting the better of it and Fortas intentionally and good-naturedly playing the unaccustomed role of second banana.

Arnold also continued his role as the absent-minded genius and paterfamilias of the firm. Even while Arnold was in the government, the press and his associates often played who could top this with the latest Thurman Arnold story. In 1939, the *Washington Times-Herald* printed an item about Arnold standing in line to retrieve his overcoat at a Brazilian diplomatic reception:

> "What kind of a coat is it?" asked the harassed coat-check maid. "Well, it had a pair of green socks in the upper left-hand pocket," replied [Arnold].
>
> "Green socks!" exclaimed Mrs. Arnold, who is almost never startled by her husband. "You see," explained Mr. Arnold, "I suddenly noticed this morning that I had on green socks. I was to appear before the Supreme Court. So somebody in the office rushed out and bought me

some black socks. I changed in my office and there the green ones are in my party overcoat."[62]

Most of the lawyers who worked with Arnold remember various office personnel rushing into his office at different times to put out garbage can fires that Arnold started when he disposed of cigars without extinguishing them. A secretary was always stationed outside his office to check that all buttons were buttoned, zippers were zipped, and ties were not stained. Edgar Brenner also recalls the day Arnold bought three of the same identical hat because he kept leaving them at meetings around town; he did not want to irritate his wife by coming home bareheaded because she thought him "more dignified in a hat." Norman Diamond in his memoir recounted the time he was summoned from a vacation in New York to return to Washington for an urgent meeting with Arnold, who absentmindedly informed him: "Glad you're here! We've got to leave for New York at once."[63] Virtually all the AF&P lawyers similarly have Thurman Arnold stories that are still vivid in their minds decades after Arnold's death and are collected and traded like baseball cards when Arnold's name comes up in conversation.

Saturdays were usually working days for Arnold, the other lawyers, and the secretaries. Arnold would take the entire secretarial crew to the nearby Cosmos Club for lunch, until he eventually resigned from the club because of its restrictive membership policies.[64]

Virtually all the Arnold & Porter lawyers also have more substantive memories of Arnold from this era. Norman Diamond describes Arnold as having two unmatched legal skills: "extraordinary creativity" and "unmatched perception of the realities of present society and of the future impact of current events." For Diamond, "Arnold was an authentic genius, the best all-around lawyer I ever knew."[65]

Eugene Gressley, the editor of Arnold's letters, described Arnold similarly:

> First, Fortas would go to Arnold with a seemingly impossible legal puzzle. After a few minutes of highly stimulating conversation, Arnold was likely to produce several ideas that at first blush appeared absolutely insane. However, after being exposed to one of Arnold's intellectual gypsy sessions, Fortas found himself several days later discovering that Arnold's deductions made sense. Arnold simply possessed an unfath-

omable depth of resourcefulness and imagination. Secondly, Fortas, particularly in the McCarthy years, found Arnold's courage a tremendous bulwark. A certain comfort and reassurance came from having ten feet down the hall an individual who plainly refused to be intimidated by the hysteria of the age.[66]

Stern recalls Arnold as teaching him to sneak up sideways on issues that did not appear to have a ready solution and, when in doubt, to "attack pomposity." He wrote in his own book *The Buffalo Creek Disaster* that Arnold taught him that sometimes "you just keep pressing ahead until the other side cracks."[67]

Arnold also stood out in the minds of several young associates who lived out in suburban Virginia near the Arnold homes, first the Summerhill estate and later the Lafayette House in Alexandria. Both Edgar Brenner and William Rogers drove in a car pool with Arnold, who was a notoriously bad driver but owned the only car among the three of them, an old Ford. The car pool continued for seven years with these and other younger lawyers taking turns keeping the car over night and picking up "Judge Arnold" in the morning for the trip to 19th and N in the District.

On the rides, Arnold would speak about his youth in Wyoming, seeing the escaped circus elephants roaming the range one summer, his unhappy years at Princeton, his legal practice in Laramie, his service in the Wyoming legislature as the only Democrat, and the other highlights of his younger days. They would also talk through the cases of the day with Arnold throwing out an endless stream of ideas and concepts to address the problems that had stumped the younger lawyers.

The car pool almost always stopped at the local drug store so Arnold could purchase his daily supply of cigars. Before, during, and after the ride, Arnold would drop burning ashes on his suits, leaving burn marks and actual rings on the suits made from polyester. Frances would then have to sew up the holes; but as she was herself color blind, she created the occasional surreal appearance to Arnold's repaired suits when she used thread that did not match the original color of the suit.[68]

As Arnold became the elder statesman of his firm, he also became the generational head of his family as well. Arnold embraced the role of grandfather and family head far more than he had done as a father. He had been a loving but distant father like so many of his generation. While his own children were growing, he was a near workaholic with frequent travels and no real hobbies. Frances had been in charge of the child rearing. Thurman Jr. recalled about both his father and Abe Fortas: "Everything they did is work, and that was their fun too. I mean when I was brought up, I never even saw my father at Christmas, he was at work, or at a bar convention, or something." Interestingly, Thurman Jr. made these remarks at an interview where his mother was present, and she did not contradict or amend his recollections. George's wife Elena observed a more cordial, but not warm, relationship between her husband and father-in-law, but noticed that she never saw the two men hug.[69]

Both Thurman Jr. and George had attended boarding school and spent college and law school away from home, Thurman Jr. attending Yale Law School and George at the University of Chicago. If it was Frances's dream that the boys practice with their father, it certainly was not Thurman's. Despite many arguments with Frances, he stuck to his guns that bringing the boys into the firm was "nepotism" and he wasn't going to do it, establishing a rule for the firm in the process.[70] Whether it was principle or questions about ability or temperament that ultimately motivated Arnold to refuse adding the boys to the firm will never be known. The matter appeared to have rankled Frances far more than the sons, leading to repeated arguments over the years and long after the sons had made their own careers elsewhere.

Both sons ended up as lawyers on the West Coast far from the professional and personal shadow of their famous father. Thurman Jr. went first to San Francisco and later Palm Springs where he practiced primarily in the tort area. George settled in Los Angeles, engaged in a broad general practice, and entered Democratic politics as chair of the area Young Democrats and a delegate to the Democratic National Convention. George's dabble with politics ended with a close but unsuccessful run for a congressional seat. While the boys were in private practice, it appears that Thurman never sent any business their way, although only Thurman Jr. seemed particularly bitter about it. Thurman Jr. recalled how Abe Fortas, and not his father, went out of his way to send him legal work on the West Coast. The combination of George's easier going nature, more cordial relationship with his father, and having his father-in-law Drew Pearson as a source of occasional referrals seemed to make him more comfortable on his own professionally.[71]

The income generated from Arnold's practice in Washington also created a new lifestyle for Frances and him. In the 1950s, the Arnolds bought Summerhill, an estate in suburban Arlington, Virginia. According to Walton Hamilton, once his faculty colleague and eventually his partner, it was "closer to the Old South than anything in Washington."[72] Frances blossomed into the role she had waited her whole life to play as social hostess and country gentlewoman, but a feisty one. She reveled in her garden and particularly her roses. She supervised the renovation of Summerhill and filled it with antiques and gracious appointments including a large mahogany dinner table seating twelve that she later donated to the Supreme Court at the suggestion of Justice Black's widow. The Arnolds also began to travel a bit more, visiting their children and grandchildren in California and taking European trips.

Frances supervised a small staff of domestics, including a most peculiar relationship with Katie, the cook. When Katie needed money beyond her salary, Frances simply turned a blind eye and let her take small items from the house. Thurman saw this as nothing more than stealing and had many loud but unsuccessful arguments with Frances over her salary supplementation program.

Frances also had a temper, especially if she had been drinking, which both she and Thurman did a fair bit. They were a loving and entertaining couple but had terrible fights. Frances's temper and stubborn streak were not, however, limited to domestic spats with her husband. Frances even argued with her daughter-in-law Elena Pearson Arnold over her choice of veil for her wedding to George and the choice of the name of Elena and George's second son, getting her way in both cases.[73]

As a grandfather, Thurman gave more of himself than he probably ever did as a father. It was much easier as grandparent just playing with the grandkids for a while or on a short visit and then sending them on their way. But Thurman and Frances also did more, taking in various grandchildren for months at a stretch when the parents were going through difficult times.

The grandchildren called Thurman "Judgie" and Frances "Deedee." Thurman never talked to his grandchildren like kids. He simply talked to them like adults, urging them to state their views and argue with him the way he did with his own friends. At bedtime, he would read them the usual stories like *Doctor Doolittle* and *Winnie the Pooh* as long as they wanted. When the grandchildren were older, he talked to them about books and whatever they were reading and would listen to his granddaughter Frances recite her poetry. He also talked to them about current events, requiring them to bone up on politics so they would be prepared for the discussions they knew were coming.

Thurman and Frances made holiday visits to the grandchildren, attended graduations and other school events, sometimes in place of an absent parent, helped them get set up in college, and financed parts of their educations. On many holidays, and particularly the summers, it was the grandkids who traveled to Judgie and Deedee, often on their own.

Judgie and Deedee's house was a place to go for comfort and protection.[74] Most of the grandchildren's memories relate to visits to the two houses. Summerhill in particular stood out as a mansionlike house with Doric columns and a large front porch. There were many rooms to explore including an attic, a basement, and a large kitchen, all fascinating to the grandchildren. The master bedroom had a large four-poster bed with thick columns carved with intricate vines. There were beautiful plantings surrounding the house and large dogwood trees in a line from the street. There was a pond in the back and off in the distance the sound of the trains passing by.

As Thurman prospered in private practice, Frances became more of a Washington hostess, holding many dinner parties for Thurman's circle of friends and clients. The grandchildren saw many of Thurman's famous friends at Summerhill and later at the Lafayette house in Alexandria, but the celebrity of the likes of Justice Douglas, Justice Black, Vice President Hubert Humphrey, and various members of Congress only registered later.[75]

When the Arnolds sold Summerhill, they moved to downtown Alexandria to the so-called Lafayette House, named for the French general who had stayed in the home in 1824 during his only visit to the United States after the American Revolution. It was a large, spacious home with eleven coal-burning fireplaces and was quite interesting to the grandchildren. But it was a town home and no match for the Summerhill grounds, which was a plus for Arnold who had no interest in the responsibilities of keeping up an estate.

Arnold only occasionally took the grandchildren on outings, but his grandson Joe remembers fondly a trip with "Judgie" to buy a new suit. It was Deedee who would escort them to Mt. Vernon, Gettysburg, Monticello, the Smithsonian, and the other museums in Washington in order to instill in the grandchildren a love of history. She was somewhat less successful at instilling her more Southern values about manners and upbringing and in getting the grandchildren to say "Yes, Ma'am."[76]

George's children remember their other grandfather, Drew Pearson, "Pazzy," being the one who took them to baseball games, Disneyland when they lived in California, or sightseeing on their trips to Washington.[77] However, they stayed with Deedee and Judgie most summers and for months at a time during the period when George and Elena were in the process of separating and divorcing.

As the 1950s grew to a close, Arnold continued to be an active lawyer and remained in the public eye much more than many of his New Deal contemporaries, who were now retired or beginning to pass from the scene. But in his final decade, he would confront the cataclysmic changes at home and abroad that would challenge the legacy of the New Deal and what it meant to be a liberal in twentieth-century America.

Edward Levi, Harold Ickes, and Thurman Arnold in NBC Radio Studios, Washington, D.C., circa 1940. Courtesy of John G. Levi.

Arnold in academic robes at Yale University, late 1940s. Courtesy of the Laramie Plains Museum, Laramie, Wyoming.

Arnold the fisherman, circa 1950. Courtesy of the Thurman Arnold Collection, American Heritage Center, University of Wyoming.

Thurman Arnold in foreground with Walter Winchell and Drew Pearson at Washington press event. Courtesy of the Thurman Arnold Collection, American Heritage Center, University of Wyoming.

Former Arnold, Fortas & Porter townhouse at 19th and N streets, Northwest, previously owned or occupied by Theodore Roosevelt and Justice Pierce Butler. Courtesy of the Thurman Arnold Collection, American Heritage Center, University of Wyoming.

Thurman Arnold at White House for celebration of his seventieth birthday with Vice President and Mrs. Johnson. Courtesy of Drew Arnold.

Thurman Arnold walking in District of Columbia, mid-1960s.
Courtesy of Drew Arnold.

10

Final Fights

Thurman Arnold's seventieth birthday was honored in many festive ways. Vice President Johnson invited him to the White House for a celebration. The alumni of the Antitrust Division threw a dinner in his honor, and lawyers from around the country returned to Washington to honor their mentor. At the firm, his partner and former student Victor Kramer edited and privately published a collection of the letters and speeches of Arnold. Kramer relied on the yellow sheets, the carbon copies of correspondence from the very beginning of the firm that were circulated to all the lawyers. Most of the letters and memos were in a humorous vein, including the 1951 memo chiding fellow partners for

> conditions of chaos, disorder and general litter in their offices which the Department [of Health and Sanitation] alleges are a menace to health and safety. . . . The Committee on Un-American Activities has informed me that the office looks like the kind of an office in which Communists congregate and multiply.

In another letter reminiscent of the famous scene involving Jack Nicholson in the movie *Five Easy Pieces,* Arnold railed to a friend about an incident on a business trip in which he ordered the breakfast special for $1.70 but without toast, only to find that he was then charged $1.80 for the remaining items because he had ordered à la carte. So, the next morning he ordered the special with toast and ordered the waiter to take it away after it arrived, then was charged the lower price.[1]

During this period, Arnold increasingly reached back into the past. In the late 1950s he sent all his papers to the University of Wyoming and periodically continued to add to the collection. In 1965, he privately published his father's poems, with Frances writing a biographical sketch of C. P. Arnold's life and long time friend Philo Calhoun serving as editor.

Arnold also privately published his own poetry and lighter works in a five copy edition called *Jingles, Jeers and Jeremiads*. He honored, but also declined, an increasing number of requests to write biographical and historical sketches of his former colleagues from the New Deal. He wrote a brief introduction for the re-publication of the TNEC hearings and final report. Arnold returned one final time to protect the reputation of Owen Lattimore, responding in writing to a particularly offensive editorial in the *Cincinnati Enquirer*.[2]

In the early sixties, Arnold also began to suffer his first major health problems. Despite a history of heavy drinking, smoking, and little exercise beyond the occasional golf game or swim, Arnold had never been seriously ill. But his streak ran out when on a business trip to New York City to argue a critical motion in a case for Peter Grace, the heir to the W. R. Grace family fortune, he suffered the first in a series of heart attacks. His associate Edgar H. Brenner had accompanied him and had carefully briefed all the cases for the argument on index cards. Brenner was ready to supply any details, while Arnold characteristically focused on the big picture of the case. The night before the argument Arnold had the heart attack but did not want to go to the hospital. He summoned Brenner to his room in the Princeton Club and told him to get help. Brenner woke up his uncle, who was president of a New York scotch whiskey importer and who had his own history of heart problems, and got his uncle's personal physician to treat Arnold. Despite having strong grounds for a continuance, at 9 o'clock a tired and pained Arnold told Brenner to go to court and give the argument. It was a direct order from the general of the firm, and the loyal associate obeyed despite his trepidations about leaving Arnold at the club where he was staying. For Arnold, it was a typical confidence-building gesture in the work of a younger colleague that Brenner never forgot.[3]

The doctors predictably told Arnold to give up smoking and drinking, cut down on food, and get some exercise. Arnold predictably agreed, but only followed the part of the doctor's advice about exercise by beginning to walk on a daily basis. He soon became a familiar sight with his walking stick in both Alexandria and around the District.

Preparing his autobiography was one of the few times that words ever failed Arnold, although only initially. He first started on an autobiography in the late 1950s but wrote only a few chapters and threw them away. "That type of writing is beyond me," and writing about himself was the "kind of thing that embarrasses me," he told an editor at Knopf who sought to secure the rights to such a project. He told former Attorney General Francis Biddle that he simply lacked the gift for "true biographical writing."[4]

But eventually he began again with a contract with Harcourt Brace for his memoirs. By December 1962 the publisher was already pressing Arnold for chapters. A January 1963 heart attack in Palm Springs, while visiting Thurman Jr., made quick completion out of the question. Arnold did not return to his Washington office until April.[5] He was able to deliver two chapters by July 1963. He sent six more chapters of the book in March 1964, but then he left the country with wife and secretary in tow to lecture at Cambridge University and to vacation in Majorca afterwards. The rest of the manuscript followed in May 1964 with the final chapter arriving at the publisher in July, entitling him to his $2000 advance.

The manuscript never entirely satisfied Arnold. Unlike past projects when he had completed lengthy books while consumed with vast amounts of legal work, the words came slowly, and then Arnold could not keep his hands off what he had written. He rearranged chapters, wrote new ones, rewrote existing ones, argued with his publisher about the mix of personal history versus commentary on public issues, fussed about the title before settling on *Fair Fights and Foul,* and generally remained unsatisfied with the whole project even after the corrected galleys were finally returned to the publisher in February 1965.

Despite the passage of time and the loose structure of the book, which alternated between personal history and public policy about now-fading events, the autobiography put Arnold back in the public eye once again. Reviews from old friends and new admirers appeared.[6] Unlike the case with any of his previous books, all published in 1940 or before, Arnold even appeared on television to promote the book, wittily chatting with Merv Griffin and turning his $256 union-scale appearance fee over to the law firm.

The year 1965 also marked another turning point in the history of the firm. On July 28, President Johnson summoned Fortas to the White House as was his custom when the president wanted political or legal advice. Fortas left an important client meeting at the firm to be informed this time by Johnson that he would be announcing Fortas's nomination to the Supreme Court later that day. As Johnson put it, there were over 75,000 troops in Vietnam, and Fortas had the duty to serve his country just as they did. Although Fortas had in fact declined an initial overture from Johnson, this time it was not an offer to think things over but the announcement of a decision that Fortas ultimately felt he had to accept.

Johnson then went into a press conference to announce he was sending more troops to Vietnam and then the Fortas appointment. Fortas claimed that he had no recollection of ever actually saying yes at any point.[7] This was a life-turning moment for Fortas but also a demonstration of both the loyalty he felt toward Johnson and the awesome ability of the president to get his way in a one-on-one conversation.

Once Fortas was confirmed to the Court, the firm dropped his name from the partnership and officially became Arnold & Porter. Abe Fortas became its most famous alum, returning for the annual Christmas dinner and occasional social visits. Justice Fortas handed off all of his clients to his partners save one. He continued his special relationship with President Johnson. Whether or not proper, Fortas continued to counsel the president while on the Supreme Court on legislative and political matters, including the conduct of the Vietnam War, which were likely to come before the Court in the future.

For the firm, it was the final evolution into an institutional firm, not beholden to its founding fathers for its livelihood and expansion. The firm had long since begun to be run like a business and not the cozy "mom-and-pop" shop of the past. Arnold was markedly slowing down, and Porter had never been involved in the day-to-day management of the firm. By and large, Fortas's clients stayed with the firm and were dispersed among the younger partners who had previously worked under Fortas's direction.

Age and the evolving practice at the law firm finally achieved what nothing else had ever been able to do, restrain Arnold from offering his opinion on certain subjects. For the first time, he declined to offer his personal views on antitrust because of the law firm's burgeoning defense practice in the area. He refused an interview with *Dun's Review* on antitrust because the firm was now engaged almost exclusively on behalf of defendants and Arnold & Porter's positions might not coincide with the views he might express. He further refused to write a blurb for a book on political economy for the same reason.[8] In private correspondence though, he was more forthright, denouncing the nonenforcement of the antitrust laws by the Kennedy administration, which now included both his former student Nicholas Katzenbach and his former local counsel Byron White.

On his traditional civil liberties issues, Arnold remained true to his liberal convictions and a staunch supporter of free speech, integration, and the work of the Warren Court. He vigorously defended the *Brown v. Board of Education* decision and responded to conservative attacks on landmark criminal procedure cases like *Miranda* and *Escobedo* both in dinner conversations and in op-eds to the newspapers. Arnold allowed his name to be used in a public statement by the socialist Norman Thomas denouncing the antisubversive efforts of the Kennedy administration. He wrote a tongue-in-cheek letter to the editor of the *Washington Post* decrying the badgering of witnesses in congressional hearings with repeated questions when it was clear the witness was asserting his constitutional rights not to answer. He facetiously proposed allowing the witness the right to refuse 1000 times, but if the committee persisted to question 1001, then the Bill of Rights would "take a breather" and the witness would have to answer. He chided conservatives opposed to public accommodations laws of the Civil Rights Act on the grounds that even under the common law innkeepers had the obligation to serve all travelers without discrimination.[9]

The evolving nature of American liberalism made Arnold's relationship with the American Civil Liberties Union increasingly prickly, despite his lengthy service on their national board. In the 1950s, he had quarreled with the group over their proposed amicus brief in the Lattimore case, which Arnold viewed as simply wrong on the law and actually contrary to Lattimore's interests and his defense strategy. He praised the ACLU's stand supporting Arthur Kinoy, a prominent liberal lawyer and former counsel to the Rosenbergs in their espionage trial, in his prosecution for disorderly conduct for his behavior in hearings before the House Un-American Activities Committee. However, Arnold protested the ACLU attempt to enjoin the HUAC hearings involving Kinoy because Arnold felt that the only way to enforce a victory would be to arrest the chairman of the committee. Arnold then declined to sign a subsequent brief on behalf of Kinoy.[10]

He also declined to represent ACLU in a suit on behalf of minor political parties excluded from federal funding through income tax checkoff:

> I am forced to agree with you on the principle that minority parties should have shares in campaign funds. However, I am completely un-

sympathetic with the idea as a practical matter since I regard parties which get less than 5,000,000 votes as an unqualified nuisance and usually represent some extremist views.[11]

A brief but stinging response from an ACLU official that "one man's 'unqualified nuisance' is another man's liberty" brought a more measured answer from Arnold: "Your criticism of my letter of November 9th is justified. Unpopular persons and organizations are certainly entitled to civil liberties as well as popular ones. . . ." Arnold remained concerned that splinter parties would lead to the type of chaos present at that time in France and beginning to occur in Germany. He admitted that his argument was potentially dangerous to the cause of civil liberties and indicated his support in principle for the suit. He was nonetheless reluctant to sign on, especially since his partner Paul Porter was on a presidential committee on campaign expenditures.

Arnold appeared increasingly conservative on Vietnam as well. His 1967 Law Day speech at Valparaiso University was his public coming out on this issue. At Valparaiso he argued that the law at home was a way of looking at society and the relations between individuals and their government, but abroad its most important aspect was to restrain lawless behavior and to prevent aggressive war.

It was an odd topic for Arnold to address in the first place. Despite the breadth of his intellect, he had never written or spoken publicly about international law and had no known interest in the subject, except for a nodding familiarity with the developing antitrust laws of the European Common Market.

Arnold began innocuously enough, recounting the typical Arnold history of law in the United States, with its battles over the legality of the New Deal, the depredations of the McCarthy era, and the rise of the Warren court as the protector of the people's liberties. As in his earlier reply to Professor Hart, he took aim against the critics of the Warren court and their hiding behind terms like "neutral principles" to cloak an attack on the new constitutional order.

Turning to international issues, Arnold inadvertently illustrated how the liberals of the prior generation had morphed into either defenders of the administration line on Vietnam or the true conservatives on foreign policy issues. He argued:

> It is in the field of international law where the greatest danger lies. We are living in a lawless world, a world where small and relatively impotent nations can nevertheless start brush fires which may spread to our own shores. We have seen it happen twice—the First World War and again in the Second. But the world is even smaller today than it was in the Second World War. It has become so small that lawless aggressive action by any nation against another can threaten world peace. It is also a world where poverty and misery in the crowded nations which cannot feed themselves threaten revolutions which upset the balance of power. In such a world we need some sort of a world constitution ever more desperately than the Thirteen Colonies needed the Constitution of the United States after the Revolutionary War. And the keystone of that world constitution is the principle that no nation must be permitted to expand its borders and its powers through an aggressive attack upon its neighbors. We are today attempting to enforce that principle in Vietnam.[12]

Arnold invoked Nuremberg as the ultimate judicial sanction against aggressive war, but he then attacked columnists like Walter Lippman, organizations of intellectuals such as Americans for Democratic Action, and "liberal professors on our college campuses" who were seeking to "prevent the enforcement of the principle that Nuremberg announced to the world." According to Arnold, these same groups and individuals were giving aid and comfort to the enemy and encouraging North Vietnam to believe that the United States would eventually abandon its attempt to enforce the Nuremberg principle in Asia.

Arnold attacked the dangers of isolationism with examples from the interwar period in the 1930s and the failed appeasement of both Japan and Germany. He then criticized public statements opposing the war by such "alienated intellectuals" as John Kenneth Galbraith, Henry Steele Commager, and Senator William Fulbright.

He concluded in a manner seemingly at odds with his own past and values:

> Here we find a new phase of disrespect for law among our alienated intellectuals, the abuse of the right to dissent and the abuse of freedom of speech. Much as I abhor the days when Senator McCarthy was in power, we did not in those dark times have to hear such nonsense from

college professors. Now that they can safely publish their dissenting views without retaliation, they have advanced a new doctrine of dissent based on the premise that dissent deserves special consideration, immunity from criticism and the right to shout down people who disagree with them.[13]

Perhaps the most quoted, but perplexing, lines from the Valparaiso speech were: "In a democratic society dissent is not sacred. Only the right to dissent is sacred." With this line alone, he earned more friends on the political right then any other action, with the possible exception of his indictments against the labor unions in the late 1930s and early 1940s.

Arnold's speech was, in fact, inconsistent with some of his prior statements on the war. When asked in 1965 by a *Washington Star* Sunday magazine reporter about his recollections of the various presidents he knew, Arnold said, "Now Lyndon Johnson could become the *great* president in history. But I worry about Viet Nam. We should get out of Asia, let them have it."[14] This was the only such past comment by Arnold and was now forgotten in his more hawkish and public comments.

The Valparaiso speech was widely covered in the press as a result of President Johnson mentioning it at a press conference as a sign of support for his policy in Vietnam. Arnold's speech was covered in daily papers throughout the country as well as *Time* magazine and the *International Herald Tribune*, inserted into the *Congressional Record* by Wyoming Republican Senator Clifford Hansen, and widely distributed by the White House. The speech was reprinted in part in such publications as *Reader's Digest* and the *National Observer*, and in its entirety in the American Bar Association *International Lawyer* journal. Arnold received praise from friends, total strangers, and public figures such as Dean Acheson, Cornelius Vanderbilt, Warren Burger, Hubert Humphrey, Earl Warren, Max Kampelman, and Senator Paul Douglas. While many of these were old friends, many were former opponents, including Colonel Robert McCormick, publisher of the *Chicago Tribune,* who had previously referred to Arnold as an "idiot in a powder mill" during his Antitrust Division days.

As Arnold made new admirers, he lost previous supporters. He was gently rebuked by his former New Deal colleague Rexford Tugwell, and more harshly so by the mother of a serviceman in Vietnam and other liberal strangers. Both the praise and criticism often came on little more than hand scribbled notes with Arnold replying to each letter as his time and health permitted. Perhaps based on his difficult experience in crafting his autobiography, he received but declined an offer to turn the speech into a book.[15]

The Vietnam War was the one subject that was a sore point with his grandchildren and many of the younger lawyers at the firm who opposed the draft and the war itself. His grandson George Jr. had applied for conscientious objector status that did not sit well with Judgie. Arnold asked younger lawyers at the firm not to represent William Sloane Coffin and others indicted for antiwar activity until Fortas, from the Supreme Court, sent word that President Johnson would not hold it against the firm if they took the case. But by this time, the defendants had found other counsel. Arnold also quietly, but firmly, resigned from the board of the Institute for Policy Studies, a left-liberal think tank that became progressively more involved in the antiwar movement.[16]

He wrote to Senator Ernest Gruening about the war, "Personally I am convinced that surrender would be disastrous and we are fortunate to have an army in Asia because otherwise Russia or Japan could go straight down the coast to Singapore."[17] Arnold saw the antiwar movement as dangerous radicals who failed to support a commitment of national honor. There is also more than a tinge of frustration with the liberal movement that had been too timid to support Arnold's lonely work on the loyalty era cases but was now vocally attacking an administration that Arnold admired for the Great Society program.

For some, Arnold's support of the war was a baffling and incongruous mixture with his lifelong liberalism. For many, there was no inconsistency in Arnold's domestic liberalism and support for the war. It was just a disagreement on the merits by a proud former veteran, an anticommunist liberal of the old school, and one with intense personal loyalty to Abe Fortas, Lyndon Johnson, and the rest of the White House that he admired more than any since the Roosevelt administration.[18]

Even on the personal side, Arnold continued to make headlines. Around two in the morning on March 8, 1966, Arnold wandered downstairs to the kitchen wearing little other than his ever-present cigar only to discover that burglars had been packing up the family silver into a couple of tablecloths. The window was open, the screen had been cut, and everything had been ransacked. Only the sounds of Arnold coming down the stairs and turning on the light scared off the burglars, thus sparing Arnold an unpleasant confrontation and the burglars the sight of a nearly naked

Arnold. While the story was reported in the papers more for its comic value, the burglars in fact had gone all the way to a second story bedroom next to where the Arnolds slept and made off with credit cards and some cash from Frances's purse.[19]

Thurman and Frances celebrated their fiftieth anniversary in Europe, leaving Washington in late August of 1967 and returning in late September. The honors and requests for Arnold as a speaker continued even in his absence as his faithful secretary Marguerite O'Brien struggled to keep up with his correspondence until he could return and decide which invitations to accept. Laramie created an Arnold Street in a new subdivision a short drive from the old Arnold house on Grand Avenue. Through Lyndon Johnson, Arnold accepted the largely ceremonial appointment as an arbitrator on international investment disputes.

One of his last great speeches was delivered at the annual dinner of the New York State Bar Association Antitrust Law Section on January 24, 1968.[20] He was introduced by former Supreme Court Justice Tom Clark, who had begun his career, as had a number of people in the room, as a young lawyer under Arnold in the Antitrust Division. After jokingly telling Don Turner, the then current head of the Antitrust Division, to bring back Clark to the division, Arnold turned serious and reviewed the past thirty years of antitrust since he had joined the Justice Department. But before doing so, he cautioned his audience with a twinkle in his eye that "some of the things I remember best never actually happened."

Arnold recalled the momentous turn of events in the New Deal that had brought him to Washington. Prior to his arrival, "no one took antitrust very seriously." He reviewed the outrage in the business community and the press as the prior policies of the NRA were reversed and prosecutions for price fixing became the norm. He recounted how the prevailing attitudes of the business community slowly gave way through the cases he and his successors brought and won.

He continued with a swipe at the academic economists, both from his government days and the late 1960s, who urged inaction and reliance on the market. To Arnold, such critics envisioned "an ideal of an economic system in an orderly organization of industry, each ruled feudally from above by the business firms already established in it, linked in associations and confederations organizing their own courts and securing and entrenching their holdings."

Arnold concluded with praise for the spread of antitrust in Europe through the Common Market and closed with his long-felt belief that "the antitrust concept is still the most effective brake against the development of a disturbed and unbalanced business structure."

Another coronary kept him confined to the hospital for much of early 1968. Matters came to a head with the ACLU shortly thereafter. The ACLU had agreed to defend an army officer who refused to comply with orders because of his personal dislike of the war in Vietnam, and they also represented Dr. Benjamin Spock and William Sloane Coffin for their destruction of draft cards. Despite impassioned pleas from the ACLU leadership and many references to Arnold's noble struggles in the loyalty cases in the 1950s, Arnold resigned from the ACLU in April 1968. Refusing a final plea from John Pemberton, the ACLU executive director, to come back to the fold, Arnold wrote,

> Today we do have freedom of speech in the sense that anyone can hire a hall or teach a course in a university or express views in Government without danger to his career. In other words, the battle for civil liberties in the sense of free expression of opinion has now been won.
>
> It is regrettable that the ACLU should be pushing the cause of civil liberties in what, in my view, amounts to a defense of civil disobedience. Interference with discipline in colleges, interference with discipline in the Army, defense of individuals who admit they are banded together to impede the draft in time of war and publicly dare the Attorney General to prosecute them—such activities are now being justified on the ground that a civil rights issue is involved.
>
> I intend to make no public issue of this. I resign privately and with regret and without any desire to cause you any more trouble than you already have with an organization which seems to be going further and further toward the extreme left.[21]

When Pemberton wouldn't leave well enough alone and persisted in writing to Arnold, enclosing the briefs in the case of the Army captain who refused orders, former Army Captain Thurman Arnold wrote back:

> Your position seems to me to be this: The late Rockwell, head of the American Fascist Party, was unquestionably a sincere believer in Hitler. This entitles him to get a commission in the Army on the implied condition that he would fight against anyone but Hitler. Your brief is so well

done that it may confuse the court. I have, therefore, decided I must do something to dissipate its impact.

I have decided upon the following course of action: Sometime at my convenience I will go to the Clerk's office of the court before which you are now appearing and begin tearing up all your petitions until someone stops me and I am arrested. I will then expect you to defend me on the ground that I was only exercising my rights of symbolic freedom of action.[22]

Arnold's fit of pique aside, his later correspondence shows a more sobering concern that the ACLU was going the way of the National Lawyers Guild in the 1930s and would be destroyed by extremists.[23]

Most of April 1968 was spent away from the office because of illness. Arnold sadly declined an invitation to attend the thirty-fifth anniversary of the signing of the Agricultural Adjustment Act of 1933, which he and Abe Fortas had defended from constitutional attack while on leave from Yale.[24]

Even while convalescing, Arnold continued his voluminous correspondence and writings. He reviewed a book by a former Antitrust Division lawyer for the *New Republic,* reviewed a political science text on American legal realism, completed galleys for his 1968 remarks given at the New York State Bar Association, prepared a foreword for a book by Professor Nicholas Kittrie of American University, became a founding member of National Citizens for Humphrey Committee, accepted another term on the largely inactive Advisory Council for Politics Department at Princeton, and dealt with various requests to translate his own books into Italian. He agreed to read a manuscript on the political and legal ideas of Jerome Frank, and again dutifully endorsed over the $25 reader's fee to the firm.

There was another coronary resulting in hospitalization in May, but Arnold still went into the office almost each day "from force of habit and lack of any other hobby." Arnold's comments on the public issues of the day and the public turmoil of 1968 sounded increasingly hawkish: "Washington is an interesting place these days. We have 3500 poor people camped near the Lincoln Memorial and raising hell generally. Everybody is for doing something for them and all of the senators from states with large Negro votes are loudly sympathizing with them. At the same time, Congress is not going to appropriate any money for anything, so all they will get is sympathy. They threaten to remain here until something is done; their permit for camping and making a mess of the Washington Mall expires on June 15. They say they are not going to go. It will probably end up in a riot. Everything seems all mixed up."[25]

There was more heart trouble in September 1968, but Arnold was back in the office by November. Arnold and Frances visited the children at Christmas in Los Angeles followed by a couple of days of vacation at Coronado Island near San Diego. Despite an additional heart attack in the winter, a frail Arnold was still able to attend the inauguration of his old friend and Antitrust Division colleague Edward Levi as president of University of Chicago, writing his former protégé afterwards: "I wouldn't have missed your Inauguration if I had had to have gone on a stretcher."[26]

At the beginning of 1969, Joseph Califano left the Johnson administration to join Arnold & Porter. Arnold viewed Califano's arrival as a passing of the torch of the public and political side of the firm and as part of a new generation of liberal lawyers taking the reins of power. In characteristic style, Arnold pressed a reluctant Califano to take his office on the main floor of the now badly overcrowded townhouse. Califano refused, despite Arnold's urgings on several occasions. Like many at the firm, he viewed Arnold's office "as a shrine" belonging to Arnold in perpetuity, despite Arnold's rapidly diminishing time in the office itself.[27]

Notes of pessimism now began to creep into Arnold's correspondence. He told his longtime friends, "While I still get to the office I am not doing very well," and "The future looks glum." Arnold felt "chained to my doctor in Alexandria, who examines me every week."[28]

His public correspondence was equally ill-tempered beyond just resigning in a huff from the ACLU. Arnold went out of his way to pick a fight with Ralph Nader over the firm's representation of General Motors in congressional hearings over auto safety. In response to Nader's accusation that Arnold & Porter was "cutting down consumer programs in their incipiency or undermining them if they mature," Arnold wrote Senator Abraham Ribicoff:

> We suspect . . . that what Mr. Nader is really objecting to is any adequate legal representation before Congress or before administrative tribunals of any organization which does not meet with his approval. Such representation, he thinks, would result in "greasing of the corporate wheels and the softening of the bureaucrat's will." By this he means that it might be possible for counsel to persuade the bureaucrat in question

that there was some merit in his client's case and thus his "bureaucrat's will" would become softened.

Perhaps a rule that counsel should not make any representation on behalf of his client without the prior approval of Mr. Nader would satisfy him. The necessity of hearing representatives of both sides of a case, even if one of them happens to be General Motors, may slow down many of Mr. Nader's praiseworthy objectives. But it is the only course consistent with the constitutional idea that adverse interests are entitled to have their claims presented by counsel of their choice.

Mr. Nader has every right to attack the claims and arguments of any group which he thinks opposes the consumers' interests. He has no right, however, to attack any group for *presenting* its claims and arguments (however wrong they may be in his eyes) to the men who must make the decisions. . . . He is saying to your Committee that we should get rid of skilled advocates because they confuse the court.[29]

He wrote an equally snide letter regarding a professor's criticism of the firm's representation of the tobacco industry, again arguing for the right to counsel and hearkening back to an era in the 1950s when, without the help of Arnold & Porter, many with unpopular views could not get lawyers to represent them. There was a more laudatory note to the president of Harvard University, supporting him against the wave of student unrest, because of that official's courageous stand on Lattimore during the McCarthy era. Arnold even went so far as to join the Alumni Committee to Involve Ourselves Now (ACTION) to fend off similar incidents at Princeton.[30] Too often the themes of most of these letters were indignant denunciations of those who disagreed with him for not being sufficiently grateful for the many lonely fights that Arnold had undertaken on behalf of unpopular causes in his lifetime.

Arnold had one last fight to wage and another unpopular cause to champion. In the waning days of the Johnson administration, after the president had declared that he would not run for reelection, Johnson announced his nomination of Fortas to succeed Earl Warren as chief justice. This would not wash politically, given Johnson's lame-duck status, a withering attack on Fortas in the press, and massive congressional criticism of Fortas's politics and decisions on the Court. Nor did Fortas help himself by giving evasive testimony at his confirmation hearing that proved later to be false in several key aspects.[31] Following a Senate filibuster on his nomination, Fortas requested that Johnson withdraw his name for chief justice.

The Nixon administration hated Fortas and what he stood for at many different levels, including being on opposite sides in the McCarthy era when Nixon had first made his public reputation as a Red hunter. Once the chief justice position was out of the question, the goal was to get Fortas off the court entirely.

The indiscretion that in the end cost Fortas his seat on the Supreme Court related to a financier named Louis Wolfson. A longtime client of the firm, Wolfson had a number of brushes with the law, primarily in the securities field. After Fortas had gone on the bench, Wolfson had been convicted of securities fraud and received a prison sentence. Wolfson also had a charitable foundation dealing with social justice issues that invited Fortas to serve as a board member in return for a lifetime honorarium of $20,000 per year. Fortas accepted, but he resigned within a year and returned the money following Wolfson's conviction.

While not illegal, and hardly unique among members of the judiciary (Douglas and Burger had similar arrangements), Fortas's relationship with Wolfson was more notorious because Wolfson was more notorious. Wolfson's continuing problems with the SEC and the courts led to the implication that Fortas was receiving money for assistance with pending government investigations through his special relationship with Lyndon Johnson. Fortas failed to give a straightforward and complete explanation of the payment and its return and the issue became a cause célèbre. At a minimum, there was the massive appearance of impropriety of a sitting justice receiving money, even indirectly, from a convicted felon who had potential business before the court or with the administration that Fortas continued to counsel on the side.

Although Fortas was in all likelihood guilty of nothing more than bad judgment, there was relentless pressure to resign both from the Nixon White House and even friends from the Johnson administration who felt betrayed by the revelations. Although Bill Douglas, who had weathered similar pressures, urged him to hang tough, other prominent Democrats like Clark Clifford urged him to resign. Fortas felt under even more pressure given his innate privacy, insecurity, and reserved nature and without many close advisers in whom he felt he could confide. Compounding the pressure was the not so subtle leaks emanating from the Nixon Justice Department that indictments for obstruction of justice in connection with the Wolfson affair were being considered against Paul Porter, other lawyers at Arnold & Porter, and possibly the firm itself. Finally in May 1969 Fortas bowed to the inevitable and announced his resignation from the court.[32]

Arnold rarely commented on the Fortas scandal but was in tears when Fortas announced his resignation. In his typical reserved and private fashion, Fortas had never consulted nor confided in Arnold about his relationship with Wolfson, why he accepted the board position or the honorarium, or his thoughts leading up to his resignation. Arnold viewed the whole episode as an attempt by the Nixon administration to destroy Fortas and the firm. In one of the few surviving bits of correspondence he observed: "Abe left the firm four years ago but he was one of the people I loved and admired most of all the friends I knew. Therefore, we are terribly disturbed by the uproar which attended his departure from the Court."[33]

The question was now whether Fortas would, or even could, return to the firm that he had cofounded and led as managing partner. Arnold was loyal to the end and immediately wrote Fortas a letter announcing the "irrevocable" decision to welcome him back to the firm. This proved to be a terrible mistake. By 1969, Arnold & Porter was no longer the firm of the founding fathers. Arnold, in particular, was elderly, ailing, and no longer even practicing on a full-time basis. When he left for the Court, Fortas had been first among equals, a stern managing partner with an iron-tight grip on the major clients and the compensation of most of the other lawyers. Four years later, things were different. The younger partners had both Fortas's clients and their own developing practices and were no longer "Abe's boys." They were respected and powerful firm partners and forces in the Washington bar in their own right.

Abe Fortas remains even today a sensitive subject for the lawyers who worked with him. Many were only willing to discuss the decision not to welcome him back to the firm obliquely or off the record. Some thought that the firm "owed it to him" to take him back. Others were shocked by his behavior or feared the reaction of clients if Fortas returned. For most though, the decision about Fortas's return was not about the merits of what he had or had not done. Having Fortas back would be a time warp, and a potentially unpleasant one at that, if Fortas was going to resume his past role as the dominant and domineering senior partner. Others simply feared that Fortas's return would hurt the firm more than it would help. The firm had changed radically and become an institution in its own right without a single dominant partner. There was a widespread feeling that it just could not go back to the way things had been.[34]

Arnold continued to fight for Fortas's return but never had the numbers on his side. By and large, the older, more senior, partners supported Fortas. A solid corps of mid-level working partners were strongly opposed. It was largely a generational dispute mirroring much of the conflict in America, with the earlier generation opposed by the lawyers of the 1960s and aided by a small number of allies from the older generation. As Joseph Califano observed, "These arguments became so heated and venomous that they stunned Thurman Arnold and reduced Paul Porter to tears on more than one occasion. These founders viewed the younger partners' reactions as selfish arrogance and ingratitude."[35]

As the partners huddled with each other to figure out their positions and the best way to proceed with this explosive issue, Arnold and another partner visited Fortas in his Georgetown home. In virtually his only display of emotion about his resignation, Fortas banged on the table and shouted that the firm needed him and would "go to hell" without him. Back at the firm, there was a concerted effort not to bring the matter to a vote, and eventually even Arnold conceded defeat, leaving another lawyer shaking at the unhappy prospect of having to inform Fortas that he could not return to the firm that had once borne his name and still included his wife as a partner.

After it was clear that Fortas was not returning to the firm he had created, time was less kind to Arnold. Although "up until his death he was able to come into the office a few days each week,"[36] there was less and less to do and less and less that he could do. There were increasing angina attacks. He had to miss funerals of friends and colleagues and began to resign from a number of his public positions, as if anticipating the end. To make matters worse, he cut a tendon in his wrist on a piece of glass, and his secretary was now signing his letters.

On the evening of November 7, Arnold went to bed early and poignantly told Frances, "I'm not sure I really want to live any longer." He then passed away so peacefully in his sleep that Frances did not even realize he was gone for several hours.[37]

In the end it was Abe Fortas, Arnold's friend and colleague for most of his adult life, who rallied to the aid of the Arnold family. It was Abe Fortas who Frances called at 2 a.m. on the night Arnold passed away, and who came from Georgetown to Alexandria in the middle of the night to comfort Frances and begin the funeral arrangements. Fortas, despite the public scandal and the still raw wounds of being denied return to the firm he started, organized the funeral and memorial services in Washington and Laramie. It was Fortas who stood with the family, and several of his former partners, when Thurman's ashes were laid to rest in the family plot in Laramie, within walking distance of the old Arnold house.

On November 20, 1969, over 500 friends and colleagues gathered for a memorial service for Thurman Arnold at the National Cathedral in Washington, D.C. Paul Porter, Justice William Douglas, Chief Justice Warren Burger, Hugh Cox, an old colleague of Arnold's from the Antitrust Division, and Abe Fortas spoke. Justice Douglas who, like Fortas, had known Arnold for almost forty years, closed the memorial by summing up the essence of Thurman Arnold:

> Here was a man of many dimensions, of tremendous vitality, of inventive genius. He was constantly at war with the forces of orthodoxy that have long been overtaking us. He made every status quo quite uncomfortable and uneasy, including traditional legal education. He was indeed the very embodiment of the spirit of dissent.
>
> Only the climate of the First Amendment could have produced him. And he did more to strengthen the spirit of the First Amendment than anyone of our time.[38]

A later obituary for members of the Association of the Bar of the City of New York captured his effect on the antitrust laws that he had done so much to shape and the people he helped shaped in the process:

> What will live long are the creations of his genius. His famous antitrust campaign in the courts and the press, and in any place where he could gather two or more together, surely shaped national economic policy as permanently and decisively as any piece of contemporaneous federal legislation. The success of his political and legal writings has been permanent, for their philosophy has passed into the intellectual climate of the times. Not least among his legacies comes from his amazing power to lift those who worked with him to achievements beyond their own unaided talents and so to shape their thoughts and aspirations that through the effects of these upon others many will feel his influence who never knew the man.[39]

Epilogue

The Arnold legacy is still felt keenly both in Laramie and Washington, D.C. The house in Laramie at 812 Grand Street where Thurman Arnold was born and raised still stands a couple of blocks west of the university. After Arnold's death, Frances Arnold surprised most of her friends in Washington moved back into the old Arnold home in Laramie, and extensively renovated it. Instead of continuing her life as a Washington society matron, she played the role of grandmother and eventually great-grandmother, living to the ripe old age of ninety-eight. In a wonderful coincidence, the current owner of the house happens to have his office in the same building in the downtown section of Laramie where Thurman practiced law with his father. Most people still refer to the house at 812 Grand Street as the Arnold house.

Laramie is still a small town with a strong connection to its past and the role of the Arnold family in its founding and development. The woman who lives across the street from the Arnold house is in the house that her great-grandfather built around the same time C. P. built the Arnold house. She and her father remember the Arnolds fondly and freely share stories of Thurman and his exploits. She is just one of numerous Laramie residents who remember the Arnolds and think of them first and foremost as belonging to Laramie, a remarkable tribute to a man who physically left Laramie for good in 1927, but never left it in his heart.

The Arnold family burial plot lies in a small well-preserved cemetery across the road from both the American Heritage Center, which houses the archives of Thurman Arnold and his father, and the University of Wyoming College of Law, which Arnold helped found. Four generations of Arnolds have influenced the law school, which continues to prosper and, in typical, puckish Arnold fashion occasionally bills itself as the "highest" rated law school in the United States.[1] C. P. Arnold lent the school his law library in the early days. Besides helping to create the school in the first place, Thurman Arnold taught as an adjunct during his years of practice in Laramie. His brother Carl Arnold served as a full-time faculty member and later dean until his death in 1941. Thurman's son George Arnold returned to Laramie in the 1970s, started the first legal clinic at the law school, and served as a full-time faculty member using memorable classroom techniques and antics that would have made his father proud. Thurman's grandson George Jr., is a graduate of the Wyoming Law School and continues to practice in the state.

At 555 12th Street in northwest Washington, D.C., just a few blocks from the main office of the Department of Justice, stands the Thurman Arnold Building. It is said to be the only office building in Washington named after a New Dealer. Its principal tenant is the firm of Arnold & Porter. Today, Arnold & Porter has over 680 lawyers and offices around the country and Europe. It also still has a garden room, albeit on the twelfth floor, with a grand piano, fireplace, and skylight where the firm's lawyers still gather for firm occasions and a drink when their time permits, although the room holds only a fraction of the current firm at one time. Portraits of both Arnold and Porter hang in an adjacent conference room called the memorabilia room, and the corridor outside is full of Arnold's collection of signed photos and newspaper accounts of the firm's cases and pro bono activities both recent and from the McCarthy era. Arnold & Porter is also an institution that values its history and traditions, and there is still an older generation of lawyers who worked with Arnold and who are always happy to take a moment and tell an Arnold story or reflect on how he influenced their lives and careers.

The firm also still values the tradition of pro bono work, which the early lawyers established in the loyalty cases. Only a few years after Arnold's death, an Arnold & Porter partner named Gerald Stern led a pro bono team of lawyers in the controversial and successful representation of the families in Buffalo Creek, West Virginia, against the coal company and its New York corporate parent following the devastating flood caused by the collapse of a dam in the narrow valleys of West Virginia coal country.[2] More recently, the firm received much attention for its lengthy and successful pro bono work by four lawyers over a five-year period to clear the name and expunge the court-martial of Lt. Henry Flipper, a nineteenth-century cavalry officer and the first African-American graduate of West Point.

Arnold & Porter continues another tradition begun by Arnold, Fortas & Porter, the hardnosed representation of large corporate interests. Gone are the days where Arnold & Porter (or any other large firm) finds its bread and butter in the representation of small companies and individual plaintiffs in courtrooms around the country. Whatever contradictions one finds in a commitment to liberal values, pro bono work, and the representation of both the underdog and the business elite, these are the contradictions embodied in Arnold himself, his firm, and his profession.

Arnold's life and career span the principal events of twentieth-century American law, the rise and fall of the Progressive era and legal realism; the Great Depression and the great experiments of both halves of the New Deal; the effect of World War II on law and legal thinking; the coming of the cold war and the McCarthy era; the Great Society and its fall from grace because of the Vietnam War. While best known as the father of modern antitrust, Arnold was front and center in all of these developments.

It is difficult to sum up the impact of the life of a man as complex and fascinating as Thurman Arnold. The task is made somewhat easier because the public side and the private side of him matched so well. Some simply believed that there was little private side to him, that what you saw and heard was the core of the man. But this only gets us part of the way home. There were many seeming contradictions even if you focused on the public life of Thurman Arnold. His was the journey of a twentieth-century liberal, but one who differed from many of his colleagues in significant ways. In the end, one of his former colleagues summed him up best when he described Arnold as being "able to laugh at the establishment and still be part of it," and what's more "relished in the contradiction."

Appendix A

Cases Decided (Opinion), Concurred, or Dissented by Judge Thurman Arnold (in Chronological Order)

(MARCH 17, 1943–JULY 10, 1945) UNITED STATES COURT OF APPEALS FOR THE DISTRICT OF COLUMBIA

1. *Cook v. Cook,* 77 U.S. App. D.C. 388; 135 F.2d 945, May 17, 1943.
2. *Neel,* Insurance Commissioner of Pennsylvania, *v. Barbra; Same v. Davis; Same v. Gustin; Same v. Warren,* 78 U.S. App. D.C. 13; 136 F.2d 269, May 29, 1943.
3. *Griffith-Consumers Co. v. Noonan* et al., 78 U.S. App. D.C. 32; 136 F.2d 271, June 4, 1943.
4. *Hurwitz v. Hurwitz,* 78 U.S. App. D.C. 66; 136 F.2d 796, June 22, 1943.
5. *Hurwitz v. Hurwitz,* 78 U.S. App. D.C. 70; 136 F.2d 800, June 22, 1943.
6. *Fox et ux. v. Ickes,* Secretary of the Interior; *Parks et ux. v. Same; Eder v. Same.,* 78 U.S. App. D.C. 84; 137 F.2d 30, June 30, 1943.
7. *De Marcos v. Overholser,* 78 U.S. App. D.C. 131; 137 F.2d 698, August 9, 1943.
8. *Hecht Co. v. Whiteford,* 78 U.S. App. D.C. 134; 137 F.2d 929, August 16, 1943.
9. *Puget Sound Power & Light Co. v. Federal Power Commission,* 78 U.S. App. D.C. 143; 137 F.2d 701, August 23, 1943.
10. *Williams et al. v. United States,* 78 U.S. App. D.C. 147; 138 F.2d 81, September 27, 1943.
11. *Childs et al. v. Radzevich,* 78 U.S. App. D.C. 235; 139 F.2d 374, December 6, 1943, (Concurring).
12. *McKay v. Parkwood Owners, Inc.,* 78 U.S. App. D.C. 260; 139 F.2d 385, December 20, 1943.
13. *Travelers Ins. Co. v. Cardillo,* Deputy Commissioner, *et al.,* 78 U.S. App. D.C. 255; 140 F.2d 10, December 20, 1943.
14. *Watson v. Massachusetts Mut. Life Ins. Co.* (two cases), 78 U.S. App. D.C. 248; 140 F.2d 673, December 20, 1943.

15. *Maloney v. Foundry Methodist Episcopal Church et al.,* 78 U.S. App. D.C. 263; 139 F.2d 388, December 27, 1943.
16. *Shokuwan Shimbakuro v. Higeyoshi Nagayama,* 78 U.S. App. D.C. 271; 140 F.2d 13, January 3, 1944.
17. *Melvin v. Melvin,* 78 U.S. App. D.C. 285; 140 F.2d 17, January 17, 1944.
18. *Potts et al. v. Coe,* Commissioner of Patents, 78 U.S. App. D.C. 297; 140 F.2d 470, January 18, 1944.
19. *Special Equipment Co. v. Coe,* Commissioner of Patents, 79 U.S. App. D.C. 133; 144 F.2d 497, January 19, 1944.
20. *Hamilton v. United States,* 78 U.S. App. D.C. 316; 140 F.2d 679, January 24, 1944.
21. *Tippitt v. Wood et al.,* 78 U.S. App. D.C. 332; 140 F.2d 689, February 7, 1944 (Dissenting).
22. *Klepinger et al. v. Rhodes,* 78 U.S. App. D.C. 340; 140 F.2d 697, February 11, 1944.
23. *Connecticut Light & Power Co. v. Federal Power Commission,* 78 U.S. App. D.C. 356; 141 F.2d 14, February 28, 1944.
24. *Rone v. Rone et al.,* 78 U.S. App. D.C. 369; 141 F.2d 23, March 6, 1944.
25. *Schneider. v. Schneider,* 78 U.S. App. D.C. 383; 141 F.2d 542, March 13, 1944.
26. *Cromer v. United States,* 78 U.S. App. D.C. 400; 142 F.2d 697, March 20, 1944.
27. *Gaston v. United States,* 79 U.S. App. D.C. 37; 143 F.2d 10, April 10, 1944.
28. *Russell v. Russell,* 79 U.S. App. D.C. 44; 142 F.2d 753, April 17, 1944.
29. *Groome et al. v. Steward,* 79 U.S. App. D.C. 50; 142 F.2d 756, April 24, 1944.
30. *Minnesota Mining & Manufacturing Co. v. Coe,* Commissioner of Patents, 79 U.S. App. D.C. 59; 143 F.2d 12, May 1, 1944.
31. *Wolpe et al. v. Poretsky et al.,* 79 U.S. App. D.C. 141; 144 F.2d 505, June 19, 1944.
32. *Vanderhuff v. Vanderhuff,* 79 U.S. App. D.C. 153; 144 F.2d 509, June 26, 1944.
33. *Monsanto Chemical Co. v. Coe,* Commissioner of Patents, 79 U.S. App. D.C. 155; 145 F.2d 18, June 26, 1944.
34. *Hill v. Hawes et al.,* 79 U.S. App. D.C. 168; 144 F.2d 511, June 30, 1944.
35. *Smith v. Schlein et al.,* 79 U.S. App. D.C. 166; 144 F.2d 257, June 30, 1944.
36. *Neely v. United States,* 79 U.S. App. D.C. 177; 144 F.2d 519, July 10, 1944.
37. *Peter J. Schweitzer, Inc., v. National Labor Relations Board,* 79 U.S. App. D.C. 178; 144 F.2d 520, July 10, 1944.
38. *Hoover Co. v. Coe,* Commissioner of Patents, 79 U.S. App. D.C. 172; 144 F.2d 514, July 10, 1944.

39. *Minnesota Mining & Manufacturing Co. v. Coe,* Commissioner of Patents, 79 U.S. App. D.C. 186; 145 F.2d 25, July 10, 1944.
40. *Potts et al. v. Coe,* Commissioner of Patents, 79 U.S. App. D.C. 223; 145 F.2d 27, August 7, 1944.
41. *Urguhart et al. v. American-LA France Foamite Co.,* 79 U.S. App. D.C. 219; 144 F.2d 542, August 7, 1944.
42. *Capital Transit Co. v. United States et al.,* 56 F. Supp. 670, August 25, 1944 (Dissenting).
43. *Lambros et al. v. Young,* President of Board of Commissioners, *et al.,* 79 U.S. App. D.C. 247; 145 F.2d 341, October 30, 1944.
44. *National Labor Relations Board v. Central Dispensary & Emergency Hospital,* 79 U.S. App. D.C. 274; 145 F.2d 852, November 13, 1944.
45. *Kraft Cheese Co. v. Coe,* Commissioner of Patents, 79 U.S. App. D.C. 297; 146 F.2d 313, December 18, 1944.
46. *O'Hara v. District of Columbia,* 79 U.S. App. D.C. 302; 147 F.2d 146, December 26, 1944.
47. *United States Rubber Co. v. Coe,* Commissioner of Patents, 79 U.S. App. D.C. 305; 146 F.2d 315, January 2, 1945.
48. *New York Life Ins. Co. v. Taylor,* 79 U.S. App. D.C. 66; 147 F.2d 297, January 10, 1945.
49. *James Heddon's Sons v. Coe,* Commissioner of Patents, 79 U.S. App. D.C. 317; 146 F.2d 865, January 15, 1945.
50. *Brotherhood of Locomotive Firemen and Enginemen et al. v. Interstate Commerce Commission,* 79 U.S. App. D.C. 318; 147 F.2d 312, January 15, 1945 (Concurring).
51. *F. J. Stokes Mach. Co. v. Coe,* Commissioner of Patents, 79 U.S. App. D.C. 325; 146 F.2d 866, January 22, 1945.
52. *Williams v. Huff,* 79 U.S. App. D.C. 326; 146 F.2d 867, January 22, 1945.
53. *Blake v. Trainer,* 79 U.S. App. D.C. 360; 148 F.2d 10, February 5, 1945.
54. *Better Business Bureau of Washington, D.C., Inc. v. United States,* 79 U.S. App. D.C. 380; 148 F.2d 14, February 19, 1945.
55. *Davy et al. v. Crawford et al.,* 79 U.S. App. D.C. 375; 147 F.2d 574, February 19, 1945.
56. *Diggs v. Welch,* Superintendent D.C. Reformatory, 80 U.S. App. D.C. 5; 148 F.2d 667, February 26, 1945.
57. *Holloway v. United States,* 80 U.S. App. D.C. 3; 148 F.2d 665, February 26, 1945.
58. *Sanders v. Bennett,* Director of Federal Bureau of Prisons, 80 U.S. App. D.C. 32; 148 F.2d 19, March 5, 1945.
59. *United States ex rel. Noel v. Carmody,* 80 U.S. App. D.C. 58; 148 F.2d 684, March 26, 1945.

60. *Strong v. Huff,* General Superintendent, D.C. Penal Institutions, 80 U.S. App. D.C. 89; 148 F.2d 692, April 23, 1945.
61. *Fisher v. United States,* 80 U.S. App. D.C. 96; 149 F.2d 28, April 23, 1945.
62. *Overholser,* Superintendent, Saint Elizabeth Hospital, *v. De Marcos,* 80 U.S. App. D.C. 91; 149 F.2d 23, April 23, 1945.
63. *Bailey v. Zlotnick,* 80 U.S. App. D.C. 117; 149 F.2d 505, May 14, 1945.
64. *Urcilio et al. v. O'Connor,* 80 U.S. App. D.C. 112; 149 F.2d 386, May 14, 1945.
65. *Railroad Retirement Board et al. v. Duquesne Warehouse Co.,* 80 U.S. App. D.C. 119; 149 F.2d 507, May 14, 1945.
66. *Holmes et al. v. Frederick W. Berens, Inc.,* 80 U.S. App. D.C. 114; 149 F.2d 388, May 14, 1945, (Dissenting).
67. *Walker,* Postmaster General of the United States, *v. Popenoe et al.,* 80 U.S. App. D.C. 129; 149 F.2d 511, May 28, 1945, (Concurring).
68. *Rainbow Dyeing & Cleaning Co., Inc. v. Bowles,* Administrator, Office of Price Administration, 80 U.S. App. D.C. 137; 150 F.2d 273, May 28, 1945, (Dissenting).
69. *Esquire, Inc. v. Walker,* Postmaster General of the United States, 80 U.S. App. D.C. 145; 151 F.2d 49, June 4, 1945.
70. *Silverfarb v. United States,* 80 U.S. App. D.C. 158; 151 F.2d 11, June 11, 1945.
71. *Waterman S. S. Co. v. Land,* Chairman of Maritime Commission, *et al.,* 80 U.S. App. D.C. 167; 151 F.2d 292, June 18, 1945, (Dissenting).
72. *Burton v. United States,* 80 U.S. App. D.C. 208; 151 F.2d 17, July 9, 1945.
73. *Reeves v. Bowles,* 80 U.S. App. D.C. 207; 151 F.2d 16, July 9, 1945.

Appendix B
Principal Writings of Thurman Arnold

BOOKS

The Symbols of Government (New Haven: Yale University Press, 1935).
Cases on Trials, Judgments and Appeals (St. Paul: West Publishing Co., 1936).
The Folklore of Capitalism (New Haven: Yale University Press, 1937).
The Bottlenecks of Business (New York: Reynal & Hitchcock, 1940).
Democracy and Free Enterprise (Norman: University of Oklahoma Press, 1942).
Cartels or Free Enterprise (New York: Public Affairs Committee, Inc., 1945).
The Future of Democratic Capitalism (Philadelphia: University of Pennsylvania Press, 1950).
Fair Fights and Foul (New York: Harcourt, Brace & World, 1965).

ARTICLES

"Changing Law of Competition in Public Service (Dissent)," *West Virginia Law Quarterly* 33 (1928): 183–88.
"Destruction of Evidence to Evade Search Warrant for Liquor as Contempt" [Burtch v. Zench, 202 NW 542], *West Virginia Law Quarterly* 34 (1928):188–92.
"Lake Cargo Rate Case of Feb. 1928," *West Virginia Law Quarterly* 34 (1928):272–82.
"Lake Cargo Rate Controversy" [Anchor Coal Co. v. United States, 25 F.2d 462], *West Virginia Law Quarterly* 34 (1928):365–66.
Book Review, Felix Frankfurter and James M. Landis, *The Business of the Supreme Court: A Study of a Judicial System*, *West Virginia Law Quarterly* 34 (1928):408–10.
Book Review, Boris Brasol, *Elements of Crime*, *West Virginia Law Quarterly* 34 (1928):410–13.
Book Review, Walter L. Summers, *A Treatise on the Law of Oil and Gas*, *West Virginia Law Quarterly* 34 (1928):413–15.

Book Review, Albert Kocourek, *Jural Relations,* West Virginia Law Quarterly 35 (1928):98–99.

"Bar and Law School Unite for Research in West Virginia," *American Bar Association Journal* 15 (1929):67–68.

Book Review, Samuel Deutsch and Simon Balicer, *How to Prove a Prima Facie Case,* West Virginia Law Quarterly 35 (1929):190–91.

Book Review, Max Isaac, *Facts about Bankruptcy,* West Virginia Law Quarterly 35 (1929):190.

Book Review, John T. Morse Jr., *Treatise on the Law of Banks and Banking,* West Virginia Law Quarterly 35 (1929):191.

Book Review, Reynolds Robertson, *Appellate Practice and Procedure in the Supreme Court of the United States,* West Virginia Law Quarterly 35 (1929):191–92.

Book Review, Elijah N. Zoline, *Federal Appellate Jurisdiction and Procedure,* 3d ed. West Virginia Law Quarterly 35 (1929):191–92.

"Judicial Councils," West Virginia Law Quarterly 35 (1929):193–238.

"Law Alumni Association" (Editorial), West Virginia Law Quarterly 35 (1929):276–77.

"Should the Jury System be Abolished?" West Virginia Law Quarterly 35 (1929):277–79.

"Success of Bar Association Amendments to the Constitution," West Virginia Law Quarterly 35 (1929):280–82.

Book Review, Laurence P. Simpson and Essel R. Dillavou, *Law for Engineers and Architects,* West Virginia Law Quarterly 35 (1929):298–99.

"Report to the Committee on Judicial Administration and Legal Reform of the West Virginia Bar Association," West Virginia Law Quarterly 36 (1929):1–102.

"The Relation of the West Virginia College of Law to the Bar," *West Virginia Bar Association* (1927):26–38.

"Inequitable Preference in Favor of Surety Companies" [Central Trust Co. v. Bank of Mullens (W.Va.) 150 SE 221], West Virginia Law Quarterly 36 (1930):278–88.

Book Review, William Harman Black, *How to Conduct a Criminal Case,* Yale Law Journal 39 (1930):1083–84.

"Criminal Attempts—The Rise and Fall of an Abstraction," *Yale Law Journal* 40 (1930):53–80.

"Collection of Judicial Statistics in West Virginia," West Virginia Law Quarterly 36 (1930):184–90.

"Review of the Work of the College of Law," West Virginia Law Quarterly, 36 (1930):319–29.

Book Review, Leon Green, *Judge & Jury,* Yale Law Journal 40 (1931):833–35.

"Restatement of the Law of Trusts," *Columbia Law Review* 31 (1931):800–823.

Book Review, Arthur L. Goodhart, *Essay in Jurisprudence and the Common Law*, *Yale Law Journal* 41 (1931):318–20.

Book Review, Charles Fairman, *Law of Martial Rule*, *Harvard Law Review* 45 (1931):400–402.

"Progress Report on Study of the Federal Courts—No. 7," *American Bar Association Journal* 17 (1931):799–802.

"Procedure" (Address), *Connecticut Bar Journal* 5 (1931):244–55.

Book Review, Judah Zelitch, *Soviet Administration of Criminal Law*, *Columbia Law Review* 32 (1932):923–25.

Book Review, Mabel A. Elliott, *Conflicting Penal Theories in Statutory Criminal Law*, *Illinois Law Review* 26 (1932):719–22.

Book Review, Clarence Darrow, *The Story of My Life*, *Yale Law Journal* 41 (1932):932–33.

"The Role of Substantive Law and Procedure in the Legal Process," *Harvard Law Review* 45 (1932):617–47.

"Law Enforcement—An Attempt at Social Dissection," *Yale Law Journal* 42 (1932):1–24.

"Code 'Cause of Action' Clarified by U.S. Supreme Court," *American Bar Association Journal* 19 (1933):215–18.

Book Review, W. P. Barrett, *The Trial of Jeanne d'Arc*, *Yale Law Journal* 42 (1933):459–62.

Book Review, Harold J. Laski, *Studies in Law and Politics*, *Columbia Law Review* 33 (1933):377–78.

"The New Deal Is Constitutional," *New Republic* (November 15, 1933).

"Trial by Combat and the New Deal," *Harvard Law Review* 47 (1934):913–47.

Book Review, A. L. Goodhart, *Precedent in English and Continental Law*, *Columbia Law Review* 35 (1935):311–13.

"Apologia for Jurisprudence," *Yale Law Journal* 44 (1935):729–53.

"Institute Priests and Yale Observers—A Reply to Dean Goodrich," *University of Pennsylvania Law Review* 84 (1936):811–24.

Book Review, George Gleason Bogert, *Trusts and Trustees*, 7 vols., *Columbia Law Review* 36 (1936):687–90.

Book Review, Roland Ford, *New York Law of Evidence*, 4 vols., *Yale Law Journal* 45 (1936):959.

"The Jurisprudence of Edward S. Robinson," *Yale Law Journal* 46 (1937):1282–89.

"A Reply," *American Bar Association Journal* 23 (1937):364–68, 393–94.

"The Folklore of Mr. Hook" (Reply to Review of *The Folklore of Capitalism* by S. Hook), *University of Chicago Law Review* 5 (1938):349–53.

"Enforcement of the Sherman Act" (Address), *Missouri Bar Journal* 9 (1938):220–26.

"Fair and Effective Use of Present Antitrust Procedure," *Yale Law Journal* 47 (1938):1294–1303.

"Prosecution Policy under the Sherman Act," *American Bar Association Journal* 24 (1938):417–20.

"An Inquiry into the Monopoly Issue," *New York Times* (August 21, 1938).

"Department of Justice: Statement," *Current History* 49 (1938):49–50.

"Must Be False in Order to Be Effective," *Saturday Evening Post* 211 (1938):22.

"Words Are Traps," *Catholic World* 146 (1938):610–11.

"What Is Monopoly?" *Vital Speeches*: (1938): 567.

"Antitrust Activities of the Department of Justice" (Address), *Oregon Law Review* 19 (1939):22–31.

"Consent Decrees and the Sherman Act," *World Convention Dates* (June 1939).

"What Can Government Offer—What Can Business Expect?" *Vital Speeches* 5 (1939):525–29.

"Feathers and Prices," *Common Sense* 8 (July 1939): 3.

"The Sherman Antitrust Act and Its Enforcement," *Law & Contemporary Problems* 7 (1940):5–23.

Address, *Georgia Bar Association* 1941:135–52.

"Anti-trust Laws and the Consumer" (Address), *Mississippi Law Journal* 12 (1940):579–88.

"Consumer Aid, Not 'Trust Busting,' Aim of Sherman Act," New York Times (July 7, 1940).

"Emergency Powers and the Anti-Trust Laws" (Address), *Missouri Bar Journal* 12 (1941):174–78.

"Free Trade within the Borders of the United States" (Address), *South Carolina Bar Association* 1940:94–102.

"Monopolies," *The Nation's Agriculture* (January 1941).

"Labor's Hidden Holdup Men," *Reader's Digest* (June 1941): 136.

"How Monopolies Have Hobbled Defense," *Reader's Digest* (July 1941).

"National Defense and Restraints of Trade," New Republic (May 19, 1941).

"Role of the Bar in War" (Address), *Illinois Bar Journal* 30 (1942):409–14, 435–36.

"Abuse of Patents," *Journal of Patent Office Society* 24 (1942):531–44.

"Confidence Must Replace Fear," *Vital Speeches* 8 (1942):557–61.

"This War Will Save Private Enterprise," *Saturday Evening Post* (1942).

"We Must Reform the Patent Law," *Atlantic Monthly* 170 (September 1942).

"The Abuse of Patents," *Atlantic Monthly* 170 (July 1942).

"How Cartels Affect You," *American Mercury* 56 (1943):321–30.

"Labor Against Itself," *Reader's Digest* (January 1944).

"Cartels Threaten Democracy," *Science Digest* (1944).

"Thoughts on Labor Day," New Republic (September 2, 1946).
"Reports and Addresses," *Forty-Seventh Nebraska Bar Association Annual Meeting*, 378 (1948):133–373.
"How Not to Get Investigated," *Harper's* 197 (1948):61–63.
"Effectiveness of Federal Antitrust Laws," *American Economic Review* 39 (1949):690.
"Bullying the Civil Service," *Atlantic Monthly* 188 (1951):45–46.
"Mob Justice and Television," *Atlantic Monthly* 187 (1951):68–70.
"The Sherman Act on Trial," *Atlantic Monthly* 192 (1953):38–42.
Conference on Freedom and the Law: 15th Anniversary Celebration, University of Chicago Law School, Conference Series No. 13 (1953).
"Economic Purpose of Antitrust Laws," *Mississippi Law Journal* 26 (1955):207–14.
"The American Ideal of a Fair Trial," *Arkansas Law Review* 9 (1955):211–17.
"Due Process in Trials," *Annals of the American Academy* 300 (1955):123–30.
"Judge Jerome Frank," *University of Chicago Law Review* 24 (1957):633–42.
"Walton Hale Hamilton," *Yale Law Journal* 68 (1959):399–400.
"Professor Hart's Theology," *Harvard Law Review* 73 (1960):1298–1317.
"The Law to Make Free Enterprise Free," *American Heritage* 11 (1960):52–55.
"A Discussion of 'The Ideologies of Taxation,'" *Tax Law Review* 18 (1962):1–22.
"The Emperor's Old Clothes: The Folklore of Capitalism Revisited," *Yale Review* 52 (1962):188–204.
"Wesley A. Sturges," *Yale Law Journal* 72 (1963):639–42.
"A Reply to 'Farewell to Grand Juries in Antitrust Litigation,'" *American Bar Association Journal* 50 (1964):925–27.
Book Review, *In Contempt of Justice, New Republic* 150 (1965):32–33.
"Fair Fights and Foul," *Antitrust Bulletin* 10 (1965):655–66.
"Growth of Awareness: Our Nation's Law and Law Among Nations," *International Lawyer* 1 (1967):534–47.
Book Review, Wilfrid E. Rumble Jr., *American Legal Realism: Skepticism, Reform, and the Judicial Process, Political Science Quarterly* 84 (1969):668–69.

Appendix C
Selected Bibliography of Works about Thurman Arnold and His Times

BOOKS

Abell, Tyler. *The Diaries of Drew Pearson, 1949–1959* (New York: Holt, Rinehart, & Winston, 1974).

Brinkley, Alan. *The End of Reform: New Deal Liberalism in Recession and War* (New York: Vintage, 1995).

Cornell, Julien. *The Trial of Ezra Pound* (New York: J. Day Company, 1992).

Diamond, Norman. *A Practice Almost Perfect: The Early Days at Arnold, Fortas & Porter* (Lanham, MD: University Press of America, 1997).

Goulden, Joseph C. *The Superlawyers* (New York: Weybright & Talley, 1971).

Gressley, Gene M. *Voltaire and the Cowboy: The Letters of Thurman Arnold* (Boulder: Colorado Associated University Press, 1977).

Hawley, Ellis W. *The New Deal and the Problem of Monopoly* (Princeton: Princeton University Press, 1966).

Hoge, Alice Albright. *Cissy Patterson* (New York: Random House, 1966).

Irons, Peter H. *The New Deal Lawyers* (Princeton: Princeton University Press, 1982).

Jackson, Robert H., and John Q. Barrett. *That Man: An Insider's Portrait of Franklin D. Roosevelt* (New York: Oxford University Press, 2003).

Kalman, Laura. *Legal Realism at Yale: 1927–1960* (Chapel Hill: University of North Carolina Press, 1986).

Kalman, Laura. *Abe Fortas: A Biography* (New Haven: Yale University Press, 1990).

Kearney, Edward N. *Thurman Arnold Social Critic: The Satirical Challenge to Orthodoxy* (Albuquerque: University of New Mexico Press, 1970).

Lattimore, Owen. *Ordeal by Slander* (Boston: Little, Brown and Co., 1950).

Leuchtenburg, William E. *Franklin D. Roosevelt and the New Deal* (New York: Harper and Row, 1963).

Lynch, David. *The Concentration of Economic Power* (New York: Columbia University Press, 1946).

Murphy, Bruce Allen. *Fortas: The Rise and Ruin of a Supreme Court Justice* (New York: William Morrow and Co., 1988).
Murphy, Bruce Allen. *Wild Bill: The Legend and Life of William O. Douglas* (New York: Random House, 2003).
Newman, Roger K. *Hugo Black: A Biography* (New York: Pantheon Books, 1994).
Schrecker, Ellen. *Many Are the Crimes: McCarthyism in America* (Boston: Little, Brown & Co., 1998).
Stocking, George W., and Myron W. Watkins. *Cartels in Action: Case Studies in International Business Diplomacy* (New York: New Twentieth Century, 1946).
Wells, Wyatt. *Antitrust and the Formation of the Postwar World* (New York: Columbia University Press, 2002).

ARTICLES

Alsop, Joseph, and Robert Kintner. "Trustbuster: The Folklore of Thurman Arnold," *Saturday Evening Post* (August 1939): 30.
Ayer, Douglas. "In Quest of Efficiency: The Ideological Journey of Thurman Arnold in the Interwar Period," *Stanford Law Review* 23 (1971):1049.
Brinkley, Alan. "The Antimonopoly Ideal and the Liberal State: The Case of Thurman Arnold," *Journal of American History* (1993):557.
Cassels, Louis. "Arnold, Fortas, Porter & Prosperity," *Harper's* 202 (1951):62.
Edwards, Corwin D. "Thurman Arnold and the Antitrust Laws," *Political Science Quarterly* 58 (September 1943):338.
Ernst, Daniel R. "Thurman Arnold," 21 *American Lawyer* (December 1999): 35.
Fenster, Mark. "The Symbols of Governance: Thurman Arnold and Post-Realist Legal Theory," *Buffalo Law Review* 51 (2003):1053.
Fortas, Abe. "Thurman Arnold and the Theater of the Law," *Yale Law Journal* 79 (1970):988.
Golden, Michael. "History of the University of Wyoming College of Law: The First Seventy-Five Years," *Land & Water Law Review* 31 (1996):1.
Gressley, Gene M. "Thurman Arnold, Antitrust, and the New Deal," *Business History* 38 (Summer 1984):217.
Hill, Warren P. "The Psychological Realism of Thurman Arnold," *University of Chicago Law Review* 22 (1955):377.
Hook, Sidney. "The Folklore of Capitalism: The Politician's Handbook—A Review," *University of Chicago Law Review* 5 (1938):341.
Johnson, Alva. "Thurman Arnold's Biggest Case," *New Yorker* 25 (January 24, 1942).
Lerner, Max. "The Shadow World of Thurman Arnold," *Yale Law Journal* 47 (1938):687.

Levi, Edward H. "The Natural Law, Precedent, and Thurman Arnold," *Virginia Law Review* 24 (1938):587.

Miller, Reed. "A Memorial to Thurman Wesley Arnold," *West Virginia Law Review* 72 (1970):203, 207.

Miscamble, Wilson D. "Thurman Arnold Goes to Washington: A Look at Antitrust Policy in the Later New Deal," *Business History* 56 (Spring 1982):5.

Rohr, Marc. "Communists and the First Amendment: The Shaping of Advocacy in the Cold War Era," *University of San Diego Law Review* 28 (1991):1.

Samuels, Warren J. "Legal Realism and the Burden of Symbolism: The Correspondence of Thurman Arnold," *Law and Society* 13 (1979):997.

Steuer, Richard M., and Peter A. Barile III. "Antitrust in Wartime," *Antitrust* 71 (Spring 2002).

Stone, I. F. "Thurman Arnold and the Railroads," *Nation* 331 (March 6, 1943).

Notes

NOTES TO CHAPTER 1

1. Mary Lou Pence, *The Laramie Story* (Wyoming: Prairie Publishing Co., 1968), 5; T. A. Larson, *History of Wyoming* (Lincoln: University of Nebraska Press, 1965), 2, 9; Lola M. Homsher, *The History of Albany County, Wyoming to 1880* (Wyoming: The Lusk Herald, 1965), 2–6 (private printing).

2. David H. Bain, *Empire Express: Building the First Transcontinental Railroad* (New York: Viking, 1999), 645–72; Larson, *History of Wyoming,* 56; Homsher, *Albany County,* 51.

3. Pence, *Laramie Story,* 5–6; Larson, *History of Wyoming,* 57.

4. Don Pitcher, *Wyoming Handbook* (California: Moon Publications, 1993), 5.

5. Larson, *History of Wyoming,* 117.

6. Ibid.; Pitcher, *Wyoming Handbook,* 95; Bain, *Empire Express,* 560–61; Homsher, *Albany County,* 52.

7. Pence, *Laramie Story,* 9–13; Homsher, *Albany County,* 53; Craig Sodaro and Randy Adams, *Frontier Spirit: The Story of Wyoming* (Boulder: Johnson Books, 1986), 87.

8. Perhaps the defining image was created in Owen Wister, *The Virginian: A Horseman of the Plains* (New York: Macmillan, 1902), which Arnold read as a boy.

9. Prior to the growth of the cattle industry, the Wyoming economy was almost entirely dependent on the Union Pacific and the largesse of the federal government. Lewis L. Gould, *Wyoming: A Political History, 1868–1896* (New Haven: Yale University Press, 1968), 11–18.

10. T. A. Larson, *Wyoming: A Bicentennial History* (New York: Norton, 1977), 112–13; Samuel Western, *Pushed off the Mountain, Sold down the River: Wyoming's Search for Its Soul* (Wyoming: Homestead Publishing, 2002), 29; Larson, *History of Wyoming,* 163–94.

11. Larson, *Bicentennial,* 87–88; Larson, *History of Wyoming,* 161; Pence, *Laramie Story,* 18, 24–25.

12. Larson, *History of Wyoming,* 127.

13. Gould, *Political History,* 36, 92. As part of the logrolling process to se-

cure support, Evanston in the southwestern corner of the state received the funds for an insane asylum and Rawlins for a new penitentiary. Larson, *History of Wyoming,* 145–46.

14. Gene M. Gressley, "The American Cattle Trust—A Study in Protest," *Pacific Historical Review* 30 (February 1961):61; Larson, *History of Wyoming,* 192–93.

15. Gould, *Political History,* 117–18.

16. Sodaro and Adams, *Frontier Spirit,* 95–97. It was only following the 1896 election that Wyoming became a solidly Republican stronghold under the leadership of Francis E. Warren. Gould, *Political History,* 228; Larson, *Bicentennial,* 77–78, 81, 84–85; Sodaro and Adams, *Frontier Spirit,* 97–100. Wyoming was not entirely alone on the suffrage issue. A similar effort in the Dakota territory failed by one vote in January 1869 and passed in the Utah territory in February 1870. Larson, *History of Wyoming,* 80.

17. This same legislature also passed, over the veto of the governor, legislation licensing gambling and uncharacteristically, given Wyoming's relative openness, also passed a statute forbidding miscegenation. Gould, *Political History,* 26.

18. Much of the Arnold family lore about Franklin Luther Arnold comes from correspondence to his grandchildren, Thurman and Carl, which was collected and arranged by their mother and privately printed in 1908 with copies still in the possession of several surviving members of the Arnold family. Mrs. C. P. Arnold, ed., *Some Letters from a Loving Grandpa to Two of His Boys Telling Stories of His Life* (Laramie: The Laramie Republican Company, 1908).

19. Thurman Arnold, *Fair Fights and Foul* (New York: Harcourt, Brace & World, 1965), 3–4. In his autobiography, Arnold refers to his grandfather as Carl Franklin and his grandmother as Elizabeth.

20. Arnold, *Fair Fights,* 4.

21. The eldest son Gottfried became a judge of the Maritime Court in Hamburg and Karl became a professor of theology at the University of Breslau. Thurman Arnold visited his German relatives during a college trip in 1910. Letter from Margaret A. Wilson to Gene Gressley, July 29, 1974, American Heritage Center.

22. Douglas Ayer, "In Quest of Efficiency: The Ideological Journey of Thurman Arnold in the Interwar Period," *Stanford Law Review* 23 (1971):1049, 1052.

23. Interview with Amy King, December 17, 2002.

24. Larson, *History of Wyoming,* 315.

25. Alfred J. Mokler, quoted in Pitcher, *Wyoming Handbook,* 34.

26. Larson, *History of Wyoming,* 100. These controversies had existed since the very organization of Wyoming as a territory. As early as 1872, President

Grant had been ready to dissolve Wyoming as a territory and distribute its lands to the surrounding states. Western, *Pushed off the Mountain,* 20–21.

27. Arnold, *Fair Fights,* 5.
28. American Heritage Center, Box 42, Folder, Correspondence: 1964.
29. Arnold, *Fair Fights,* 9–15.
30. Arnold, *Fair Fights,* 10.
31. Pence, *Laramie Story,* 28.
32. Arnold, *Fair Fights,* 3.
33. Gene M. Gressley, *Voltaire and the Cowboy: The Letters of Thurman Arnold* (Boulder: Colorado Associated University Press, 1977), 14.
34. In 1966, he corresponded warmly with the president of Wabash College and eventually made a visit and spoke there.
35. The changes that made Princeton a center of true intellectual thought, particularly in the sciences and mathematics, are discussed in Sylvia Nasar, *A Beautiful Mind* (New York: Simon & Schuster, 1998), 49–103.
36. F. Scott Fitzgerald, *This Side of Paradise* (New York: Charles Scribner's Sons, 1920), 36.
37. Arnold, *Fair Fights,* 16; Interview with Barbara Hauer Oliver, September 16, 2002; Interview with Abe Krash, Washington, D.C., April 24, 2002.
38. Arnold, *Fair Fights,* 17–18.
39. T. W. Arnold to Mrs. C. P. Arnold, September 3, 1910.
40. Arnold, *Fair Fights,* 20.
41. See Joel Seligman, *The High Citadel: The Influence of Harvard Law School* (Boston: Houghton Mifflin, 1978), 20–67; Stephen A. Siegel, "John Chipman Gray and the Moral Basis of Classical Legal Thought," *Iowa Law Review* 86 (2001):1513.
42. Compare Roscoe Pound, "The Need for a Sociological Jurisprudence," *The Green Bag* 19 (1907):612, and Roscoe Pound, "Mechanical Jurisprudence," *Columbia Law Review* 8 (1908):605, with Roscoe Pound, "The Call for a Realist Jurisprudence," *Harvard Law Review* 44 (1931):697.
43. Joseph Beale, *A Treatise on the Conflict of Laws* (New York: Baker, Voorhis & Co., 1935).
44. Arnold, *Fair Fights,* 21–22.
45. Interview with Abe Krash, Washington, D.C., April 24, 2002; Interview with Barbara Hauer Oliver, September 16, 2002.
46. Letter to Mrs. C. P. Arnold, December 19, year undated, Box 1, C. P. Arnold collection, American Heritage Center.
47. Letter to C. P. Arnold, Cambridge, MA, October 6, 1912, AHC, Box 7, Folder: Correspondence 1910–1927.
48. Letter to Mr. and Mrs. C. P. Arnold, Cambridge, MA, November 16, 1913, AHC, Box 7, Folder: Correspondence 1910–1927.

49. Letter to Mrs. C. P. Arnold, Cambridge, MA, June 8, 1912, AHC, Box 7, Folder: Correspondence 1910–1927.
50. Letter to Mrs. C. P. Arnold, undated, AHC, Box 1, C. P. Arnold Collection.
51. Ibid.
52. Letter to C. P. Arnold, June 15, 1911, Box 2, C. P. Arnold Collection.
53. Letter to Mrs. C. P. Arnold, Cambridge, MA, November 23, 1913, AHC, C. P. Arnold Collection, Box 3, File: Correspondence: 1913 May–December.
54. Letter to C. P. Arnold, January 27, 1913, Box 3, C. P. Arnold Collection.
55. T. W. Arnold to C. P. Arnold, Cambridge, MA, February 15, 1914, reprinted in Gressley, *Voltaire*, 118.
56. T. W. Arnold to C. P. Arnold, February 24, 1913, Box 3, C. P. Arnold Collection. Italics mine.

NOTES TO CHAPTER 2

1. Letter to Mrs. C. P. Arnold, June 19, 1914, reprinted in Gressley, *Voltaire*, 120.
2. Ibid.
3. Letter to Mr. and Mrs. C. P. Arnold, Chicago, IL, September 2, 1914, reprinted in Gressley, *Voltaire*, 121.
4. Herman Kogan, *The First Century: The Chicago Bar Association, 1874–1974* (Chicago: Rand McNally, 1974), 101, 125.
5. Gressley, *Voltaire*, 10.
6. Letter to Mrs. C. P. Arnold, Springfield, IL, October 6, 1914, reprinted in Gressley, *Voltaire*, 122.
7. Letters to C. P. Arnold, Chicago, IL, May 5, 1915; Mrs. C. P. Arnold, October 11, 1915; C. P. Arnold, Chicago, IL, November 2, 1915, AHC, C. P. Arnold Collection, Box 4, File, Correspondence: 1915.
8. Letter to Mrs. C. P. Arnold, Chicago, IL, January 13, 1916, AHC, C. P. Arnold Collection, Box 4, File, Correspondence: 1916.
9. Letters to C. P. Arnold, Chicago, IL, November 19, 1914; to C. P. Arnold, January 7, 1915, AHC, Box 4, C. P. Arnold Collection, File, Correspondence: 1914, 1915.
10. Letter to C. P. Arnold, November 2, 1915, AHC, C. P. Arnold Collection, Box 4, File, Correspondence: 1915.
11. C. P. Arnold to T. W. Arnold, May 3, 1916, Box 4, C. P. Arnold Collection, File, Correspondence: 1916.
12. Letter to C. P. Arnold, March 4, 1916, AHC, C. P. Arnold Collection, Box 4, File, Correspondence: 1916.
13. Letter to C. P. Arnold, June 17, 1916, AHC, C. P. Arnold Collection, Box 4, File, Correspondence: 1916.

14. Letters to Mrs. C. P. Arnold, April 8, 1916; to C. P. Arnold, June 7, 1916; to C. P. Arnold, June 17, 1916, AHC, C. P. Arnold Collection, Box 4, File, Correspondence: 1916.

15. Letter to C. P. Arnold, June 7, 1916, AHC, C. P. Arnold Collection, Box 4, File, Correspondence: 1916.

16. Letter to C. P. Arnold, June 17, 1916, AHC, C. P. Arnold Collection, Box 4, File, Correspondence: 1916.

17. Letters to Mrs. C. P. Arnold, June 19, 1916; July 12, 1916; February 7, 1916, AHC, C. P. Arnold Collection, Box 4, File, Correspondence: 1916.

18. Letter to C. P. Arnold, Chicago, IL, November 2, 1915, AHC, C. P. Arnold Collection, Box 4, File, Correspondence: 1915.

19. Arnold, *Fair Fights*, 24.

20. New York Times Oral History Program, Columbia University Oral History Collection, Part IV, No. 7, Thurman W. Arnold, Paul Greenberg Interview, June 1962, Franklin D. Roosevelt Library, Fiche 1 at 1.

21. Letter to C. P. Arnold, June 14, 1916, AHC, C. P. Arnold Collection, Box 4, File, Correspondence: 1916.

22. Letter to Mrs. C. P. Arnold, June 19, 1916, AHC, C. P. Arnold Collection, Box 4, File, Correspondence: 1916.

23. Arnold, *Fair Fights*, 25–26.

24. Gressley, *Voltaire*, 12.

25. Letter to C. P. Arnold, December 24, 1916.

26. Letters to Mrs. C. P. Arnold, Feb. 7, 1917; to C. P. Arnold, March 26, 1917, AHC, C. P. Arnold Collection, Box 5, File, Correspondence: 1917.

27. Interview with Barbara Hauer Oliver, September 16, 2002.

28. Ibid.

29. T. W. Arnold to Mrs. C. P. Arnold, June 9, 1917, Box 5, C. P. Arnold Collection.

30. Raymond Waite to C. P. Arnold, C. P. Arnold Collection, Box 1.

31. Arnold, *Fair Fights*, 27–28.

32. Preston Slosson to C. P. Arnold, September 3, 1917, Box 5, C. P. Arnold Collection.

33. Gressley, *Voltaire*, 13. Frances's niece, Barbara Hauer Oliver confirms this anecdote but adds that Mother Longan was already unwell by this point in time. Interview with Barbara Hauer Oliver, September 16, 2002.

34. Mrs. Preston Slosson to Mrs. C. P. Arnold, September 4, 1917, Box 5, C. P. Arnold Collection.

35. Letters to Frances Arnold, October 5, 1917; C. P. Arnold, October 4, 1917; to Frances Arnold, October 5, 1917, AHC, Box 5, C. P. Arnold Collection.

36. Letter to C. P. Arnold, October 4, 1917, AHC, Box 5, C. P. Arnold Collection.

37. T. W. Arnold to Mrs. C. P. Arnold, December 10, 1917, Box 4, C. P. Arnold Collection.

38. Letters to Mrs. C. P. Arnold, December 10, 1917; to Mrs. C. P. Arnold, December 16, 1917, Box 4, C. P. Arnold Collection.

39. Letters to Mrs. C. P. Arnold, December 10, 1917; to Mrs. C. P. Arnold, January 10, 1918; to Mr. and Mrs. C. P. Arnold, March 4, 1918; to C. P. Arnold, March 14, 1918, Box 4, C. P. Arnold Collection.

40. Letter to Frances Arnold, February 11, 1918, Box 4, C. P. Arnold Collection.

41. Letter to Mr. and Mrs. C. P. Arnold, March 4, 1918, Box 4, C. P. Arnold Collection.

42. Ibid.

43. Interview with G. Duane Vieth, April 24, 2002.

44. Larson, *History of Wyoming*, 398.

NOTES TO CHAPTER 3

1. Gressley, *Voltaire*, 14.

2. Larson, *History of Wyoming*, 452.

3. Undated letter, Frances Arnold to Robert Woodruff, Special Collections and Archives, Robert Woodruff Library, Emory University, Box 12.

4. Gressley, *Voltaire*, 14–16.

5. Western, *Pushed off the Mountain*, 46–52; Larson, *History of Wyoming*, 452.

6. Arnold, *Fair Fights*, 32–33.

7. Ayer, "Quest," 1053.

8. Ayer, "Quest," 1053; Larson, *History of Wyoming*, 453.

9. Gressley, *Voltaire*, 20.

10. Ayer, "Quest," 1055–57.

11. Arnold, *Fair Fights*, 32.

12. Joseph Alsop and Robert Kintner, "Trustbuster—The Folklore of Thurman Arnold," *Saturday Evening Post* 4 (August 1939):30.

13. Gressley, *Voltaire*, 22.

14. Western, *Pushed off the Mountain*, 49.

15. Arnold, *Fair Fights*, 33.

16. From *The Buffalo Creek Disaster* by Gerald M. Stearn, copyright 1976 by Gerald M. Stern. Used by permission of Random House, Inc. pp. 135–36.

17. See *State v. Snyder*, 29 Wyo. 163, 212 P. 758 (1923); *State v. Hoskins*, 29 Wyo. 198, 212 P. 766 (1923).

18. *State v. Carter*, 31 Wyo. 401, 226 P. 690 (1924).

19. Ibid. at 409–12; 226 P. at 692–94.

20. See generally Michael Golden, "History of the University of Wyoming

College of Law: The First Seventy-five Years," *Land & Water Recreation* 31 (1996):1.

21. Letter to Russell Wilbur, December 21, 1938, reprinted in Gressley, *Voltaire*, 282.

22. Alsop and Kintner, "Trustbuster," 30.

23. Commencement Address, June 7, 1943, University of Wyoming, AHC, Box 4, Thurman Arnold Collection.

NOTES TO CHAPTER 4

1. Arnold, *Fair Fights*, 35.

2. West Virginia University Catalogue and Announcements, 1927–1932; Summer Sessions 1930.

3. January 8, 1930, AHC, Box 8, Folder 1.

4. Letter to John R. Turner, April 29, 1930, AHC, Box 8, File 1.

5. See Thurman W. Arnold, "The Collection of Judicial Statistics in West Virginia," *West Virginia Law Quarterly and the Bar* 36 (1930):184; Thurman W. Arnold, "Review of the Work of the College of Law," *West Virginia Law Quarterly and the Bar* 36 (June 1930):319; Thurman W. Arnold, "Judicial Councils," *West Virginia Law Quarterly and the Bar* 35 (April 1929):193; Thurman W. Arnold, "Bar and Law School United for Research," *American Bar Association Journal* 15 (1929):67; Thurman W. Arnold, "The Relation of the West Virginia College of Law to the Bar," *Representative to the West Virginia Bar Association* (1927):26.

6. See "Report to the Committee on Judicial Administration and Legal Reform of the West Virginia Bar Association," *West Virginia Law Quarterly and the Bar* 36 (1929):1.

7. See T. W. Arnold, "An Inequitable Preference in Favor of Surety Companies," *West Virginia Law Quarterly and the Bar* 36 (April 1930):278; T. W. Arnold, Review of *Law of Engineers and Architects,* by Lawrence P. Simpson and Essel R. Dillavou, *West Virginia Law Quarterly and the Bar* 35 (April 1929):298; T. W. Arnold, Review of *Appellate Practice and Procedure in the Supreme Court of the United States, West Virginia Law Quarterly and the Bar* 35 (Feb. 1929):191; T. W. Arnold, Review of *Treatise on the Law of Banks and Banking,* by John T. Morse Jr. *West Virginia Law Quarterly and the Bar* 35 (Feb. 1929):191; T. W. Arnold, Review of *Facts about Bankruptcy,* by Max Isaac, *West Virginia Law Quarterly and the Bar* 35 (Feb. 1929):190; T. W. Arnold, Review of *How to Prove a Prima Facie Case,* by Samuel Deutsch and Simon Balicer, *West Virginia Law Quarterly and the Bar* 35 (Feb. 1929):190; T. W. Arnold, Review of *Jural Relations,* by Albert Kocourek," *West Virginia Law Quarterly and the Bar* 35 (Dec. 1928):98; T. W. Arnold, Review of *A Treatise on the Law of Oil and Gas,* by Walter L. Summers, *West Virginia Law*

Quarterly and the Bar 34 (June 1928):413; T. W. Arnold, Review of *The Elements of Crime,* by Boris Brasol, *West Virginia Law Quarterly and the Bar* 34 (June 1928):410; T. W. Arnold, Review of *The Business of the Supreme Court,* by Felix Frankfurter and James Landis, *West Virginia Law Quarterly and the Bar* 34 (June 1928):408; T. W. Arnold, "The Lake Cargo Rate Controversy," *West Virginia Law Quarterly and the Bar* 34 (June 1928):365; T. W. Arnold, "The Lake Cargo Rate Case of February 1928," *West Virginia Law Quarterly and the Bar* 34 (April 1928):272; T. W. Arnold, Review of *Destruction of Evidence to Evade Search Warrant for Liquor as Contempt, West Virginia Law Quarterly and the Bar* 34 (Feb. 1928):188; T. W. Arnold, "The Changing Law of Competition in Public Services—A Dissent," *West Virginia Law Quarterly and the Bar* 34 (Feb. 1928):183; T. W. Arnold, "Contempt-Evasion of Criminal Process as Contempt of Court," *West Virginia Law Quarterly and the Bar* 34 (Feb. 1928):188.

8. See Thurman W. Arnold, "Judicial Councils," *West Virginia Law Quarterly and the Bar* 35 (1929):193; Thurman W. Arnold, "Bar and Law School United for Research," *American Bar Association Journal* 15 (1929):67.

9. Letter to Charles E. Clark, October 12, 1929; Arnold, "Judicial Councils," 209–10.

10. Letter to John R. Turner, Morgantown, WV, May 29, 1928.

11. Letter to Fred Nussbaum, Morgantown, WV, February 2, 1929, reprinted in Gressley, *Voltaire,* 167.

12. See Reed Miller, "A Memorial to Thurman Wesley Arnold," *West Virginia Law Review* 72 (1970):203, 207.

13. Laura Kalman, *Legal Realism at Yale* (Chapel Hill: University of North Carolina Press, 1986), 67–68, 117.

14. Letter to Charles E. Clark, Morgantown, WV, October 12, 1929, reprinted in Gressley, *Voltaire,* 169. Clark's study eventually included the law faculties of California, Columbia, Harvard, Michigan, Yale, Ohio State, Tulane, Chicago, Colorado, Kansas, and North Carolina. John Henry Schlegel, *American Legal Realism and Empirical Social Science* (Chapel Hill: University of North Carolina Press, 1995), 87 and n. 59 (1995).

15. Yale University, The School of Law, Reports of the Dean and of the Librarian, July 1, 1928–June 30, 1929 at 13.

16. Letter to Charles E. Clark, March 23, 1930, AHC, Box 8, File 2.

17. Letters to Charles E. Clark, March 18, 1930, AHC, Box 8, File 2; to Mother and Father, March 26, 1930, AHC, Box 30, file 1.

18. Letters to John R. Turner, May 5, 1930; to John R. Turner May 15, 1930, AHC, Box 8, File 2.

19. Letter to John R. Turner, New Haven, CT, December 23, 1930, reprinted in Gressley, *Voltaire,* 175–76; John R. Turner to Arnold, January 14, 1931, AHC, Box 8, File 4.

20. Arnold to Fred Nussbaum, Morgantown, WV, February 2, 1929, reprinted in Gressley, *Voltaire,* 167.

21. Gressley, *Voltaire,* 28.

NOTES TO CHAPTER 5

1. Letter to Roscoe Pound, January 23, 1931, reprinted in Gressley, *Voltaire,* 176; Letter to Wilson Clough, March 17, 1931, reprinted in Gressley, *Voltaire,* 178; Letter to Glenn Frank, April 18, 1931, reprinted in Gressley, *Voltaire,* 182.

2. See generally Kalman, *Legal Realism.*

3. William Twining, *Karl Llewellyn and the Realist Movement* (London: Weidenfeld and Nicolson, 1973); Robert L. Hale, "Coercion and Distribution in a Supposedly Non-Coercive State," *Political Science Quarterly* 38 (1923):470; Morris R. Cohen, "Property and Sovereignty," *Cornell Law Quarterly* 13 (1927):8; Leon A. Green, *The Litigation Process in Tort Law* (Indianapolis: Bobbs-Merrill, 1965). For Arnold's own thoughts on Green, see Thurman Arnold, "Leon Green: An Appreciation," *Illinois Law Review* 43 (1948):1.

4. See Seligman, *High Citadel,* 32–46.

5. See, e.g., Leon Green, *Cases on Injuries to Relations* (Rochester, NY: The Lawyers Co-operative Publishing Company, 1940) (not even including *Palsgraf*); Leon Green et al., *Cases on the Law of Torts* (Saint Paul: West Publishing Company, 1968), 618.

6. See Schlegel, *American Legal Realism.*

7. The classic example of the rule and fact skeptic realist is Jerome Frank, whose *Law and the Modern Mind* and *Courts on Trial* best embody this approach.

8. Letter to Frank P. Kenan, November 7, 1931, reprinted in Gressley, *Voltaire,* 191; Kalman, *Legal Realism,* 34–35.

9. Arnold, *Fair Fights,* 63.

10. William O. Douglas, *Go East Young Man: The Early Years* (New York: Random House, 1974), 172.

11. John Henry Schlegel, "American Legal Realism and Empirical Social Science: From the Yale Experience," *Buffalo Law Review* 28 (1979):512, n. 264; Schlegel, *American Legal Realism,* 200, n. 516.

12. For more on Arnold's break with the realists, see Mark Fenster, "The Symbols of Governance: Thurman Arnold and Post-Realist Legal Theory," *Buffalo Law Review* 51 (2003):1053.

13. Interview with Victor Kramer, July 2, 2002; Remarks of Hon. Gerhard A. Gessell, in Thurman Arnold Remembered: A Centennial Celebration, 11, 12 (October 30, 1991); Kalman interview with Norman Diamond, undated.

14. Kalman interview with Norman Diamond, 19–20; Interview with Victor Kramer, July 2, 2002; Interview with Robert Nitzche, January 20, 2004.

15. *Washington Herald,* March 18, 1938; Bruce Allen Murphy, *Fortas: The Rise and Ruin of a Supreme Court Justice (*New York: William Morrow and Co., 1988), 10.

16. Alsop and Kintner, "Trustbuster," 4, 33.

17. Kalman interview with Norman Diamond, 17.

18. Thurman W. Arnold, "Institute Priests and Yale Observers—A Reply to Dean Goodrich," *University of Pennsylvania Law Review* 84 (1936):811; Thurman W. Arnold, "Apologia for Jurisprudence," *Yale Law Journal* 44 (1935):729; Thurman W. Arnold, "Law Enforcement—An Attempt at Social Dissection," *Yale Law Journal* 42 (1932):1; Thurman W. Arnold, "The Restatement of the Law of Trusts," *Columbia Law Review* 32 (1932):840; Thurman W. Arnold, "Criminal Attempts—The Rise and Fall of an Abstraction," *Yale Law Journal* 40 (1930):53.

19. Thurman W. Arnold, "Trial by Combat and the New Deal," *Harvard Law Review* 47 (1934):926 n. 21.

20. See Thurman W. Arnold, "Apologia for Jurisprudence," 931, 935; Thurman W. Arnold, "Trial by Combat," 913, 919–20, 923–26; Thurman W. Arnold, "Law Enforcement—An Attempt at Social Dissection," 1, 5–6; Thurman W. Arnold, "The Code 'Cause of Action' Clarified by United States Supreme Court," *American Bar Association Journal* 19 (1933): 215; Thurman Arnold, "Criminal Attempts—The Rise and Fall of an Abstraction," 57–58, 79–80; Thurman W. Arnold, "Restatement of the Law of Trusts," 800. See generally Kalman, *Legal Realism,* 4–5, 22–23.

21. See, e.g., Thurman W. Arnold, Book Review of *Precedent in English and Continental Law,* by Arthur L. Goodhart, *Columbia Law Review* 35 (1935):311, 312–13; Arnold, "Apologia," passim; Arnold, "Law Enforcement," 13; Arnold, "Criminal Attempts," 79.

22. Arnold borrowed heavily from his earlier work, particularly "Trial by Combat," 926; Thurman W. Arnold, "The Role of Substantive Law and Procedure in the Legal Process," *Harvard Law Review* 45 (1932): 617; Arnold, "Law Enforcement," 1.

23. Edward S. Robinson, *Law and Lawyers* (New York: Macmillan, 1935). Robinson passed away shortly thereafter. See Thurman W. Arnold, "The Jurisprudence of Edward S. Robinson," *Yale Law Journal* 46 (1937):1282.

24. Thurman Arnold, *Symbols of Government* (New York: Harcourt, Brace & World, 1962), xiv.

25. Ibid., 2 (emphasis added).

26. Ibid., 10.

27. Ibid., 17, 29.

28. Ibid., 6, 42–44, 53. Arnold had already made this point in "Apologia," 733.

29. Arnold, "Institute Priests and Yale Observers," 811, 819.

30. Arnold, *Symbols,* 60–64, 68.
31. Ibid., 72, 80–81, 93.
32. Ibid., 94.
33. Ibid., 111–12.
34. Ibid., 114–15, 118, 120–24.
35. Arnold, "Criminal Attempts," 53.
36. Arnold, *Symbols,* 130.
37. Ibid., 129, 130, 134.
38. Ibid., 142–43.
39. Ibid., 144–45.
40. Ibid., 150–51.
41. Ibid., 150–64.
42. Ibid., 172–73. See *Schechter Poultry Corp. v. United States,* 295 U.S. 495 (1935); *Panama Refining Co. v. Ryan,* 293 U.S. 495 (1935).
43. Arnold, *Symbols,* 174–77.
44. Ibid., 197–98.
45. Murphy, *Fortas,* 36–39; Peter H. Irons, *The New Deal Lawyers* (Princeton: Princeton University Press, 1982), 137–39.
46. Arnold, *Symbols,* 201–09
47. Ibid., 217–18, 226.
48. Ibid., 232, 235–40, 263.
49. Ibid., 270–71.
50. K. N. Llewellyn, "Book Review," *Brooklyn Law Review* 5 (1936):219, 221. Llewellyn also observed correctly that the book was loosely written and "only about 45 percent thought-through" but that it would "take ten years more" to think through another 45 percent.
51. Harold J. Laski, "Book Reviews," *Yale Law Journal* 45 (1936):951, 953. Arnold had favorably reviewed Laski's own book *Studies in Law and Politics* in *Columbia Law Review* 33 (1933):377.
52. Morris R. Cohen, "Book Reviews," *University of Illinois Law Review* 31 (1936):411.
53. Max Radin, "Book Review," *Harvard Law Review* 49 (1936):1397, 1401; C. B. Spaeth, "Book Reviews," *Yale Law Journal* 45 (1936):737, 738; Frederick E. Hines, "Book Reviews," *Southern California Law Review* 9 (1936):288, 291; Cohen, "Book Reviews," 415.
54. T. Munford Boyd, "Book Reviews," *Virginia Law Review* 22 (1936):969; Justin H. Folkerth, "Book Review," *Ohio State Law Journal* 3 (1936):119.
55. Radin, "Book Review," 1399.
56. Cohen, "Book Reviews," 412–13. Later commentators have described Arnold's social science as amateurish or simplistic. Fenster, "Symbols of Governance," 1109.

57. Felix S. Cohen, "Book Reviews," *New York University Law Quarterly Review* 13 (1936):636–37.

58. Julius Stone, "Book Reviews," *Georgetown Law Journal* 25 (1936):224.

59. Harold S. Bowman, "Book Review," *Boston University Law Review* 16 (1936):798, 800.

60. William Anderson, "Book Review," *Minnesota Law Review* 20 (1936):328, 329. See also Stone, "Book Reviews" at 226 (linking Arnold as detached observer to the failure of Italian and German experiences).

61. Peter H. Odegard, "Book Review," *Cornell Law Quarterly* 21 (1936):686.

62. See Jon Blackwell, *1941: Off to War, Prisoner of War*, available at http://www.capitalcity.com/1941.html.

63. Interview with Nicholas Deb. Katzenbach, September 9, 2002.

64. Thurman W. Arnold and Fleming James Jr., *Cases and Materials on Trials, Judgments and Appeals* (Saint Paul: West Publishing Company, 1936).

65. Arnold and James, *Cases*, vi.

66. Philip Werner Amram, "Book Reviews," *Temple Law Quarterly* 11 (1937):458, 459.

67. Kalman, *Legal Realism*, 81.

68. Ibid., 137–39.

69. Letter from W. N. Stokes Jr., to Jess McNeel, October 15, 1965, contained in T. W. Arnold Collection, AHC, Box 43. See also Douglas, *Go East*, 171.

70. Arnold, *Fair Fights*, 134; Irons, *New Deal*, 137–39; *New York Times*, March 19, 1933, Sec. 2 at p.1.

71. Arnold, *Fair Fights*, 134–135; *Helvering v. Tex-Penn Oil Co.*, 300 U.S. 481 (1937); *Elmhurst Cemetery Co. of Joliet v. Commissioner of Internal Revenue*, 300 U.S. 37 (1937); *DuPont v. United States*, 300 U.S. 150 (1937); *Helvering v. Illinois Life Insurance Co.*, 299 U.S. 88 (1936).

72. Letter to Frank Murphy, September 3, 1935, AHC, Box 9; Letter to Mr. and Mrs. C. P. Arnold, September 19, 1937.

73. Douglas, *Go East*, 168.

74. Bruce Allen Murphy, *Wild Bill: The Legend and Life of William O. Douglas* (New York: Random House, 2003), 91–92; Douglas, *Go East*, 168–69; James F. Simon, *Independent Journey, The Life of William O. Douglas* (New York: Harper & Row, 1980), 116–19.

75. Thurman W. Arnold, *The Folklore of Capitalism* (New Haven: Yale University Press, 1937).

76. Ibid., 10–11, 16.

77. Ibid., 10, 22–23.

78. Ibid., 35, 107, 110.

79. Ibid., 35–37, 43, 63.

80. Ibid., 38.
81. Ibid., 46–47.
82. Ibid., 48–55, 61.
83. Ibid., 121–22.
84. Ibid., 122.
85. Ibid., 127.
86. Charles Reich, "The New Property," *Yale Law Journal* 73 (1964): 733.
87. Letter to Jack T. Graham, December 5, 1938; reprinted in Gressley, *Voltaire,* 281.
88. Arnold, *Folklore,* 136–39, 188–89, 190–91.
89. Ibid., 207.
90. Ibid., 207–09.
91. Ibid., 211.
92. Ibid., 211, 212, 214, 217. See chapter 6 in *Folklore* for the confrontation between Borah and Arnold during Arnold's confirmation hearing as head of the Antitrust Division.
93. Ibid., 221–28.
94. Ibid., 231.
95. Ibid., 263, 267–68, 304.
96. Ibid., 300–310.
97. Ibid., 311, 313–16, 321.
98. Ibid., 321.
99. Ibid., 329.
100. Ibid., 393.
101. *New York Herald Tribune Books,* January 23, 1938 at p. 19.
102. *New Yorker,* January 15, 1938 at p. 69; *Nation,* January 1, 1938 at p. 735; *New Republic,* December 8, 1937 at p. 141.
103. Philip Mechem, "Review," *Iowa Law Review* 23 (1938): 443–44.
104. J. Leo Sullivan, "The Speculations of Thurman Arnold," *Polamerican Law Journal* 1 (1938):3; Harold J. Laski, "Book Reviews," *Brooklyn Law Review* 7 (1938):535.
105. Sidney Hook, "The Folklore of Capitalism, The Politician's Handbook —A Review," *University of Chicago Law Review* 5 (1938):341, 346, 348.
106. Thurman Arnold, "The Folklore of Mr. Hook—A Reply," *University of Chicago Law Review* 5 (1938):349–51. Hook remained unconvinced. Sidney Hook, "Neither Myth nor Power—A Rejoinder," *University of Chicago Law Review* 5 (1938):354.
107. Max Lerner, "The Shadow World of Thurman Arnold," *Yale Law Journal* 47 (1938):687, 691, 694, 702–03.
108. Letter to Jack T. Graham, December 5, 1938, reprinted in Gressley, *Voltaire,* 281.

109. Letters to Porter Sargent, August 6, 1937, reprinted in Gressley, *Voltaire,* 263; to Mr. and Mrs. C. P. Arnold, July 1, 1937, reprinted in Gressley, *Voltaire,* 255.

110. Arnold, "Folklore of Mr. Hook," 349, 350.

111. Compare Jerome Frank, *Save America First: How to Make Our Democracy Work* (New York: Harper & Bros., 1938), which came out slightly afterward and discussed many of the same themes.

112. Edward N. Kearney, *Thurman Arnold Social Critic: The Satirical Challenge to Orthodoxy* (Albuquerque: University of New Mexico Press, 1970); Fenster, "The Symbols of Governance," 1053.

113. "I never read Veblen until after *Folklore* was published. The sole influence on *Folklore* was my experience in Government investigations," Letter to Rick Tillman, April 3, 1968; AHC, Box 44.

114. Ayer, "Quest," 1049. This is highly implausible. See chapter 6 in this book.

115. Stanley Fish, "Dennis Martinez and the Uses of Theory," *Yale Law Journal* 96 (1987):1773.

116. Letter to Mr. and Mrs. C. P. Arnold, July 1, 1937, reprinted in Gressley, *Voltaire,* 255, 259–60.

NOTES TO CHAPTER 6

1. Alan Brinkley, *The End of Reform: New Deal Liberalism in Recession and War* (New York: Vintage, 1995), 111; Wilson D. Miscamble, "Thurman Arnold Goes to Washington: A Look at Antitrust Policy in the Later New Deal," *Business History* 56 (Spring 1982):6–7.

2. Letter to Mr. and Mrs. C. P. Arnold, July 1, 1937, reprinted in Gressley, *Voltaire,* 255, 257.

3. Franklin D. Roosevelt, *Looking Forward* (New York: Da Capo Press, 1933), 26.

4. See Bernard Sternsher, *Rexford Tugwell and the New Deal* (New Brunswick, NJ: Rutgers University Press, 1964), 342–43.

5. See, e.g., Ellis W. Hawley, *The New Deal and the Problem of Monopoly* (Princeton: Princeton University Press, 1966), 123–24; Rexford G. Tugwell, *The Democratic Roosevelt* (Garden City, NY: Doubleday, 1957), 563; Raymond Moley, "Roosevelt's Refusal to Make a Choice," in *New Deal Thought,* Howard Zinn, ed. (Indianapolis: Bobbs Merrill, 1966), 135–50; Miscamble, "Thurman Arnold Goes to Washington," 5.

6. Robert H. Jackson and John Q. Barrett, *That Man: An Insider's Portrait of Franklin D. Roosevelt* (New York: Oxford University Press, 2003), 124.

7. New York Times Oral History Project, Columbia University Oral History

Collection, Part IV, No. 7, Thurman W. Arnold, Paul Greenberg Interview, June 1962, Franklin D. Roosevelt Library, Fiche 1.

8. Hawley, *New Deal,* passim; William E. Leuchtenburg, *Franklin D. Roosevelt and the New Deal* (New York: Harper and Row, 1963), 56–60, 64–70, 163–65, 248–49, 258; Charles R. Geist, *Monopolies in America* (Oxford: Oxford University Press, 2000), 92–106; Rudolph J. R. Peritz, *Competition Policy in America 1888–1992* (Oxford: Oxford University Press, 1996), 76–78; Ellis W. Hawley, *The Great War and the Search for a Modern Order* (New York: St. Martin's Press, 1979); Richard M. Steuer and Peter A. Barile III, "Antitrust in Wartime," *Antitrust* 16 (Spring 2002):71.

9. Leuchtenburg, *Franklin D. Roosevelt,* 34–35.

10. Geist, *Monopolies,* 140–43; Hawley, *New Deal,* 189; Brinkley, *End of Reform,* 18; Charles F. Roos, *NRA Economic Planning* (Bloomington, IN: Principia Press, 1937). The NRA contained its own contradictions; in some ways it was merely a continuation of the battle between those who favored industrial self-government, national economic planning, and competition enforced through the antitrust laws. Hawley, *New Deal,* 51.

11. Hawley, *New Deal,* 57–60; David Lynch, *The Concentration of Economic Power* (New York: Columbia University Press, 1946), 150–54; Peter H. Irons, *The New Deal Lawyers* (Princeton: Princeton University Press, 1982); Christopher R. Leslie, "Trust, Distrust, and Antitrust," *Texas Law Review* 82 (2004):517, 664–68; Jonathan Baker, "The Case for Antitrust Enforcement," *Journal of Economic Perspectives* 17 (2003):27, 37.

12. Hawley, *New Deal,* 136.

13. U.S.C. § 703(a) (1933).

14. Letter to Ellen Stevenson, late July 1933, in T*he Papers of Adlai E. Stevenson,* Walter Johnson, ed. (Boston: Little, Brown & Co., 1972), 248–49.

15. Hawley, *New Deal,* 72–90, 361.

16. "Symposium: In Commemoration of the Sixtieth Anniversary of the Establishment of the Antitrust Division," *Antitrust Bulletin* 39 (1994):813–940; Irons, *New Deal Lawyers,* 35–57, 133–55.

17. *Appalachian Coals v. United States,* 288 U.S. 344 (1933).

18. *A.L.A. Schechter Poultry Corp. v. United States,* 295 U.S. 553 (1935).

19. Arnold, *Fair Fights,* 146.

20. Franklin D. Roosevelt and Samuel Rosenman, *The Public Papers and Addresses of Franklin D. Roosevelt* 129 (New York: Random House, 1938), 129; Brinkley, *End of Reform,* 56–57; Hawley, *New Deal,* 392–93.

21. Hawley, *New Deal,* 374–76; Homer Cummings and Carl Brent Swisher, *Selected Papers of Homer Cummings, Attorney General of the United States, 1933–1939* (New York: Charles Scribner's Sons, 1939), 17.

22. March 9, 1938.

23. Arnold, *Folklore,* 217. After confirmation, Arnold in fact apologized to Borah for this passage. Letter to William Borah, March 16, 1938, reprinted in Gressley, *Voltaire,* 268.

24. Letter to Mr. and Mrs. C. P. Arnold, undated, C. P. Arnold Collection, AHC, Box 45, Correspondence.

25. Nomination of Thurman W. Arnold, Hearings before a Subcommittee of the Committee on the Judiciary, United States Senate, Seventy-Fifth Congress, Third Session on the Nomination of Thurman W. Arnold to be Assistant Attorney General, March 11, 1938 (G.P.O., 1938); Arnold, *Folklore,* 141.

26. Lerner, "The Shadow World of Thurman Arnold," 687, 701. For Lerner, this wasn't necessarily a bad thing, and the moral of the story was "that you don't take your dissecting instruments into the Senate chamber." Ibid.

27. *New York Times,* March 15, 1938; *Washington Herald,* March 16, 1938.

28. *Hartford Times,* March 23, 1938; Brinkley, *End of Reform,* 118.

29. Ibid.

30. Peritz, *Competition Policy,* 75–89; Hawley, *New Deal,* 166–68.

31. Arnold, *Fair Fights,* 133.

32. Ibid., 113.

33. Brinkley, *End of Reform,* 106–36; Thurman W. Arnold, *The Bottlenecks of Business* (New York: Reynal & Hitchcock, 1940), 122, 202, 211–12; Thurman Arnold, "Labor's Hidden Holdup Men," *Reader's Digest* (June 2, 1941):136, 139–40; Thurman Arnold, "Antitrust Law Enforcement, Past and Future," *Law & Contemporary Problems* 7 (1940):5, 12; *New York Sun,* August 9, 1940; Thurman W. Arnold, "Feathers and Prices," *Common Sense* 8 (July 1939):3, 5; Thurman Arnold, "What Can Government Offer—What Can Business Expect?" *Vital Speeches* 5 (1939):525; Thurman Arnold, "Address at Banquet," *Mississippi Bar Journal* 9 (1938):219, 223; Thurman Arnold, "An Inquiry into the Monopoly Issue," *New York Times,* August 21, 1938, Sec. 7 at 1, 14.

34. Arnold, *Symbols,* 149–71, 199–228.

35. Letter to Dexter M. Keezer, August 1, 1947, AHC, Box 37, File 4.

36. Arnold, *Bottlenecks,* 103–07, 164–89; Thurman Arnold, "Antitrust Law Enforcement," 5, 14; Letter to William L. Chenery, May 5, 1939, reprinted in Gressley, *Voltaire,* 284–85; Thurman W. Arnold, "Consent Decrees and the Sherman Act," *World Convention Dates* 12 (June 1939); Report of the Assistant Attorney General, Thurman Arnold, in Charge of the Antitrust Division 1–2 (G.P.O., 1939); Arnold, "Address at Banquet," 219–21.

37. Thurman Arnold, "Cartels Threaten Democracy," *Science Digest* (1944):78, 80.

38. Arnold, *Bottlenecks,* 97, 119–21, 134–35, 191, 212, 272–73; Report of the Assistant Attorney General, Thurman Arnold, in Charge of the Antitrust Di-

vision 6–7 (G.P.O., 1939); Letter to Helen Rogers Reid, December 2, 1938, reprinted in Gressley, *Voltaire,* 278–79; Letter to Frank Knox, July 6, 1939, reprinted in Gressley, *Voltaire,* 286; Letter to Arthur Sulzberger, August 25, 1939, reprinted in Gressley, *Voltaire,* 291; Letter to Robert H. Jackson, September 2, 1942, reprinted in Gressley, *Voltaire,* 330.

39. Richard Lee Strout, "The Folklore of Thurman Arnold," *New Republic,* April 27, 1942, 570.

40. Arnold, *Bottlenecks,* 156–58 (reprinting critical cartoon).

41. Arnold, *Bottlenecks,* 141–89; Thurman W. Arnold, "Consent Decrees and the Sherman Act."

42. Interview with Victor Kramer, July 2, 2002.

43. Thurman W. Arnold, "Prosecution Policy under the Sherman Act," *American Bar Association Journal* 24 (1938):417.

44. Strout, "Folklore," 570–71; Miscamble, "Thurman Arnold Goes to Washington," 5, 13.

45. Report of the Assistant Attorney General, Thurman Arnold, in Charge of the Antitrust Division 4–6 (G.P.O., 1939); Arnold, "Antitrust Law Enforcement," 5, 10; Arnold, "Feathers," 3–4; Arnold, "Address at Banquet," 219, 222; Arnold, *Bottlenecks,* 171, 276; Corwin D. Edwards, "Thurman Arnold and the Antitrust Laws," *Political Science Quarterly* 58 (September 1943):338; Antitrust Division, Summary of Cases under the Antitrust Laws, February 19, 1941 (Inclusive), AHC Box 103.

46. Hawley, *New Deal,* 432. Recruiting standards were so high that Arnold had to fend off charges that he would only hire men from Yale, Harvard, and Columbia. To Gordon Dean, October 15, 1938, reprinted in Gressley, *Voltaire,* 276. Wendell Berge himself led the Antitrust Division after Tom Clark from September 1943 until April 1947. Like Arnold, both Berge and Clark were Westerners.

47. S. Doc. 173, 75th Cong., 3d Sess.

48. Drew Pearson, "Washington Merry-Go-Round," *Washington Herald,* May 5, 1938.

49. Hawley, *New Deal,* 405.

50. Brinkley, *End of Reform,* 122–31.

51. Lynch, *Concentration,* 21–22.

52. *Washington Post,* May 5, 1938.

53. Lynch, *Concentration,* 35–43.

54. Douglas left shortly after the creation of the TNEC to join the Supreme Court. He was replaced by SEC Commissioners Jerome Frank and then Sumner Pike. For more on Oliphant as an antitrust scholar and a legal realist, see Spencer Weber Waller, "The Language of Law and the Language of Business," *Case West Law Review* 52 (2001):283, 286–87; Kalman, *Legal Realism,* 9–10, 19–20, 29–32, 68–74, 109–113; Schlegel, *American Legal Realism,* passim. Oliphant died

within a year of the beginning of the TNEC's work. For the backgrounds of the other executive branch members, see Lynch, *Concentration*, 43–46.

55. Brinkley, *End of Reform*, 83, 124–31.
56. Lynch, *Concentration*, 71–90.
57. Department of Justice Release, July 14, 1938.
58. *Christian Science Monitor*, March 31, 1941.
59. Final Report and Recommendations of the Temporary National Economic Committee (1941). See Lynch, *Concentration*, 337–53.
60. Arnold, *Fair Fights*, 139–43.
61. Lynch, *Concentration*, 338.
62. TNEC Final Report and Recommendations, 77th Cong., 1st Sess., Sen. Doc. 35 (1941); Arnold, *Fair Fights*, 140–41; Lynch, *Concentration*, 273–79; *Hartford-Empire Co. v. United States*, 323 U.S. 386, clarified, 324 U.S. 570 (1945).
63. U.S.C. §§ 18, 18a.
64. *South Bend Tribune*, May 17–18, 1938.
65. Arnold, *Bottlenecks*, 123.
66. Hawley, *New Deal*, 436.
67. Ibid., 435–36; Arnold, *Bottlenecks*, 194.
68. Hawley, *New Deal*, 439; Memo from George P. Comer to Johnston Avery, December 18, 1939, AHC Box 103; Arnold, *Bottlenecks*, 48, 77.
69. *United States News*, August 1, 1938.
70. Alva Johnson, "Thurman Arnold's Biggest Case," *New Yorker* (January 24, 1942), 25.
71. George David Smith, *From Monopoly to Competition: The Transformation of Alcoa, 1888–1986* (Cambridge: Cambridge University Press, 1988), 205–6; *United States v. Aluminum Co. of Am.*, 44 F. Supp. 97 (S.D.N.Y. 1941).
72. *United States v. Aluminum Co. of Am.*, 148 F.2d 416 (2d Cir. 1945).
73. A special provision of the antitrust laws applies to the District of Columbia without the need to show an effect on interstate commerce. 15 U.S.C. § 3. This was still a potentially thorny issue for an investigation in the medical profession in the 1930s. The issue of the effect of the practice of medicine on interstate commerce was only resolved by the Supreme Court decades later by a closely divided Supreme Court in *Pinhas v. Summit Health, Ltd.*, 500 U.S. 322 (1991).
74. Statement by Assistant Attorney General Thurman Arnold, Chief of the Antitrust Division of the Department of Justice, *Current History* 49 (1938).
75. See Kurt Eichenwald, *The Informant* (New York: Broadway Books, 2000).
76. *La Crosse Tribune*, August 5, 1938. They were eventually right as mandatory price schedules and certain restrictions on lawyer advertising fell to

attack under the antitrust laws and the First Amendment. See *Goldfarb v. Virginia State Bar,* 421 U.S. 773 (1975).

77. *Washington Times,* Aug. 2, 1938; *Chicago Daily Tribune,* August 2, 1938.

78. Gressley, *Voltaire,* 514 n. 139.

79. *United States v. Am. Med. Ass'n,* 110 F.2d 703 (D.C. Cir. 1940) (reinstating indictment); *United States v. Am. Med. Ass'n,* 28 F. Supp. 752 (D.D.C. 1939) (dismissing indictment).

80. *Am. Med. Ass'n v. United States,* 317 U.S. 519 (1943).

81. *United States v. South-eastern Underwriters Ass'n,* 322 U.S. 533 (1944), reversed by statute, McCarran Ferguson Act, 15 U.S.C. § 1011 *et seq.*

82. Internal DOJ Memos, Box 88, File 1, AHC, Box 88, File 3.

83. The key provisions restricting the sales of so-called hot oil had been declared unconstitutional in January 1935 in *Pan. Ref. v. United States,* 293 U.S. 388 (1935).

84. Arnold, *Bottlenecks,* 208.

85. *United States v. Socony-Vacuum Oil Co.,* 105 F.2d 809 (7th Cir. 1939).

86. *New York Herald Tribune,* February 7, 1940.

87. *United States v. Socony-Vacuum Oil Co.,* 310 U.S. 150 (1940). Chief Justice Hughes and Justice Murphy did not participate in the case. Justice Roberts wrote a dissent in which Justice McReynolds concurred.

88. Ibid., 200–221.

89. Ibid., 223–24.

90. Ibid., 224 n. 59.

91. Ibid., 225–28.

92. Arnold, *Bottlenecks,* 173–81; Thurman W. Arnold, "We Must Reform the Patent Law," *Atlantic Monthly* 170 (September 1942):47. Thurman W. Arnold, "The Abuse of Patents," *Atlantic Monthly* 170 (July 1942):14; Statement of Honorable Thurman W. Arnold, Assistant Attorney General of the United States Before the Committee on Patents of the Senate of the United States (Bone Committee), 77th Cong., 2d Sess, Washington, D.C., July 31, 1942; Statement of Honorable Thurman W. Arnold, Assistant Attorney General of the United States Before the Committee on Patents of the Senate of the United States (Bone Committee), 77th Cong., 2d Sess, Washington, D.C., April 23, 1942; The Abuse of Patents, Speech by Thurman Arnold, Assistant Attorney General of the United States, Before the American Business Congress, Hotel Pennsylvania, New York City, July 28, 1942; Letter to Isador Lubin, September 20, 1943, Walton Hamilton Collection, Box J11, Folder 2, Rare Books and Special Collections, Tarlton Law Library, University of Texas at Austin.

93. Many of these cases were postponed because of the advent of World War II and came to fruition long after Arnold had left the Justice Department. See, e.g., *United States v. Timken Roller Bearing Co.,* 341 U.S. 593 (1951).

94. Statement of Honorable Thurman W. Arnold, Assistant Attorney General of the United States Before the Committee on Patents of the Senate of the United Sates (Bone Committee), 77th Cong., 2d Sess, Washington, D.C., April 25, 1942.

95. *United States v. Hartford-Empire Co. v. United States,* 323 U.S. 386, clarified, 324 U.S. 570 (1945); *Ethyl Gasoline Corp. v. United States,* 309 U.S. 436 (1940); *United States v. Univis Lens Co., Inc.,* 316 U.S. 241 (1942).

96. Thurman Arnold, "Defense and Restraints of Trade," *New Republic,* May 19, 1941; Thurman W. Arnold, "How Monopolies Have Hobbled Defense," *Reader's Digest* 51 (July 1941); Thurman W. Arnold, "Labor's Hidden Holdup Men," *Reader's Digest* 136 (June 1941); Thurman Arnold, "Free Trade within the Borders of the United States," *South Carolina Bar Association* 94 (1941); "Address by Hon. Thurman W. Arnold," *Georgia Bar Association* 135 (1941); Thurman W. Arnold, "The Anti-Trust Law and the Consumer," *Mississippi Law Journal* 12 (1940):57; Arnold, "Feathers," 3; Thurman Arnold, "An Inquiry into the Monopoly Issue," *New York Times Magazine,* August 21, 1938; Arnold, "Prosecution Policy," 417; Thurman Arnold, "Fair and Effective Use of Present Antitrust Procedure, *Yale Law Journal* 47 (1938):1294.

97. August 12, 1939.

98. Ibid., 34.

99. "Arnold vs. Clean Rest Rooms," *Collier's,* August 30, 1941.

100. Kalman, *Legal Realism,* 140–49.

101. Arnold, *Fair Fights,* 136; Interview with Charles A. Reich, December 20, 2002.

102. Arnold, "Introduction," *Bottlenecks,* x–xi.

103. Arnold, *Fair Fights,* 120. In fairness, Arnold in his autobiography notes, "I no longer believe that this is true."

104. Arnold, *Bottlenecks,* 20–45, 97; Arnold, "Antitrust Law Enforcement," 5, 12–13; Arnold, "Prosecution Policy," 417; Thurman Arnold, "An Inquiry into the Monopoly Issue," Sec. 7, at 1, 14; Thurman Arnold, "What Is Monopoly?" *Vital Speeches* 5 (1938):567.

105. AHC, Box 87, File 1.

106. Department of Justice Release, August 28, 1942, AHC Box 60, Associated Press Folder.

107. Cissy Patterson's biography recalls this incident quite differently with Patterson trying to get Arnold to file suit and Arnold refusing unless Patterson's paper more strongly supported President Roosevelt editorially for reelection in 1940. There is no support offered for this supposed direct quid pro quo, particularly at a time when Patterson's *Washington Herald* had not definitively broken with the Roosevelt administration. See generally Alice Albright Hoge, *Cissy Patterson* (New York: Random House, 1966).

108. Arnold, *Fair Fights,* 114.

109. *Associated Press v. United States*, 326 U.S. 1 (1945).

110. Thurman Arnold, "Labor against Itself," *Reader's Digest* 37 (January 1944):38–39.

111. Arnold could not have been unaware of this point. Many of the reviewers of *Bottlenecks* pointed this out even when otherwise sympathetic to the rest of Arnold's mission. See Paul M. Sweezy, "Book Review," *Harvard Law Review* 54 (1941):530, 532.

112. Letters to Robert H. Jackson, January 23, 1940, reprinted in Gressley, *Voltaire*, 300; to Freda Kirchwey, December 14, 1939, reprinted in Gressley, *Voltaire*, 298.

113. 15 U.S.C. § 17; 29 U.S.C. § 52.

114. Department of Justice Release, November 20, 1939 (releasing letter from Arnold to Secretary of Central Labor Union of Indianapolis).

115. Letter to Arthur Krock, February 27, 1958, reprinted in Gressley, *Voltaire*, 424.

116. Letter to Robert H. Jackson, January 23, 1940, reprinted in Gressley, *Voltaire*, 300.

117. Arnold, *Fair Fights*, 116.

118. *United States v. Hutcheson*, 312 U.S. 219 (1941); *United States v. Int'l Hod Carriers & C.L. Dist. Council*, 313 U.S. 539 (1941) (per curiam); *United States v. Local 807 Int'l Brotherhood of Teamsters*, 315 U.S. 521 (1942).

119. Arnold's original March 21, 1942, testimony was simply reprinted; 22 *Congressional Digest* 176 (1943).

120. Franklin D. Roosevelt, President's Personal Files 8319, Thurman Arnold, Franklin D. Roosevelt Library; *Pittsburgh Press*, April 28, 1940.

121. Arnold, *Fair Fights*, 115–119; Letter to Reed Powell, April 19, 1941, reprinted in Gressley, *Voltaire*, 318; Letter to Reed Powell, February 21, 1941, reprinted in Gressley, *Voltaire*, 315.

122. *United States v. Aluminum Co. of Am.*, 148 F.2d 416 (2d Cir. 1945). Later, the sale of government smelting facilities created new competitors to Alcoa that broke Alcoa's monopoly in the aluminum industry. Even then the litigation continued until 1950, when the courts held that no further remedies would be required. *United States v. Aluminum Co. of Am.*, 91 F. Supp. 333 (S.D.N.Y. 1950).

123. *Associated Press v. United States*, 326 U.S. 1 (1945); *Am. Tobacco Co. v. United States*, 328 U.S. 781 (1946).

124. Clayton Act, ch. 323, 38 Stat. 731–32 (1914), codified at 15 U.S.C. § 18 (1933).

125. Report of the Federal Trade Commission on the Merger Movement—A Summary Report (G.P.O., Washington, 1948); 15 U.S.C. § 18 (1950).

126. Gressley, *Voltaire*, 49.

127. Thurman W. Arnold, *Democracy and Free Enterprise* (Norman: University of Oklahoma Press, 1942); Arnold, *Bottlenecks*, 15, 60–90; Thurman

Arnold, "How Cartels Affect You," *American Mercury* 56 (1943): 321; Arnold, "We Must Reform," 47; Thurman Arnold, "This War Will Save Private Enterprise," *Saturday Evening Post* (May 30, 1942), 24; Thurman W. Arnold, "The Role of the Bar in War," *Illinois Bar Journal* 30 (1942):409, 411; Thurman Arnold, "Concerning the War Effort," Sales Management in War and After Victory (1942), AHC, Box 107; The Abuse of Patents, Speech by Thurman Arnold, Assistant Attorney General of the United States, before the American Business Congress, Hotel Pennsylvania, New York City, July 28, 1942, AHC Box 106; "Postwar Issue: State Controls or Competition, Why Thurman Arnold Believes Antitrust Prosecutions Necessary," *The United States News* 16, April 7, 1942, AHC Box 107; Thurman Arnold to Robert H. Jackson, May 18, 1940, in Gressley, *Voltaire,* 305; Arnold, "Antitrust Law Enforcement, 5, 7, 19; Arnold, "Feathers" 3, 6; Thurman W. Arnold, "Antitrust Activities of the Department of Justice," *Oregon Law Review* 19 (1939):22; Thurman Arnold, "What Can Government Offer—What Can Business Expect?" *Vital Speeches* 5 (1939):525.

128. Arnold, *Bottlenecks,* 74.

129. Memorandum on the Board of Economic Warfare Work of the Antitrust Division, Department of Justice, Washington, D.C., Memo 60-0-28, August 11, 1942, Franklin D. Roosevelt Library, Francis Biddle File, Container 1.

130. Arnold, *Bottlenecks,* 70–71.

131. The Abuse of Patents, Speech by Thurman Arnold, Assistant Attorney General of the United States, before the American Business Congress, Hotel Pennsylvania, New York City, July 28, 1942, AHC, Box 106, Patent Abuse Folder 1 of 3.

132. George W. Stocking and Myron W. Watkins, *Cartels in Action: Case Studies in International Business Diplomacy* (New York: Twentieth Century Fund, 1946), 491–505; Christopher R. Leslie, "Trust, Distrust and Antitrust," *Texas Law Review* 82 (2004):515, 561–62. For an account of the case more sympathetic to Standard Oil see Wyatt Wells, *Antitrust and the Formation of the Postwar World* (New York: Columbia University Press, 2002), 67–81.

133. *United States v. Standard Oil Co.* 1940–43 Trade Cas. (CCH) ¶ 56, 198 (D.N.J. 1942), as amended, 1940–43 Trade Cas. (CCH) ¶ 56, 269 (D.N.J. 1943).

134. I. F. Stone, "Thurman Arnold and the Railroads," *Nation* 331 (March 6, 1943); "Arnold vs. Standard Oil," *Newsweek* (June 8, 1942), 46.

135. Remarks of Edward H. Levi, Thurman Arnold Remembered: A Centennial Celebration (October 30, 1991):3, 7.

136. The Abuse of Patents, Speech by Thurman Arnold, Assistant Attorney General of the United States, Before the American Business Congress, Hotel Pennsylvania, New York City, July 28, 1942, AHC, Box 106; Arnold, *Fair Fights,* 145; Supplemental Statement of the Honorable Thurman W. Arnold, Assistant Attorney General of the United States before the Special Senate Committee Investigating the National Defense Program of the United States, Washing-

ton, D.C., June 1, 1942; Statement of the Honorable Thurman W. Arnold, Assistant Attorney General of the United States before the Committee on Patents, Washington, D.C., April 23, 1942; Statement of the Honorable Thurman W. Arnold, Assistant Attorney General of the United States before the Special Senate Committee Investigating the National Defense Program of the United States, Washington, D.C., March 26 and 27, 1942.

137. Arnold, "Cartels," 321, 326.

138. Arnold, *Bottlenecks,* 73; Letters to Robert H. Jackson, September 9, 1942, reprinted in Gressley, *Voltaire,* 330; to Miss C. Warriner, April 28, 1942, reprinted in Gressley, *Voltaire,* 326; to Hugh Johnson, February 7, 1941, reprinted in Gressley, *Voltaire,* 310. See generally Richard M. Steuer and Peter A. Barile III, "Antitrust in Wartime," *Antitrust* (Spring 2002):71.

139. More on the abortive investigation of the railroads can be found in Corwin D. Edwards, "Thurman Arnold and the Antitrust Laws," *Political Science Quarterly* 58 (September 1943):338, 349–53; I. F. Stone, "Thurman Arnold and the Railroads," *Nation* (March 6, 1943), 331.

140. Arnold, *Fair Fights,* 145.

141. Wyatt Wells, *Antitrust and the Formation of the Postwar World* (New York: Columbia University Press, 2002); Kingman Brewster, James R. Atwood, and Spencer Weber Waller, *Antitrust and American Business Abroad,* § 2.12–.13 (Eagan, MN: West Group, 1997 & supp.).

142. Remarks of Janet Reno, Attorney General of the United States, "Symposium," *Antitrust Bulletin* supra at 831; Email from John Shenefield, September 30, 2003, June 10, 2003; Email from James R. Rill, December 11, 2003; Email from Anne Bingaman, October 1, 2003.

NOTES TO CHAPTER 7

1. Arnold, *Fair Fights,* 156.

2. Franklin D. Roosevelt to Thurman W. Arnold, Washington, D.C., January 28, 1943, Box 45, C. P. Arnold Collection, American Heritage Center, University of Wyoming.

3. To the Honorable Thurman W. Arnold, A Tribute from his Friends and Associates of the Antitrust Division, Department of Justice, Presidential Room, Statler Hotel, Washington, D.C., March 9, 1943, Box 6, Thurman W. Arnold Collection, American Heritage Center, University of Wyoming; An Address by the Honorable Thurman W. Arnold, Mutual Broadcasting Network, March 9, 1943, Box 6, Thurman W. Arnold Collection, American Heritage Center, University of Wyoming.

4. Cong. Rec. 1724 (March 9, 1943).

5. *United States v. Alum. Co. of America,* 148 F.2d 416 (2d Cir. 1945) (on remand and certification from the Supreme Court for lack of a quorum).

6. Arnold, *Fair Fights*, 157.
7. Franklin D. Roosevelt, President's Personal Files 8319, Justice Department Endorsements (A-B), Franklin D. Roosevelt Library.
8. Pub. L. 91-358, 84 Stat. 473; D.C. Code Title 11.
9. 28 U.S.C. §§ 1331, 1332, 1367.
10. See Appendix A for a full list of Justice Arnold's opinions; *Waterman Steamship Corp. v. Land*, 151 F.2d 292 (D.C. Cir. 1945) (dissent claiming lack of jurisdiction to reverse Federal Maritime Commission decision investigating fleet's profits from charter with British government); *Rainbow Dyeing & Cleaning v. Bowles*, 150 F.2d 273 (D.C. Cir. 1945) (dissenting from affirmance of maximum price regulation on grounds of ambiguity); *Tippitt v. Wood*, 140 F.2d 689 (D.C. Cir. 1944) (concurring in result over power of district court to direct concurrent running of unexpired portion of sentence imposed by Parole Commission); *Holmes v. Frederick W. Berens, Inc.*, 149 F.2d 388 (D.C. Cir. 1945) (dissenting in contract case over meaning of word "eventual").
11. 146 F.2d 865 (D.C. Cir. 1945).
12. Ibid.
13. 149 F. 2d 505 (D.C. Cir. 1945).
14. 28 U.S.C. § 1295(a)(4)(A) & (B).
15. 145 F.2d 18, 20–21 (D.C. Cir. 1944).
16. 144 F.2d 497, 501–02 (D.C. Cir. 1944).
17. See, e.g., *Hartford-Empire Co. v. United States*, 324 U.S. 570 (1945) (successful monopolization case against acquisition and misuse of patents for glass technology).
18. Letter to Homer Bone, September 28, 1944, AHC, Box 34.
19. Arnold also decided *Williams v. United States*, 138 F.2d 81 (D.C. Cir. 1943), which affirmed a criminal conviction of a doctor for providing abortion service where the issue was which party had the burden for showing the necessity of the abortion for the life or health of the woman.
20. 137 F.2d 698 (D.C. Cir. 1943).
21. See also *Fisher v. United States*, 149 F.2d 29 (D.C. Cir. 1945); *Holloway v. United States*, 148 F.2d 665 (D.C. Cir. 1945) (rejecting challenges to convictions based on insanity grounds).
22. 137 F.2d at 699.
23. Ibid., 700.
24. Arnold, *Fair Fights*, 236–42. See also Julien Cornell, *The Trial of Ezra Pound* (New York: J. Day Company, 1992), 123–29. Arnold's eventual law partner, Abe Fortas, also ventured into these waters in a famous pro bono case that altered the definition of the insanity defense. *Durham v. United States*, 214 F.2d 862 (D.C. Cir. 1954).
25. 149 F.2d 511 (D.C. Cir. 1945).
26. Ibid., 513.

27. Ibid., 514.
28. 151 F.2d 49, 50 (D.C. Cir. 1945).
29. Ibid.
30. 250 U.S. 616, 630 (1919).
31. 395 U.S. 444 (1969). Interestingly, the Supreme Court's *Brandenburg* opinion was drafted by Arnold's former law partner Abe Fortas immediately prior to his resignation from the Court and was issued as a per curiam opinion. Geoffrey R. Stone, Louis M. Seidman, Cass R. Sunstein, and Mark V. Tushnet, *The First Amendment* (Gaithersburg: Aspen Law & Business, 1999), 32.
32. 151F.2d at 52.
33. Ibid.
34. Ibid., 53.
35. H. L. Mencken to Arnold, June 7, 1945, AHC, Box 35; Francis Biddle to Arnold, June 5, 1945, AHC, Box 35.
36. 151 F.2d 16 (D.C. Cir. 1945).
37. Arnold continued to publish on this theme throughout the remainder of his life, showing that this issue rankled far more than otherwise acknowledged. Thurman Arnold, "Why We Have a Housing Mess," *Look*, April 1, 1947.
38. Arnold, *Fair Fights*, 159.
39. T. W. Arnold to Mrs. Elizabeth Schmidt Ranke, June 7, 1947, in William O. Douglas, *Selections from the Letters and Legal Papers of Thurman Arnold*, Victor Kramer, ed. (Washington, D.C.: Merkle Press, 1961), 3.
40. Letter to J. D. Hyman, April 21, 1960, reprinted in Gressley, *Voltaire*, 435.
41. William O. Douglas, "Foreword," *Selections from the Letters and Legal Papers of Thurman Arnold*, viii.
42. Abe Fortas, "Thurman Arnold and the Theatre of Law," *Yale Law Journal* 79 (1970):988, 990.
43. Tyler Abell, *Drew Pearson Diaries 1949–1959* (New York: Holt, 1974), 514; Arnold, *Fair Fights*, 158.
44. See, e.g., Jerome Frank, *Courts on Trial: Myth and Reality in American Justice* (Princeton: Princeton University Press, 1949).
45. Interview with Joseph Arnold, March, 19, 2002.

NOTES TO CHAPTER 8

1. Arne C. Wiprud, *Justice in Transportation: An Expose of Monopoly Control* (Chicago: Ziff-Davis, 1945).
2. Reed Miller, "A Memorial to Thurman Wesley Arnold," *West Virginia Law Review* 72 (1970):203.
3. T. W. Arnold to Westbrook Pegler, September 18, 1945, reprinted in Gressley, *Voltaire*, 362–63.

4. Most accounts describe the Pullman litigation as the only matter Arnold and Wiprud handled together. See, e.g., Fortas, "Theatre of Law," 988, 990. *Reynolds Int'l Pen Co. v. Eversharp, Inc.,* 63 F. Supp. 423 (D. Del. 1945).

5. *United States v. Pullman Co.,* 330 U.S. 806 (1947).

6. Wiprud eventually returned to government legal service as assistant solicitor with the Post Office until 1952 when he reentered private practice. From 1960 to 1963, he served as director of the New York State Office of Transportation and then practiced law in Washington, D.C., until his retirement in 1968. He passed away at the age of ninety-three in 1987.

7. Following his retirement from Arnold & Porter, Diamond wrote a memoir about the firm. Norman Diamond, *A Practice Almost Perfect: The Early Days at Arnold, Fortas & Porter* (Lanham, MD: University Press of America, 1997).

8. Fortas, "Theatre of Law," 988, 990.

9. See chapter 5 in this book.

10. A Memorial Service for Paul A. Porter (1904–1975) Thursday, December 11, 1975, A&P Files.

11. Diamond, *Practice,* 97; Kalman interview with Milton Freeman, June 23, 1989.

12. Hawley, *New Deal,* 172, 205–12.

13. Kalman interview with Frances Arnold and Thurman Arnold Jr. (undated).

14. Interview with Patricia Wald, January 17, 2003; Interview with Charles Reich, December 20, 2002; Interview with Edgar Brenner, October 24, 2002; Interview with Victor Kramer, July 2, 2002; Interview with G. Duane Vieth, July 1, 2002; Interview with Robert Herzstein, January 4, 2002; Kalman interview with Milton Freeman, June 23, 1989; Kalman interview with Victor Kramer; Kalman interview with G. Duane Vieth; Kalman interview with Norman Diamond; Kalman interview with Reed Miller (all undated).

15. Laura Kalman, *Abe Fortas: A Biography* (New Haven: Yale University Press, 1990), 37; Kate Loucheim interview with Fortas, September 29, 1981.

16. Murphy, *Fortas,* 77.

17. Interview with Patricia Wald, January 17, 2003; Interview with Edgar Brenner, October 24, 2002; Interview with Victor Kramer, July 2, 2002; Interview with G. Duane Vieth, April 26, 2002, and July 1, 2002; Interview with Abe Krash, April 24, 2002; Interview with Robert Herzstein, January 4, 2002; Kalman interview with Milton Freeman, June 23, 1989; Kalman interview with Victor Kramer; Kalman interview with G. Duane Vieth; Kalman interview with Norman Diamond; Kalman interview with Reed Miller. A considerably softer portrait of Fortas can be found in Diamond, *Practice,* 93–100.

18. Kalman, *Fortas,* 146.

19. Diamond, *Practice,* 100.

20. Kalman interview with Nicholas Katzenbach; Interview with Nicholas Katzenbach, September 30, 2002.

21. Ellen Schrecker, *Many Are the Crimes: McCarthyism in America* (Boston: Little, Brown & Co., 1998), 90–91; Leuchtenburg, *Roosevelt,* 280–81.

22. Executive Order No. 9835, March 21, 1947, 12 Fed. Reg. 1935 (March 25, 1947).

23. See David McCullogh, *Truman* (New York: Simon & Schuster, 1992), 551–54. *See* also Schrecker, *Many Crimes,* 209.

24. The FBI had been screening federal employees since 1939. Schrecker, *Many Crimes,* 209.

25. Part II (6).

26. Part V.

27. Statement by the president on the government's Employee Loyalty Program, November 14, 1947.

28. Ibid.

29. Kalman interview with Norman Diamond.

30. *Freidman v. Schwellenbach,* 159 F.2d 22 (D.C. Cir. 1946), cert. denied, 330 U.S. 838 (1947), reh'g. denied, 331 U.S. 865 (1947).

31. Kalman interview with G. Duane Vieth; Interview with William Rogers, July 2, 2002.

32. Letter to George Gardner, April 19, 1950, reprinted in Gressley, *Voltaire,* 388.

33. Brief for Appellant, *Bailey v. Richardson,* No. 10382, United States Court of Appeals for the District of Columbia Circuit at 9, 15, 16, 18.

34. *Washington Star,* May 12, 1949.

35. *Bailey v. Richardson,* 182 F.2d 46 (D.C. Cir. 1950).

36. Ibid., 66.

37. Ibid., 67.

38. Ibid., 74.

39. *Bailey v. Richardson,* 339 U.S. 977 (1950).

40. Petitioner's Brief, 15.

41. Reply Brief for Petitioner, *Bailey v. Richardson,* Supreme Court of the United States, October Term 1950, Case No. 49, 1–2.

42. Paul Porter to Edward F. Pritchard Jr., October 13, 1950, A&P Office Files, Box 5, Edward F. Pritchard Jr., Folder; Letter to Arthur Krock, December 20, 1950, reprinted in Gressley, *Voltaire,* 394.

43. *Bailey v. Richardson,* 341 U.S. 918 (1951).

44. See Schrecker, *Many Crimes,* 281.

45. Motion for Disposition of Appeal without Formal Briefs or Argument, *Peters v. Hobby,* United States Court of Appeals for the District of Columbia, No. 12, 246.

46. Arnold, *Fair Fights,* 209–10; Joseph H. Rauh Jr., "Historical Perspectives: An Unabashed Liberal Looks at a Half-Century of the Supreme Court," *North Carolina Law Review* 69 (1990): 213, 235–36.

47. *Peters v. Hobby,* 349 U.S. 331 (1954).

48. Ibid., 349, 350, 353. The Supreme Court never opined on the overall constitutionality of the Truman loyalty program although the Ninth Circuit eventually held the program unconstitutional the same year as the Peters case. *Parker v. Lester,* 227 F.2d 708 (9th Cir. 1955). By that time, subsequent legislation allowed key federal departments to summarily dismiss employees considered a threat to national security, shifting the focus away from individual loyalty. Schrecker, *Many Crimes,* 288.

49. Arnold, *Fair Fights,* 210–13.

50. Thurman Arnold, "The American Ideal of a Fair Trial," *Arkansas Law Review* 9 (1955):311–12. See also Thurman Arnold, "Due Process in Trials," *Annals of the American Academy of Political and Social Science* 300 (1955):123.

51. *United States v. Lattimore,* 127 F. Supp. 405 (D.D.C. 1955), aff'd 232 F.2d 334 (D.C. Cir. 1955); 215 F.2d 847 (D.C. Cir. 1954), modifying, 112 F. Supp. 507 (D.D.C. 1953); 125 F. Supp. 295 (D.D.C. 1954).

52. Schrecker, *Many Crimes,* 247.

53. Interview with Patricia Wald, January 17, 2003.

54. Owen Lattimore, *Ordeal by Slander* (Boston: Little, Brown & Co., 1950), 59.

55. Arnold, *Fair Fights,* 215.

56. T. W. Arnold to Joseph Hergeshimer, February 3, 1953, reprinted in Victor Kramer, ed., *Selections from the Letters and Legal Papers of Thurman Arnold* (Washington, D.C.: Merkle Press, 1961), 77; Letter to B. M. McKelway, Feb. 4, 1955, in Kramer, *Selections,* 85, 86.

57. *United States v. Lattimore,* 215 F.2d 847 (D.C. Cir. 1954), aff'g, 112 F. Supp. 847 (D.D.C. 1953).

58. Interview with William Rogers, July 2, 2002; Interview with Pat Wald, January 17, 2003.

59. *United States v. Lattimore,* 125 F. Supp. 295 (D.D.C. 1955) (dismissing motion to disqualify as scandalous); *United States v. Lattimore,* 127 F. Supp. 405 (D.D.C. 1955) (dismissing principal perjury counts in indictment).

60. *United States v. Lattimore,* 232 F.2d 334 (D.C. Cir. 1955).

61. Kalman, *Fortas,* 150; Letter to Harry Barnard, April 3, 1950, A&P Files, Box 1, Loyalty Cases (returning check to author of biography of Illinois Governor Altgeld, sent in support of Dorothy Bailey).

62. Letter from Abe Fortas to Edwin M. Reiskind, March 21, 1951, A&P Files. Paul Porter also represented Uta Hagen, Ferrer's ex-wife, in connection with her appearance before HUAC and protested her being boycotted as a stage actress.

63. Lillian Hellman, *Scoundrel Time* (New York: Bantam Books, 1976), 50–55, 98–99.

64. Letters to Dr. Stringfellow Barr, August 20, 1951; to Graham C. Miller, December 30, 1948, A&P Files.

65. Thurman Arnold, "How Not to Get Investigated: Ten Commandments for Government Employees," *Harper's Magazine* 197 (1948):61.

66. Ibid., 61–62.

67. Special Study—How to Spot a Communist, Ordinance Corps, Watertown Arsenal, Watertown 72, Massachusetts, 7 January, 1955, A&P Files.

68. Arnold, "Ten Commandments," 62.

69. Fortas, "Theatre of Law," 988, 994. See also Gressley, *Voltaire*, 86.

70. Kalman, *Fortas*, 90, 97–98.

71. FBI Response to Daniel Ernst Freedom of Information Act Request re: Thurman Arnold, dated February 27, 2002.

72. Arnold, *Bottlenecks*, 274.

73. Stone, "Arnold and the Railroads," 331.

74. Schrecker, *Many Crimes*, 303; Interview with William Rogers, July 2, 2002.

75. Schrecker, *Many Crimes*, 81.

76. Letter to Rockwell Kent, September 3, 1941, reprinted in Gressley, *Voltaire*, 325.

77. AF&P letter to *Washington Post*, November 24, 1950, A&P Files; Kalman, *Fortas*, 135–37.

78. For the full scope of the legal campaign against alleged Communists see Marc Rohr, "Communists and the First Amendment: The Shaping of Freedom of Advocacy in the Cold War Era," *San Diego Law Review* 28 (1991):1.

79. Letter from Thurman Arnold, Adrian Scott Papers, American Heritage Center, Box 7, File 3.

80. Kalman interview with Milton Freeman, June 23, 1989.

NOTES TO CHAPTER 9

1. Arnold also spoke highly of Ford Motor Company during this era, praising Henry Ford as persevering to enter and succeed in an automobile industry previously characterized by collusion and misuse of patents. Arnold also spoke of Ford as the victim of cartelization that prevented him from efficiently building cars made of light metals and plastics. See Arnold, *Bottlenecks*, 119–21; Thurman Arnold, "How Cartels Affect You," *The American Mercury* 56 (1943):321.

2. Thurman Arnold, "The Economic Purpose of Antitrust Laws," *Mississippi Law Journal* 26 (1955):207, 212–14; Thurman Arnold, "A Reappraisal of the Antitrust Laws," in Conference on Freedom and the Law, at 98, 101–02, May 7, 1953, University of Chicago Law School, Conference Series No. 13; Thurman Arnold, "Depression—Not in Your Lifetime," *Colliers* (April 25, 1953):24, 26–

28; Talk Made by Judge Thurman Arnold at Dinner of Coca-Cola Men, December 4, 1948, in Atlanta, Georgia, on file with author.

3. Letter to J. R. Sullivan, November 17, 1944, reprinted in Gressley, *Voltaire*, 355; to R. W. Woodruff, December 16, 1944, reprinted in Gressley, *Voltaire*, 356; to J. R. Sullivan, December 21, 1944, reprinted in Gressley, *Voltaire*, 357; to J. R. Sullivan, June 26, 1945, reprinted in Gressley, *Voltaire*, 358.

4. Letter to Maury Maverick, July 11, 1945, reprinted in Gressley, *Voltaire*, 361.

5. Robert A. Caro, *The Years of Lyndon Johnson: Means of Ascent* (New York: Vintage 1990), 11–15.

6. Caro, *Lyndon Johnson*, 317.

7. Robert Dallek, *Lone Star Rising: Lyndon Johnson and His Times, 1908–1960* (New York: Oxford University Press, 1991), 333.

8. Caro, *Lyndon Johnson*, 368.

9. Caro, *Lyndon Johnson*, 370–73.

10. Dallek, *Lone Star*, 339.

11. Roger K. Newman, *Hugo Black: A Biography* (New York: Pantheon Books, 1994); Interview with William Rogers, July 2, 2002.

12. Caro, *Lyndon Johnson*, 379–84.

13. Kalman, *Fortas*, 161.

14. See, e.g., Statement by Thurman Arnold before House Committee on the District of Columbia on H.R. 7375 (July 29, 1959) (opposing the introduction of resale price maintenance for the sale of liquor in the District of Columbia).

15. Letters to Mrs. C. P. Arnold, July 24, 1947, AHC, Box 37, File 4; to Mrs. C. P. Arnold, June 25, 1947, AHC, Box 37, File 3.

16. Interview with Ted Janger, former law clerk to Judge Irving Goldberg, October 12, 2002.

17. Dennis J. Hutcheson, *The Man Who Was Whizzer White* (New York: Free Press, 1998).

18. *Loew's Inc. v. Cinema Amusements, Inc.*, 210 F.2d 86 (10th Cir. 1954), cert. denied, 347 U.S. 976 (1954).

19. The brief can be found in substantial part in Arnold, *Fair Fights*, 172–86.

20. Kalman interview with Norman Diamond (undated); Interview with Stuart Land, July 2, 2002.

21. Interview with Nicholas Katzenbach, September 30, 2002; Diamond, *Practice*, 63; Interview with Dennis Lyons, April 24, 2002.

22. Diamond, *Practice*, 63.

23. *In the Matter of Rodale Press, Inc., et al.*, Docket 8619, Federal Trade Commission, 71 F.T.C. 1184 (1968), following remand from the Court of Appeals, 407 F.2d 1252 (D.C. Cir. 1968).

24. Kalman, *Fortas*, 194.
25. Interview with Lewis Dabney, January 8, 2003.
26. Henry Hart Jr. and Albert M. Sacks, *The Legal Process: Basic Problems in the Making and Application of Law* (New York: Foundation Press, 1994); Anthony J. Sebok, "Reading the Legal Process," *Michigan Law Review* 94 (1996):1571.
27. Henry Hart, "Foreword: The Time Chart of the Justices, The Supreme Court, 1958 Term," *Harvard Law Review* 73 (1959):84, 85–93.
28. Ibid., 99–100, 124–25.
29. Ibid., 99–101.
30. Schlegel, "American Legal Realism," 459, 514 and n. 273.
31. Interview with Charles Reich, December 20, 2002.
32. Thurman Arnold, "Professor Hart's Theology," *Harvard Law Review* 73 (1960):1298, 1299, 1314–15.
33. Ibid., 1300–1304.
34. Ibid., 1302.
35. Ibid., 1304.
36. Ibid., 1307–8.
37. Hart, *Legal Process*, 100.
38. Arnold, "Professor Hart's Theology," 1311, 1312.
39. Ibid., 1313.
40. Nathaniel Weyl, "Correspondence: Pound and U.S. Treason Law," *New Republic*, June 27, 1959, 22; Arnold, *Fair Fights*, 238; William D. Rogers, "Ezra Pound and the Law," *New Republic*, June 1, 1959, 20.
41. Humphrey Carpenter, *A Serious Character: The Life of Ezra Pound* (London: Faber, 1988), 840.
42. See Carpenter, *Serious Character*, 841; Arnold, *Fair Fights*, 239; see generally Julien Cornell, *The Trial of Ezra Pound* (New York: The Notable Trials Library Gryphon Editions, 1992), 124–25.
43. Arnold, *Fair Fights*, 240.
44. Anthony Lewis, "U.S. Asked to End Pound Indictment," *New York Times*, April 15, 1958, at sect. 9d; Carpenter, *Serious Character*, 842–43.
45. Carpenter, *Serious Character*, 841; William Van O'Connor, *A Casebook on Ezra Pound* (New York: Crowell, 1959), 136.
46. Anthony Lewis, "Court Drops Charge against Ezra Pound," *New York Times*, April 19, 1958, at sect. 5c; Carpenter, *Serious Character*, 843. Arnold's motion, brief, and all attachments including Frost's statement are reproduced in their entirety in Cornell, *Trial of Ezra Pound*, 125–34.
47. Lewis, "Court Drops Charge against Ezra Pound"; Letter to Westbrook Pegler, April 29, 1958, reprinted in Kramer, *Selections*, 37, 38; "Pound to Live with Daughter," *New York Times*, May 18, 1958.
48. See generally Hoge, *Cissy Patterson*.

49. Interview with Joseph Arnold, March 19, 2002.

50. Edgar H. Brenner, "Reflections: Thurman Arnold, the Hope Diamond, and the Cigar Box," *Yale Law Report* (1980–1981):9. For Walsh's account of the history and acquisition of the Hope diamond and the rest of her immense jewel collection, see Evalyn Walsh McLean, *Father Struck It Rich* (Boston: Little, Brown & Company, 1936).

51. Brenner, "Reflections," 10.

52. Letter to Mrs. C. P. Arnold, May 21, 1947, AHC, Box 37, File 3, reprinted in Kramer, *Selections*, 35–37; Brenner, "Reflections," 10–11.

53. Interview with Edgar H. Brenner, November 6, 2002. Diamond, *Practice*, 133–34.

54. Diamond, *Practice*, 133.

55. Hoge, *Cissy Patterson*, 231–33.

56. Interview with Lewis Dabney, January 8, 2003.

57. Kalman interview with Victor Kramer; Interview with G. Duane Vieth, July 1, 2002.

58. Interview with William P. Rogers, April 26, 2002; Interview with Gerald M. Stern, July 12, 2002.

59. Diamond, *Practice*, 82–83; Interview with G. Duane Vieth, April 26, 2002.

60. Diamond, *Practice*, 95.

61. Ibid., 100. Remarks of Justice Abe Fortas and Thurman Arnold, (Holiday Party 1967), A&P Files.

62. Helen Essary, "Dear Washington," *Washington Times-Herald*, November 18, 1939.

63. Interview with Patricia Wald, January 17, 2003; Interview with Edgar H. Brenner, November 6, 2002; Diamond, *Practice*, 86–87, 95, 111.

64. Kalman interview with G. Duane Vieth.

65. Diamond, *Practice*, 2, 3.

66. Gressley, *Voltaire*, 68.

67. Interview with Gerald M. Stern, July 12, 2002; Stern, *Buffalo Creek*, 136.

68. Interview with Edgar H. Brenner, October 24, 2002; Interview with William Rogers, July 2, 2002.

69. Kalman interview with Frances Arnold and Thurman W. Arnold Jr.; Interview with Elena Pearson Arnold, July 2, 2003.

70. Kalman interview with G. Duane Vieth.

71. Kalman interview with Frances Arnold and Thurman W. Arnold Jr.; Interview with Frances Arnold Stern, January 9, 2003; Abell, *Diaries*, 36, 59, 82.

72. Walton Hamilton to Frances Arnold, May 19, 1953, Walton Hamilton Collection, Rare and Special Collections, Tarlton Law Library, University of Texas at Austin, Box J26, Folder 1.

73. Interview with Elena Pearson Arnold, July 18, 2003.

74. Interview with Frances Arnold Stern, January 9, 2003; Interview with Barbara Hauer Oliver, September 16, 2002.

75. Interview with Drew Arnold, December 19, 2002; Interview with Joe Arnold, March 19, 2002.

76. Interview with Frances Arnold Stern, January 9, 2003; Interview with Joe Arnold, March 19, 2002.

77. Interview with Joe Arnold, March 19, 2002.

NOTES TO CHAPTER 10

1. Victor Kramer, ed., *Selections from the Letters and Legal Papers of Thurman Arnold* (Washington, D.C.: Merkle Press, 1961), 17–18, 27–28.

2. Letters to Stuart A. Rice, July 28, 1966, AHC Box 44; to Robert B. Goldman, April 30, 1969, AHC Box 45.

3. Interview with Edgar H. Brenner, October 24, 2002.

4. Letters to Henry Robbins, June 7, 1962, AHC Box 42, File 1; to Francis Biddle, September 20, 1965, in Gressley, *Voltaire,* 460.

5. Jeannette E. Hopkins to Thurman Arnold, December 18, 1962, AHC, Box 42, File 1; Letter from Marguerite O'Brien to Philo Calhoun, January 11, 1963, Box 42, File 2.

6. See, e.g. Joseph Featherstone, "The Machiavelli of the New Deal," *New Republic,* August 7, 1965, 22; Arthur Miller, "Book Review," *American University Law Review* 15 (1965):160; James H. O'Keefe, "Book Reviews," *North Dakota Law Review* 42 (1965–1966):248; "Review," *New Jersey Bar Journal* 10 (1966):1568.

7. Fortas interview with Joe B. Frantz, August 14, 1969.

8. Letter to David T. Bazelon, June 11, 1962, AHC, Box 42, File 2.

9. Diamond, *Practice,* 9; Letters to the *Washington Post,* March 20, 1966 E7; to Norman Thomas, June 28, 1963, AHC, Box 42, File 2; to the *Washington Post,* February 27, 1964, AHC, Box 42, File 3; to Vermont Royster, June 22, 1964, AHC, Box 42, File 3.

10. Letters to James Lawrence Fly, March 14, 1953, Kramer, *Selections,* 77–81; to Herbert Monte Levy, October 29, 1953, Kramer, *Selections,* 81–83; Letter to Melvin Wulf, August 30, 1966, AHC, Box 44; Letter to John de J. Pemberton Jr., September 7, 1966, reprinted in Gressley, *Voltaire,* 466.

11. Letter to Melvin Wulf, November 9, 1966, AHC, Box 44.

12. Thurman Arnold, "The Growth of Awareness: Our Nation's Laws and Law among Nations," *International Law* 1 (1967):534, 538–39.

13. Ibid., 544.

14. Scott Smith, "The Old Trustbuster," Sunday Magazine, *The Washington Star* 7 (June 13, 1965).

15. Rexford Tugwell to Arnold, May 17, 1967, AHC, Box 44; Mrs. William P. Gilmore to Thurman Arnold, May 3, 1967, AHC, Box 44; James A. Skardon, Literary Associates, Inc., to Thurman Arnold, May 16, 1967, AHC, Box 44.

16. Interview with Robert Herzstein, January 4, 2002; Interview with Frances Arnold Stern, January 9, 2003.

17. Letter to Ernest Gruening, June 27, 1967, reprinted in Gressley, *Voltaire,* 472.

18. Interview with William Rogers, July 2, 2002.

19. *Washington Daily News,* March 9, 1966.

20. "Antitrust, Then and Now—A Reminiscence," Speech of Thurman Arnold at the Annual Dinner of the Antitrust Law Section of the New York State Bar Association, Wednesday, January 24, 1968, Hotel Commodore, New York City.

21. Letter to John de J. Pemberton Jr., May 27, 1968, AHC, Box 45.

22. Letter to John de J. Pemberton Jr., June 6, 1968, Box 45.

23. Letter to Roger Baldwin, October 29, 1968, AHC, Box 45.

24. Letter to Orville Freeman, May 3, 1968, AHC, Box 45.

25. Letter to Robert W. McKisson and George R. Lindblom May 27, 1968, AHC, Box 45.

26. Letter to Edward H. Levi, December 11, 1968, Series II, Subseries 2, Box 12, Folder 1, Edward H. Levi Papers.

27. Interview with Joseph Califano, January 7, 2004.

28. Letter to Stanley Zimmerman, February 24, 1969, AHC, Box 45; Letter to Robert P. Goldman, February 24, 1969, AHC, Box 45; Letter to Paul Montgomery, February 25, 1969, AHC, Box 45.

29. Letter to Abraham Ribicoff, April 3, 1969, reprinted in Gressley, *Voltaire,* 480.

30. Letter to Julian Sturtevant, July 1, 1969, reprinted in Gressley, *Voltaire,* 482. The letter to Professor Sturtevant was widely circulated, and Arnold received congratulatory letters from Lewis Powell, Lloyd Cutler, and other leaders in the bar; Letter to Nathan M. Pusey, April 14, 1969, reprinted in Gressley, *Voltaire,* 481.

31. Kalman, *Fortas,* 336–42; Joseph A. Califano Jr., *Inside: A Public and Private Life* (New York: Public Affairs 2004), 192–93.

32. Kalman, *Fortas,* 370–76; Diamond, *Practice,* 277–281.

33. Interview with Edgar H. Brenner, October 24, 2002; Letter to Lawrence Kiplinger, May 26, 1969.

34. Califano, *Inside,* 192–93; Interview with Edgar H. Brenner, October 24, 2002; Interview with Robert Herzstein, January 4, 2002; Kalman interview with Milton Freeman, June 23, 1989.

35. Califano, *Inside,* 192.

36. Marguerite O'Brien to Alan D. Harper, February 5, 1970, AHC, Box 45.

37. Undated letter from Frances Arnold to Kate and Ed Levi, Series II, Subseries 2, Box 12, Folder 1, Edward H. Levi Papers.

38. William Douglas, Memorial Service for Thurman Arnold, (November 20, 1969):12.

39. Fowler Hamilton, "Thurman Wesley Arnold," *Memorial Book*, The Association of the Bar of the City of New York, 1970:8.

NOTES TO THE EPILOGUE

1. At an altitude of more than 7,000 feet, this is of course a truthful statement.

2. Gerald M. Stern, *The Buffalo Creek Disaster* (New York: Vintage, 1976).

Index

AAA (Agricultural Adjustment Act), 54, 57, 64, 80, 192
Abrams v. United States, 120
Acheson, Dean, 188
ACLU (American Civil Liberties Union), 69, 145, 149, 185–186, 191–192
ACTION (Alumni Committee to Involve Ourselves Now), 194
Adams, Follansbee, Hawley & Shorey, 20–22
Administrative agencies, 48, 81
Agger, Carolyn, 172
Agricultural Adjustment Act (AAA), 54, 57, 64, 80, 192
Agricultural Adjustment Administration: boss of, 113; Fortas and, 127, 128; Frank and, 113, 126; New Deal, 79; Porter and, 127; TA on, 56
Alcoa, 93–94, 105, 113, 235n122
Alsop, Joseph, 49, 99–100
Aluminum industry, 80
Alumni Committee to Involve Ourselves Now (ACTION), 194
AMA (American Medical Association), 95–96, 100
American Bar Association Journal, 99
American Civil Liberties Union (ACLU), 69, 145, 149, 185–186, 191–192

American Law Institute, 42, 50
American Medical Association (AMA), 95–96, 100
American Mercury (magazine), 99, 120
Americans for Democratic Action, 187
Anti-Communism, 28
Anti-war movement, 28
Antitrust Division (of the Department of Justice), 78–112; administrative agencies, 81; as backwater of the Justice Department, 80; budget, 86, 87, 88, 109; caseload, 87; Clark (Tom) and, 87; enforcement activities (*see* antitrust enforcement); goal, 80; investigations, number of, 87; Jackson and, 64, 77, 80, 97, 105; large business, 85; Levi and, 106; low-hanging fruit, 84; proposed conduct, 86; regional offices, 87; staff, 87, 109, 231n46; TA and, 1, 64, 78–112; Transportation Section, 121; war effort, 106–107; Wiprud and, 121
Antitrust enforcement: in 1920s, 79, 83–84; Alcoa, 93–94, 105, 113, 235n122; aluminum industry, 80; AMA investigation, 95–96, 100; *Appalachian Coals v. United States*, 80; Associated Press (AP),

251

252 | Index

Antitrust enforcement (*Continued*) 102–103, 105, 170; automobile industry, 80, 91–92; bar associations, 95, 232n76; "bottlenecks," 92; cartels, 110; case-by-case method, 85; codes of fair competition, 79–80, 83; consent decrees, 85–86, 92; construction industry, 93; dairy/milk industry, 92–93, 100; damage awards, 158; D.C. Medical Society, 96; Douglas (William) and, 97–98; FBI agents in, 95; First Amendment, 103; free market competition, 79; glass container market, 91, 99; Great Depression, 102; Hartford-Empire Company, 91, 99; housing industry, 93; insurance industry, 96; Kennedy administration, 184–185; labor unions, 103–105; length and size of cases, 105; local firms, 96; mandate for, 110; mergers and acquisitions, 105–106; motion picture industry, 92; New Deal, 79; NRA, 83–84, 85, 106; oil industry, 96–98, 100; overseas, 94, 109–110; patents, 90, 98–99, 107, 117–118; peach industry, 128; press leaks, 107; price-fixing, 96–98, 109, 110, 190; railroads, 109; Roosevelt (Franklin) and, 78, 80, 88, 89; rubber market, 107–108; Second Circuit, 94, 101, 105; Seventh Circuit, 100; TA on, 102; TA's first exposure to, 31; threat of indictment, 86; TNEC, 88–91, 105–106; tobacco industry, 105; war planning and production, 106–109; World War I, 79
Antitrust laws: District of Columbia, 232n73; oil industry case, 97–98; TA on, 69–70, 78, 82–83, 157–158, 191

AP (Associated Press), 102–103, 105, 170
Appalachian Coals v. United States, 80, 98
Arizona, Miranda v., 185
Arnell, Ellis, 152
Arnold, C. P. (Constantine Peter, TA's father): Arnold (Frances) and, 25, 26, 36, 181; business interests/connections, 20; cars, 11; Christian name, 9; death, 115; Democratic Party, 9; estate, 115; homestead allotments, 29; Laramie home, 10; law practice, 9, 28, 33; Millbrook ranch, 9, 30; Mondell and, 9, 24; occupations, 9; older brothers, 9; oratorical skills, 9; poems by, 181; property tax exemption, 29; reputation as lawyer, 33; TA and, 20, 22–23, 28, 181; TA's letters to, 16, 18–19, 23, 44; University of Wyoming law school, 199; Wabash College, 9; Wyoming Congressional election (1898), 24; Wyoming State Bar Association, 9, 21
Arnold, Carl (TA's brother): father's will, 115; law practice, 36; military service, 24, 36; Princeton, 17, 24; TA and, 17; West Virginia University College of Law, 41; Wyoming law faculty, 37, 41, 200; Yale University, 37
Arnold, Elena Pearson (TA's daughter-in-law), 169, 177, 178, 180
Arnold, Fortas & Porter, 127–160, 172–176; ACLU, 145; Bailey and, 138; *Bailey v. Richardson*, 133–138, 140; banana industry, 128; Black and, 173; Christmas party, 174, 184; Cinema Amusements, 156–158; Clark (Charles)

and, 173; clients, 152, 155–156, 160; decision to not represent admitted Communists, 149–150; defending homosexuals and Communists, 148; Diamond and, 174; Douglas (William) and, 173; Ferrar case, 144–145; Fifth Amendment, invocation of, 150; first woman associate, 172; Fort Monmouth ten, 140; Fortas and, 148, 152, 172, 173, 174, 183–184; founding, 125–126; growth, 172–173; Hellman case, 145; Johnson (Lyndon) and, 155; loyalty cases, 130–150, 173; luncheons, 174; Madden and, 146; most important unofficial client, 153; office location, 143, 173; partners' offices, 173–174; partners' styles, 128–129; *Peters v. Hobby*, 138–140; *Playboy* defense, 158–159; Porter (Paul) and, 126–127, 147–148, 172, 174, 184; Pound's release from Saint Elizabeth's, 166–169; pro bono work, 133, 143–144, 147, 150; profit-sharing, 172–173; Reich and, 163; renamed Arnold & Porter, 184; reputation, 150, 173; Rodale Press, 160; Screen Writers Guild, 150; subcontracting cases, 146; Supreme Court appeals, 159; TA's role, 155–160, 166–169, 174–176; TA stories, 175–176; as targets of investigation, 148; Texas Senate primary race (1948), 153–155; typical loyalty case clients, 145

Arnold, Frances (née Longan, TA's wife): Arnold (C. P.) and, 25, 26, 36, 181; child rearing, 177; color-blindness, 176; courtship of, 25; daughter-in-law, 178; as "Deedee," 178–180; Douglas (William) and, 64–65; elopement and marriage, 24–26; father, 26; Fortas and, 197–198; French accent, 25; in Georgia, 26; Hogg (Ima) and, 25; Hollins College, 24, 26; in Laramie (Wyoming), 29, 30, 37, 38; longevity, 199; mother, 26, 219n33; Patterson ("Cissy") and, 170; preferred name, 24; schooling, 24–25; as seamstress, 176; sister, 24–25; TA on, 25; TA's death, 197–198, 199; TA's letters to, 26–27; in Virginia, 26, 114; in Washington, D.C., 178; on West Virginia University law faculty, 44; Woodruff and, 29

Arnold, Franklin Luther (TA's grandfather), 8–9, 10, 216n18, 216n19

Arnold, George (TA's son): birth, 36; marriage, 169, 180; military service, 115; Pearson (Drew) and, 177, 179–180; Wyoming law faculty, 37, 200

Arnold, George, Jr. (TA's grandson), 37, 189, 200

Arnold, Patterson & Arnold, 30, 33–36

Arnold, Thurman ("TA" elsewhere)
– **antitrust enforcement:** first exposure to, 31. *See also* Antitrust Division
– **appearance:** clothes, 48–49, 174–175, 176; physical appearance, 127
– **birth,** 10
– **cars owned by,** 85, 100, 176
– **childhood/early life,** 10–11
– **clients:** Chesapeake & Ohio Railroad, 152; Cinema Amusements, 156–158; Coca Cola Company, 125, 151; Cyrus Eaton, 124, 156,

Arnold, Thurman (*Continued*)
160; German clients, 160; Howard (Dave), 37–38; Justice Department, 64; loss of Wyoming clients, 33; loyalty to, 140; McLean estate, 170–171; Otis & Company, 124, 152; *Playboy*, 158–159; Pound (Ezra), 166–169; Reo Automobile company, 21; Rodale Press, 160; typical clients, 155–156; United States Supreme Court, 75
– **compared to:** Colman, 83; a cowboy, 100; Fields, 77; Frank, 116, 123; Frankfurter, 59; Hemingway, 159; Hitler, 100; Hook, 74; Hoover (J. Edgar), 87, 171; an idiot in a powder mill, 103, 188; a madman, 100; Marx Brothers, 109; Marx (Groucho), 77; Mencken, 76; Rabelais, 100; a store clerk, 100; Veblen, 77; Voltaire, 100
– **court venues:** state courts, 35; United States Supreme Court, 64, 75, 81, 96, 99, 137, 159; Wyoming Supreme Court, 35–36
– **death,** 63, 197–199
– **Democratic Party,** 30
– **education:** *Harvard Law Review*, 16; Harvard Law School, 13–17, 38; high school, 11; Latin classes, 22; Phi Beta Kappa, 12, 17; Princeton University, 12–14; Reserve Officers' Training Corps (ROTC), 11; University of Wyoming, 11; Wabash College, 11–12, 217n34
– **elopement and marriage,** 24–26
– **family:** brothers (*see* Arnold, Carl); cook, 178; daughter-in-law, 177, 178, 180; dog, 49; father (*see* Arnold, C. P.); father-in-law, 26; grandfather, 8–9, 10, 216n18, 216n19; grandmother, 8–9, 216n19, 216n21; grandmother's brother, 8; grandson, 37, 189, 200; mother, 17, 23, 25, 27, 115; mother-in-law, 26; sister-in-law, 24–25; sons (*see* Arnold, George; Arnold, Thurman, Jr.); uncles, 13, 216n21; wife (*see* Arnold, Frances)
– **FBI investigation of,** 148
– **finances:** investments, 41–42; retainers, 152; salary, 41, 45, 85; wealth, 68; Yale University Law School, 44, 64
– **government service:** Agricultural Adjustment Administration, 56; Antitrust Division of Justice Department (*see* Antitrust Division); brain trust, 78; D.C. Circuit court of appeals (*see* D.C. Circuit court of appeals); Laramie mayor, 31–33, 37; part-time service, 64; Philippines administration, 64; SEC, 64; Tax Division of Justice Department, 78; Treasury Department, 78; Wyoming House of Representatives, 30–31
– **health:** cut tendon, 197; heart problems, 24, 182, 183, 192–193, 197
– **hobbies,** 177
– **homes/residences:** burglars, 189–190; Chicago, 19–23; homesteading, 29; Lafayette House (Alexandria, Virginia), 176, 179; Laramie (Wyoming), 1, 8, 10, 11–12, 28–38, 44, 114–115; McLean (Virginia), 114; Morgantown (West Virginia), 44; New Haven (Connecticut), 64, 65, 77, 114; Summerhill estate (near Arlington, Virginia), 114, 176,

177–178, 179; Washington, D.C., 64, 65
- honors: arbitrator on international investment disputes, 190; Arnold Street (Laramie), 190; seventieth birthday celebrations, 181; Thurman Arnold Building (Washington, D.C.), 200
- intellectual interests: bureaucracies and administrative agencies, 48; government regulation of the economy, 48; international law, 186; natural science, 76; psychology, 50; regulatory side of law, 48; symbolic functions of law, 48, 50
- judgeship of D.C. Circuit court of appeals, 112–123
- as "Judgie," 123, 178–180
- law firms/legal practices: Adams, Follansbee, Hawley & Shorey, 20–22; Arnold, Fortas & Porter, 155–160, 166–169, 174–176; Arnold, Patterson & Arnold (family law practice), 28, 30, 33–36; Arnold & Fortas, 125–126; Arnold & Porter, 196–197; challenging governments/powerful interests, 36; divorce cases, 17; Harvard Legal Aid Society, 21; legal clinic, 17–18; O'Bryan, Waite & Arnold, 22–23; pro bono work, 1
- legal opinions written/concurred/dissented by: *Bailey v. Zlotnick*, 116; *De Marcos v. Overholser*, 118–119; *Esquire v. Walker*, 119–121, 158; *James Heddon's Sons v. Coe*, 116; *Monsanto Chemical Co. v. Coe*, 117–118; *Reeves v. Bowles*, 121; *Special Equipment Co. v. Coe*, 117–118; *Walker v. Popenoe*, 119; *Williams v. United States*, 238n19. See also Appendix A
- legal profession: Connecticut procedures, 42, 47; empirical studies of procedure, 42, 47, 52; legal statistics, 47–48; main blemish on his record, 103; use of FBI agents as data gatherers, 95; West Virginia procedural reform, 42–43; Wickersham Study, 47
- legal realism, 16, 46–48, 50, 52, 59, 60. See also Folklore of Capitalism; Symbols of Government
- letters/correspondence: collection of, 2, 181; to editor of *Washington Post*, 185; to his father, 16, 18–19, 23, 44; to his wife, 25–26; to a tie company, 34–35; World War I letters home, 27
- military service, 23, 24, 26–28
- opinions (his) of: admitted Communists, 149; Agricultural Adjustment Act, 54; Agricultural Adjustment Administration, 56; analyzing the good life, 74; anti-Communism, 28; anti-war movement, 28; antitrust enforcement, 102; antitrust laws, 69–70, 78, 82–83, 157–158, 191; bad decisions, 57; baseball, 16; the best time to get married, 25; bureaucracies, 57; business, 66–67; capitalism, 82; cartels, 85; Caruso, 16; civil liberties, 191–192; Civil Rights Act, 185; civil trials, 55–56; Coca Cola Company, 151; Communist Party – USA, 149; corporate reorganization, 70–71; courts, 57, 84–85; creeds/myths, 66–68, 70; criminal trials, 54–55; critics of the New Deal, 54–59; dissent, 186–187; economic colonization of the West,

Arnold, Thurman (*Continued*)
33–34, 151; economic competition, 3, 70, 78, 84; economic planning, 78, 102; economics, 58; economists, 190; expert testimony, 55; fair trials, 55, 56; First Amendment, 143; Ford, 243n1; free speech, 3; freedom of action, 191–192; government, 51, 58, 66–67, 72; government censorship, 119–121; groups uncurbed by legal authority, 103; habeas corpus, 118; Hart's critique of the Supreme Court, 162–166, 186; his academic skills, 43; his father, 18–19; his wife, 25, 26; inconsistency in law, 50; independent thought, 132; international law, 187; Jewish students taking bar exam, 21; judges, 122; labor unions, 103–105, 150, 188; Laramie (Wyoming), 10, 12, 18; law, 52–53, 58; law enforcement, 55–56, 84–85; legal realists, 52; legal statistics, 47–48; legal theory, 52; loyalty program (Truman's), 132, 137, 141, 147, 159; minor political parties, 185–186; misuse of power, 3; monopolies, 85, 99, 102; Morgantown (West Virginia), 44; myths/creeds, 66–68, 70; Nader, 193–194; nepotism, 177; NRA, 54, 57, 84; obscenity, 119; patriotism, 28; personification of the corporation, 69–70; poor people, 192–193; price controls, 84, 108; price-fixing, 102; Princeton University, 12–13; principles, 51–52, 53, 55, 73; private enterprise, 57; private property, 67–68; production quotas, 84; Prohibition, 32, 56, 81; public works, 53–54; Roosevelt (Franklin), 79, 80; secondary boycotts, 104; Securities and Exchange Act, 54; Sherman Act, 84, 85, 112; social sciences, 51; Social Security Act, 54; Springfield (Illinois), 21; state law schools, 40–41; Supreme Court, 82; symbols, 51–52; taxation (public and private), 70–72; TNEC, 91; Vietnam War, 28, 188; wealth, 68; Wyoming, 38

– opinions (others of him/his work): Acheson's, 188; AFL general counsel's, 105; Bingaman's, 110; Burger's, 188; Diamond's, 49; Douglas's (Paul), 188; Douglas's (William), 122, 198; Fortas's, 123, 129; his antitrust efforts, 109, 110; his antitrust suits against labor unions, 105; his contribution to modern jurisprudence, 59, 198; his Court of Appeals tenure, 122; his D.C. Circuit court judgeship, 109, 123; his encounter with Borah, 82; his personality, 43, 111, 123, 129, 173, 198; his radicalism, 148; his teaching skills, 49; his Valparaiso speech, 188; his workaholism, 176–177; Humphrey's, 188; Jackson's, 111; Johnson's (Lyndon), 188; Kampelman's, 188; Laski's, 59; Lerner's, 82; McCormick's (Robert), 188; Pearson's (Drew), 109, 123; Reno's, 110; Rill's, 110; Shenefield's, 110; Stern's, 173; Stone's (I. F.), 148; Thurman Jr.'s, 177; Tugwell's, 109, 188; Vanderbilt's, 188; Warren's (Earl), 188; West Virginia University College of Law colleague's, 43

– organizational relationships: ACLU, 185–186, 191–192; ACTION, 194; American Business

Congress, 99; American Law Institute, 50; Americans for Democratic Action, 187; Cosmos Club, 175; Elks Club, 100; FBI, 148, 171; Institute for Policy Studies, 189; National Citizens for Humphrey Committee, 192; National Lawyers Guild, 149, 192; New Haven Hunt Club, 65; Potter Law Club, 37; Rockefeller Foundation, 47; Senate National Defense Committee, 107; Senate Patent Committee, 107; Sisters of the Centurion, 32–33; TNEC, 90–91, 182; West Virginia Bar Association, 42

– personal relationships with: Arnell, 152; Arnold (C. P., his father), 20, 22–23, 28, 181; Arnold (Carl, his brother), 17; Berge, 87; Biddle, 105, 183; Black, 127, 172; Bone, 107; Borah, 81–83; Burger, 139; Califano, 193; Caruso, 17; Clark (Charles), 39, 41, 43–44, 45, 47, 59, 65; Clark (Tom), 87, 121–122, 159–160, 190; Cook, 41; Dabney, 161; Diamond, 125, 175; Donovan, 97; Douglas (William), 45, 47, 48, 63, 65, 97, 112, 113, 127, 172; Fortas, 21, 65, 121, 125–126, 127, 128, 129, 172, 174, 189, 197–198; Frank, 65, 123, 192; Frankfurter, 65, 113, 139, 162; Freeman, 125; Goldberg, 156; Green, 41; Griffin, 183; Gruening, 139; Hamilton, 125, 177; Hart, 162–163; Howard, 37, 41, 42; Jackson, 64, 77, 87, 111, 113; James, 61–62; Johnson (Lyndon), 181, 190; Kramer, 48; Lerner, 63; Levi, 87, 107–108; Llewellyn, 43; Maverick, 152; McCormick (Charles), 43; Mencken, 121; Miller, 124, 125; Murphy, 64, 104, 111, 113; O'Brien, 114, 124, 125, 163, 190; O'Mahoney, 36, 81, 82, 112, 113–114, 142; Patterson ("Cissy"), 127, 169–170, 234n107; Patterson ("Cissy") and, 102–103; Pearson (Drew), 99, 127; Porter (Paul), 127, 198; Pound (Ezra), 119; Pound (Roscoe), 37–38; Reich, 68; Robinson, 51; Roosevelt (Franklin), 77, 78, 109, 111–112, 113; Stern, 34, 173, 176; Sturges, 65; Thayer, 18; Truman, 107, 122, 170; Turner (John), 43–44; White, 156; witnesses to his marriage, 25; Woodruff, 151–152; Youngdahl, 158

– personality: accomplishments, 2; ambitiousness, 18, 20; bad driver, 176; big picture conceptualist, 128; car pooler, 176; comedian, 77; confidence-builder, 182; conservatism, 186–189; cynic, 77; dislike of pomposity, 2; drinker, 182; East Coast polish, 17; forgetfulness, 25, 32; genius or its equivalent, 128; as grandfather, 178–180; his one true professional love, 111; homesickness for the West, 13, 38; humor/wit, 2, 32, 34–35, 50, 116, 120, 181, 190; imaginativeness, 175–176; ironist, 76–77; lack of interest in sports, 16–17; lavish in praise, 128; liberalism, 148, 180, 185–189, 201; love of cigars, 16, 49, 175, 176, 189; love of opera, 17; loyalty, 140, 189; pessimism, 193; prankster, 160–161; preference for partisan argument rather than impartial decision, 122; preference for talking rather than listening, 123; radicalism, 77, 148;

Arnold, Thurman (*Continued*)
renown, 112; salesmanship, 86–87; sarcasm, 18, 25, 120; self-promotion, 86, 99, 183; sense of decorum, 139; smoker, 182; social bonds of students, 16; social critic, 76; walker, 182; workaholic, 176–177
– **political campaigns:** run for Wyoming prosecuting attorney (1924), 37
– **popularity of,** 87
– **press coverage of,** 99–100
– **press leaks by,** 107
– **speeches:** about not playing with chorus girls, 63–64; to American Business Congress, 99; collection of, 181; farewell speech to Antitrust Division, 112; to Legal Aid Society, 173; to New York State Bar Association, 190, 192; to Sisters of the Centurion, 32–33; "The Man from Mexico," 23; University of Wyoming commencement address, 38, 114; at Valparaiso University, 186–189; in Wyoming House of Representatives, 30–31
– **teaching career:** Cambridge University, 183; co-teaching, 129; English to Italian immigrants, 21–22; law school at night, 22; offers rejected, 45; teaching skills, 48–49, 76; teaching style, 49; University of Wyoming College of Law, 36–37; West Virginia University College of Law, 37–44; Yale University Law School, 43–50, 62–65, 68, 77, 101, 129
– **travels:** Coronado Island, 193; Europe, 13, 190; Majorca, 183
– **writings about:** *Buffalo Creek Disaster* (Stern), 1, 176; *Voltaire and the Cowboy* (Gressley), 2. See also Appendix C
– **writings by:** autobiography/memoirs, 182–183; book reviews, 42, 192; *Bottlenecks of Business*, 101–102, 106; casebook of trials and appeals, 61–62; course notes, 42; early Yale articles, 13; *Fair Fights and Foul*, 183; fees for, 121; *Folklore of Capitalism* (see *Folklore of Capitalism*); in *Harper's Magazine*, 146; "How Not to Get Investigated: Ten Commandments for Government Employees," 146–147; *Jingles, Jeers and Jeremiads*, 182; in law reviews, 50, 76; life experience in, 76; "London," 13; in miscellaneous magazines, 99; in *Nassau Literary Magazine*, 13; poem about Conflict of Laws class, 14–15; *Professor Hart's Theology*, 163–166; royalties, 62, 73; style, 51, 58, 60, 71, 159; *Symbols of Government* (see *Symbols of Government*); "The Prairie," 13; "The Wanderlust," 13; in *University of Chicago Law Review*, 75; in *West Virginia Law Quarterly*, 42, 50; "Why Women Marry," 13. See also Appendix B

Arnold, Thurman, Jr. ("Turno," TA's son): birth, 36; as infant, 29; military service, 115; on TA, 177; TA's heart attack, 183
Arnold & Fortas, 125–126
Arnold & Porter (previously Arnold, Fortas & Porter), 194–197, 200–201; corporate clients, 200–201; Diamond and, 240n7; Fortas's nomination as chief justice, 194–196; Fortas's return to,

196–197; General Motors, 193–194; Johnson (Lyndon) and, 189; memoir about, 240n7; offices of, 200; Porter (Paul) and, 184, 195–196; pro bono work, 200; size, 200; TA's role, 196–197; tobacco industry, 194
Arnold & Wiprud, 124–125
Associated Press (AP), 102–103, 105, 170
Association of the Bar of the City of New York, 198
Atlantic (magazine), 99
Auden, W. H., 167
Automobile industry, 80, 91–92

Bad decisions, 57
Bailey, Dorothy, 133–138
Bailey v. Richardson, 133–138, 140
Bailey v. Zlotnick, 116
Baldwin, Roger, 69
Baltimore Sun (newspaper), 81
Banana industry, 128
Baruch, Bernard, 79
Beale, Joseph, 14–15
Bentham, Jeremy, 73
Berge, Wendell, 87
Berle, Adolph, 78, 79
Biddle, Francis, 105, 121, 155, 183
Bingaman, Anne, 110
Bingham, Alfred, 73
Black, Hugo: Arnold, Fortas & Porter, 173; Associated Press suit, 103; *Bailey v. Richardson*, 137; celebrity of, 179; Johnson (Lyndon) and, 155; nomination to Supreme Court, 81; *Peters v. Hobby*, 140; Reich and, 163; Roosevelt (Franklin) and, 81; Senator, 113; TA and, 127, 172; Texas Senate primary race (1948), 154–155
Blair, Frank, 31

Board of Economic Warfare, 106–107
Board of Education, Brown v., 162, 185
Bone, Homer, 107, 118
Boomerang (newspaper), 30
Borah, William, 70, 81–83, 89
"Bottlenecks," 92
Bottlenecks of Business (Arnold), 101–102, 106
Bowles, Reeves v., 121
Brandeis, Louis, 59, 113
Brandenburg v. Ohio, 120
Brenner, Edgar, 170–171, 175, 176, 182
Brinkley, Alan, 84
Brooks, Rupert, 27
Brown v. Board of Education, 162, 185
Brownell, Herbert, 166
Buffalo Creek Disaster (Stern), 1, 176
Bureaucracies, 48, 57
Burger, Warren, 139, 188, 195, 198
Burke, Edward, 81
Burton, Harold Hitz, 140
Bush, George H. W., 110
Business, 66–67
Butler, Pierce, 173
Byrnes, James Francis, 94

Calhoun, Philo, 181–182
Califano, Joseph, 193, 197, 198
Cambridge University, 183
Capitalism, 82
Capone, Al, 55
Cardozo, Benjamin, 59
Caro, Robert, 153, 154
Cartels, 85, 110
Caruso, Enrico, 17
Cary, Joseph, 7
Cavers, David, 39
Chaplin, Charlie, 92
Chesapeake & Ohio Railroad, 152

Chesterton, G. K., 13
Cheyenne (Wyoming), 6–7
Chiang Kai-shek, 141
Chicago, 19–23
Chicago Bar Association, 21
Chicago Daily News (newspaper), 22
Chicago Sun (newspaper), 102, 170
Chicago Tribune (newspaper), 102, 169, 170, 188
Chorus girls, 63–64
Chrysler Corporation, 92
Cincinnati Enquirer (newspaper), 170, 182
Cinema Amusements, 156–158
Civil Aeronautics Board, 87
Civil liberties, 119–121, 191–192
Civil Rights Act, 185
Civil Service Commission, 131
Civil trials, 55–56
Clark, Charles: Arnold, Fortas & Porter, 173; Connecticut study, 43; empirical studies of procedure, 47; Hart and, 162–163; *Peters v. Hobby*, 139; Second Circuit appeals court, 101, 113; TA and, 39, 41, 43–44, 45, 47, 59, 65; Yale University Law School, 39, 43, 45
Clark, Tom, 87, 121–122, 137–138, 159–160, 190
Clayton Act, 91, 105–106
Clifford, Clark, 195
Coca Cola Company, 125, 151, 155
Coe, James Heddon's Sons v., 116
Coe, Monsanto Chemical Co. v., 117–118
Coe, Special Equipment Co. v., 117–118
Coffin, William Sloane, 189, 191
Cohen, Ben, 88, 154
Cohen, Felix, 60
Cohen, Morris, 59–60

Collier's (magazine), 100
Colman, Ronald, 83
Columbia Law School, 14, 45, 46, 89
Commager, Henry Steele, 187
Commerce Department, 89–90
Commercial law, 45
Common Sense (magazine), 99
Communist Party – USA, 149
Communists, 149–150
Communists, distinctive speech patterns of, 147
Congressional Record (newspaper), 188
Connecticut, 42, 43, 47
Consent decrees, 85–86, 92, 107
Construction industry, 93
Contract law, 45
Cook, Walter Wheeler, 41
Coolidge, Calvin, 94
Coral Gables (Florida), 72
Corbin, Arthur, 45
Corcoran, Tommy, 153, 154
Corporate reorganization, 70–71
Corporations: personification of, 69–70
Corwin, E. S., 13
Cosmopolitan (magazine), 121
Cosmos Club, 175
Countryman, Vern, 139
Courts, 57, 84–85
Cox, Hugh, 154, 198
Creeds, 66–68
Criminal trials, 54–55
Cummings, e. e., 166
Cummings, Homer, 81, 87, 88, 92, 95
Cyrus Eaton, 124, 156, 160

Dabney, Lewis, 161, 172
Daily News (New York newspaper), 144
Dairy/milk industry, 92–93, 100
Darwin, Charles, 73

D.C. Circuit court of appeals, 112–123; assigned judges, 115; *Bailey v. Richardson,* 135–136; cases heard, 115–116; civil liberties, 119–121; *Esquire v. Walker,* 119–121; insanity defense, 118–119; opinions, 115; patents, 116–118; presidential patronage, 113; senatorial prerogative, 113; TA's judgeship, 112–123; *Walker v. Popenoe,* 119

D.C. Medical Society, 96

De Marcos v. Overholser, 118–119

"Deedee," 178–180

Democratic Party, 9, 30

Diamond, Norman: Arnold, Fortas & Porter, 152, 174; Arnold & Fortas, 125; Arnold & Porter, 240n7; on TA, 49; TA and, 175

Dissent, 186–187

Donovan, William "Wild Bill," 97

Douglas, Paul, 188

Douglas, William (Bill): antitrust enforcement, 97–98; Arnold, Fortas & Porter, 173; Arnold (Frances) and, 64–65; *Bailey v. Richardson,* 137; celebrity of, 179; citations of own work, 65, 116; empirical studies of procedure, 47; Fortas and, 63, 126, 195; Frank and, 231n54; government service, 64; influence on Roosevelt administration, 111; lifetime honorarium, 195; New Deal, 89; oil industry case, 97–98; *Peters v. Hobby,* 140; regulatory side of law, 48; SEC, 89, 126, 231n54; Supreme Court, 111; on TA, 122; TA and, 45, 47, 48, 63, 65, 97, 112, 113, 127, 172; TA's death, 198; TNEC, 89, 231n54; Yale University Law School, 45, 46, 48

Dowd, Irvin v., 164

Duffy (TA's dog), 49

Dun's Review, 184

Economic competition, 3, 70, 79, 84

Economic planning, 78, 102, 127

Economics, 58

Economists, 190

Edgerton, Henry W., 135–136

Eicher, Edward C., 89

Eisenhower, Dwight David, 172

Eliot, T. S., 166, 167

Elks Club, 100

Encyclopedia Britannica, 94

Escobedo v. Illinois, 185

Esquire (magazine), 119–121

Esquire v. Walker, 119–121, 158

Ethyl Gasoline Corp. v. United States, 99

European Economic Community, 111

Executive Order 9835, 131

Expert testimony, 55

Fair Fights and Foul (Arnold), 183

Fair trials, 55, 56

Fairbanks, Douglas, 92

Farouk (King of Egypt), 171

FBI (Federal Bureau of Investigation), 95, 134–135, 148, 171

FCC (Federal Communication Commission), 81, 127, 152

Federal Communication Commission (FCC), 81, 127, 152

Federal Trade Commission (FTC), 81, 89

Ferrar, Jose, 144–145

Field, Marshall, 102

Fields, W. C., 77

Fifth Amendment, 150

First Amendment, 103, 143

First Restatement of Conflicts of Law (Beale), 14

Fish, Stanley, 76
Fitzgerald, F. Scott, 12, 13
Flipper, Henry, 200
Folklore of Capitalism (Arnold), 65–76; argument in, 65–73; Borah in, 82; critical reception, 73–76; Mencken and, 76; Roosevelt (Franklin) and, 78; sales, 82; *Symbols of Government* and, 65, 69, 72; TA's legacy, 65; Veblen and, 76; writing of, 75
Follansbee, George, 21
Follansbee, Mitchell, 21
Ford, Henry, 85, 243n1
Ford Motor Company, 92, 243n1
Fordham, Jeff, 39
Fort Monmouth ten, 140
Fort Sanders (Wyoming), 4, 6
Fort Sheridan (Illinois), 23
Fortas, Abe: academic career, 125–126; Agricultural Adjustment Act, 57, 64, 192; Agricultural Adjustment Administration, 127, 128; appearance, 127; Arnold, Fortas & Porter, 148, 152, 172, 173, 174, 183–184; Arnold & Fortas, 125; Arnold & Porter, 194–197; Arnold (Frances) and, 197–198; Arnold (Thurman, Jr.) on, 177; *Brandenburg v. Ohio*, 239n31; clients, 152, 160; Clifford and, 195; Department of the Interior, 127, 148; Douglas (William) and, 63, 126, 195; economic planning, 127; Ferrar case, 144; Frank and, 126; government service, 127, 148; Hellman case, 145; Ickes and, 126; insanity defense, 238n24; investigation of his organizational memberships, 148; Johnson (Lyndon) and, 63, 153, 155, 183–184, 194; Katzenbach on, 129–130; liberal causes, 148; Nixon administration, 195–196; personality, 125, 128; Porter (Paul) and, 127, 172, 197; Public Works Administration, 126; representation for admitted Communists, 149; SEC, 126; social life, 127; style as litigator, 127–128, 129; Supreme Court, 173, 183–184, 194–196, 239n31; on TA, 123, 129; TA and, 21, 65, 121, 125–126, 127, 128, 129, 172, 174, 189, 197–198; TA's death, 197–198; Texas Senate primary race (1948), 154–155; *United States v. Lattimore*, 141; Wallace and, 127; wife, 172, 197; work to, 177; *Yale Law Journal*, 125; Yale University Law School, 63
Frank, Jerome: Agricultural Adjustment Act, 57, 64; Agricultural Adjustment Administration, 113, 126; brain trust, 78; citations of own work, 116; Douglas (William) and, 231n54; economic planning, 127; Fortas and, 126; SEC, 231n54; Second Circuit appeals court, 113; TA and, 65, 123, 192; TA compared to, 116, 123
Frankfurter, Felix: *Bailey v. Richardson,* 137; brain trust, 78; Hart and, 161, 162; *Peters v. Hobby,* 139; Sacco and Vanzetti, 69; TA and, 65, 113, 139, 162; TA compared to, 59
Free market competition, 79
Freeman, Milton, 125, 132, 134, 139
Fremont, Charles, 4
Frost, Robert, 166–167
FTC (Federal Trade Commission), 81, 89
Fulbright, William, 187

Galbraith, John Kenneth, 187
General Motors, 92
Germany, 110
Gessell, Gerhard, 48–49
Glass container market, 91, 99
Goldberg, Irving, 156
Gone with the Wind (Mitchell), 94
Government, 51, 58, 66–67, 72
Government censorship, 119–121
Grace, Peter, 182
Grant, Cary, 144
Grant, Ulysses S., 7
Great Depression, 30, 102
Great Escape (film), 61
Green, Leon, 41, 45, 46
Greening of America (Reich), 163
Gressley, Eugene, 2, 29, 95, 175–176
Grey, Zane, 7
Griffin, Merv, 183
Gruening, Ernest, 189

Habeas corpus, 118
Hamilton, Walton, 45, 65, 125
Hammarskjöld, Dag, 166
Hand, Augustus, 113
Hand, Learned, 113
Hansen, Clifford, 188
Harlan, John Marshall, II, 139
Harper, Fowler, 139
Harper's Magazine, 146
Harriman, Averell, 109
Harrison, Benjamin, 10
Hart, Henry, 161–166
Hartford-Empire Company, 91, 99
Harvard Law Review, 16, 161
Harvard Law School, 13–17, 38, 45, 46
Harvard Legal Aid Society, 21
Havighurst, Harold, 39
Hawley, Ellis, 79
Hellman, Lillian, 145
Hemingway, Ernest, 159, 166, 167
Henderson, Leon, 90

Hitler, Adolph, 73, 100, 102
Hobby, Peters v., 138–140, 159
Hogg, Ima, 25
Hogg, James, 25
Holliday, Judy, 144
Hollins College, 24, 26
Holmes, Oliver Wendell, 59, 120
Hook, Sidney, 73–74, 75
Hoover, Herbert, 79
Hoover, J. Edgar, 87, 171
Hope diamond, 170, 171, 172
Horn, Tom, 10–11
House Un-American Activities Committee (HUAC), 144, 145, 185
Housing industry, 93
Howard, David (Dave), 37–38, 41, 42
HUAC (House Un-American Activities Committee), 144, 145, 185
Hughes, Charles Evan, Jr., 93
Humphrey, Hubert, 179, 188
Hutcheson, United States v., 105
Hutcheson, William, 104–105

ICC (Interstate Commerce Commission), 81
Ickes, Harold, 80, 126
I.G. Farben, 107–108
Illinois, Escobedo v., 185
Illinois National Guard, 23
Insanity defense, 55, 118–119, 238n24
Institute for Policy Studies, 189
Institute of Pacific Relations (IPR), 141, 142
Insurance industry, 96
Interior Department, 127, 148
International Herald Tribune (newspaper), 188
International law, 186–187
International Lawyer (journal), 188
Interstate Commerce Commission (ICC), 81

IPR (Institute of Pacific Relations), 141, 142
Irvin v. Dowd, 164

Jackson, Robert: Alcoa, 94; Antitrust Division, 64, 77, 80, 97, 105; Assistant Attorney General, 77; *Bailey v. Richardson,* 137; influence on Roosevelt administration, 111; monopolies, 80, 87–88; Richberg and, 88; on Roosevelt (Franklin), 78; solicitor general nomination, 81, 83; Supreme Court, 111; on TA, 100; TA and, 64, 77, 87, 111, 113
James, Fleming, 61–62
James Heddon's Sons v. Coe, 116
Japan, 111
Jingles, Jeers and Jeremiads (Arnold), 182
Johnson, Hugh, 109
Johnson, Lyndon: Arnold, Fortas & Porter, 155; Arnold & Porter, 189; Black and, 155; Fortas and, 63, 153, 155, 183–184, 194; Roosevelt (Franklin) and, 153; TA and, 181, 190; TA's Valparaiso speech, 188; Texas Senate primary race (1948), 153–155; Truman and, 153
Judges, 122
"Judgie," 123, 178–180
Justice Department, 64, 78. *See also* Antitrust Division
Justice in Transportation (Wiprud), 124

Kalman, Laura, 62
Kampelman, Max, 188
Katie (TA's cook), 178
Katzenbach, Nicholas, 61, 129–130, 185
Keller, Helen, 170

Kennedy, John F., 156
King, William H., 81, 82–83, 89
Kinoy, Arthur, 185
Kintner, Robert, 49, 99–100
Kittrie, Nicholas, 192
Knight, Samuel H., 28
Kramer, Victor, 48, 181
Krash, Abe, 173

La Follette, Robert, 112
Labor unions, 103–105, 150, 188
Landon, Alf, 127, 169
Langdell, Christopher Columbus, 14, 46, 62
Laramie Daily Bugle (newspaper), 9, 11
Laramie (Wyoming), 4–8, 10–12, 29–38; American Heritage Center, 199; Arnold (C. P.) in, 10; Arnold (Frances) in, 29, 30, 37, 38; Arnold family in, 9, 10, 199; Arnold Street, 190; crime, 5; Great Depression, 30; settlement/development, 4–5, 10–11; TA home/residency, 1, 8, 10, 11–12, 28–38, 44, 114–115; TA on, 10, 12, 18; TA's mayoralty, 31–33, 37; Union Pacific Railroad, 4–5, 6, 30; University of Wyoming, 6
Larson, T. A., 5, 29
Laski, Harold, 59, 73, 115
Lattimore, Owen, 141–143, 182, 194
Lattimore, United States v., 141–143, 185
Law, 48, 50, 52–53, 58
Law and economics movement, 76
Law and Lawyers (Robinson), 51
Law enforcement, 55–56, 84–85
Laws, Bolitha J., 167, 168
Legal Aid Society, 173
Legal education, 46
Legal formalism, 14, 45

Legal process school of jurisprudence, 161, 165
Legal realism, 45–77; approaches to, 46, 60–61; casebooks, 46, 61–62; Columbia Law School, 14, 45, 46; commercial law, 45; contract law, 45; dean of, 45, 59; focus, 45; legal education, 46; legal formalism, 14, 45; legal science, 46; principal target, 45; private property, 45; replacement as principle American legal philosophy, 161; schools associated with, 14; TA and, 16, 46–48, 50, 52, 59, 60; tort law, 46; Yale University Law School, 14, 45, 46, 101
Legal science, 46
Legal theory, 52
Lerner, Max, 59, 63, 73, 74–75, 82
Levi, Edward, 87, 106, 107–108, 193
Lexington Herald (newspaper), 126
Liberalism, 148, 180, 185–189, 201
Lippman, Walter, 187
Llewellyn, Karl, 43, 45, 47–48, 59
Long, Hugh, 139
Long Island Newsday (newspaper), 169
Long Island R.R. Company, Palsgraf v., 46
Longan, Agnes (TA's sister-in-law), 24–25
Longan, Frances. *See* Arnold, Frances (née Longan, TA's wife)
Longworth, Alice Roosevelt, 169
Looking Forward (Roosevelt), 78
Loyalty Board, 133, 134–135, 138–139, 140
Loyalty Review Board, 131, 132, 138–139, 140

Machiavelli, Niccoló, 73
MacLeish, Archibald, 166

Madden, Murdaugh, 146
Mao Tse-Tung, 130
Marx, Groucho, 77
Marx, Karl, 73
Marx Brothers, 109
Maverick, Maury, 152
McCarran, Pat, 86–87, 142
McCarthy, Joseph, 130, 140, 141, 187
McCormick, Charles T., 43
McCormick, Robert, 102–103, 169, 172, 188
McCullough, David, 131
McLean, Evalyn Walsh, 127, 169, 170–172
McQueen, Steve, 61
McWhinnie, Ralph E., 28
Mellon, Andrew, 93
Mencken, H. L., 76, 121
Mergers and acquisitions, 105–106
Militia Contingency Fund, 35–36
Miller, Reed, 124, 125, 173
Miller-Tydings Act, 90
Minton, Sherman, 138
Miranda v. Arizona, 185
Mondell, Frank W., 9, 24
Monopolies, 85, 99, 102
Monsanto Chemical Co. v. Coe, 117–118
Moore, Underhill, 45
Morgantown (West Virginia), 44
Motion picture industry, 92
Murphy, Frank: Alcoa, 94; influence on Roosevelt administration, 111; McLean and, 170; sugar production quota, 64; Supreme Court, 111; TA and, 64, 104, 111, 113
Myths, 66–68

Nader, Ralph, 193–194
Nation (magazine), 148

National Citizens for Humphrey Committee, 192
National Industrial Recovery Act (NIRA), 56, 79, 80
National Labor Relations Board, 64
National Lawyers Guild, 149, 150, 192
National Observer (newspaper), 188
National Recovery Administration. *See* NRA (National Recovery Administration)
Nation's Agriculture (magazine), 99
Natural law tradition, 14
New Deal, 54–59, 79, 87, 89
New Haven (Connecticut), 64, 65, 77
New Haven Hunt Club, 65
New Property, The (Reich), 68, 163
New Republic (magazine), 99
New York Illustrated Daily News (newspaper), 169
New York Independent, 25
New York State Bar Association, 190, 192
New York Sun (newspaper), 82
New York Times Magazine, 99
New York Times (newspaper), 82
New Yorker (magazine), 73, 94
Nicholson, Jack, 181
NIRA (National Industrial Recovery Act), 56, 79, 80
Nixon administration, 195–196
No-fault automobile insurance, 61
NRA (National Recovery Administration): antitrust enforcement, 83–84, 85, 106; contradictory nature, 229n10; endorsement of wholesale cartelization, 88; head of, 87, 109; *Schechter Poultry Corp. v. United States*, 79; self-regulation, 88; TA on, 54, 57, 84
Nussbaum, Fred, 43
Nye, Bill, 11

O'Brien, Marguerite, 114, 124, 125, 163, 190
O'Bryan, Waite & Arnold, 22–23
Obscenity, 119
Ohio, Brandenburg v., 120
Oil industry, 96–98, 100
Oliphant, Herman, 78, 89
O'Mahoney, Joseph: TA and, 36, 81, 82, 112, 113–114, 142; TNEC, 89, 90, 91
Ordeal by Slander (Lattimore), 142
Origin of the Species (Darwin), 73
O'Sullivan, Joe, 124
Otis & Company, 124, 152, 155–156
Overholser, De Marcos v., 118–119
Overholser, Winfred, 119, 167–168

Palsgraf v. Long Island R.R. Company, 46
Patents, 90, 91, 98–99, 107, 116–118
Patterson, Eleanor "Cissy": Arnold (Frances) and, 170; brother, 169; death, 172; granddaughter, 169; inheritance, 169; lifestyle, 169; McCormick (Robert) and, 102, 169; Pearson (Drew) and, 169; TA and, 102–103, 127, 169–170, 234n107; *Washington Times-Herald*, 102
Patterson, Joseph, 169
Peach industry, 128
Pear-cutting devices, 117
Pearson, Drew: Arnold (George) and, 177, 179–180; Patterson ("Cissy") and, 169; as "Pazzy," 179; TA and, 99, 127; TA's nomination to D.C. Circuit court, 109; on TA's resignation from D.C. Circuit court, 123
Pearson, Ellen (Elena), 169, 177, 178, 180
Pemberton, John, 191
Perlman, Philip, 137

Pershing, John Joseph, 23, 24
Personification of the corporation, 69–70
Peters, John, 138–140
Peters v. Hobby, 138–140, 159
Philadelphia Record (newspaper), 81
Pickford, Mary, 92
Pike, Sumner, 231n54
Playboy (magazine), 158–159
Political parties, 185–186
Popenoe, Walker v., 119
Porter, Fred, 29
Porter, Paul: Agricultural Adjustment Administration, 127; appearance, 127; Arnold, Fortas & Porter, 126–127, 147–148, 172, 174, 184; Arnold & Porter, 184, 195–196; *Bailey v. Richardson*, 134, 135, 137; clients, 152; on defending homosexuals and Communists, 148; Federal Communications Commission, 127, 152; Fortas and, 127, 172, 197; government service, 127, 186; home town, 129; humor, 147–148; law school, 126; liberal causes, 148; Office of Price Administration, 127; personality, 128–129; social life, 127; style as litigator, 128, 129; TA and, 127, 198; Texas Senate primary (1948), 154, 155; *United States v. Lattimore*, 141; Wallace and, 127; Wolfson affair, 195–196
Potter Law Club, 37
Pound, Dorothy, 167
Pound, Ezra, 119, 166–169
Pound, Roscoe, 14, 37–38
Prettyman, E. Barrett, 135
Price controls, 84, 108
Price-fixing, 96–98, 102, 110, 190
Princeton University, 12–14, 17, 24
Principles, 51–52, 53, 55, 73

Private enterprise, 57
Private property, 45, 67–68
Proctor, James, 135
Production quotas, 84
Professor Hart's Theology (Arnold), 163–166
Prohibition, 32, 56, 81
Public Affairs (journal), 141
Public Utility Holding Company Act, 88
Public works, 53–54
Public Works Administration, 126
Pullman Co., United States v., 124–125, 159

Rabelais, 100
Radin, Max, 59–60
Railroads, 109
Ramsauer, Gottfried (TA's uncle), 13, 216n21
Ramsauer, Johannes (TA's grandmother's brother), 8
Ramsauer, Karl (TA's uncle), 216n21
Ramsauer, Maria (TA's grandmother), 8–9, 216n19, 216n21
Rauh, Joseph, 145, 155
Reader's Digest (magazine), 99, 102, 121, 188
Reed, Stanley: Alcoa, 94; *Bailey v. Richardson*, 137, 138; nomination to Supreme Court, 81; *Peters v. Hobby*, 140; Roosevelt (Franklin) and, 81
Reese, B. Carroll, 89
Reeves v. Bowles, 121
Reich, Charles, 68, 163
Remarque, Erich Maria, 27
Reno, Janet, 110
Republican (newspaper), 30
Republican Party, 7, 8, 9, 30, 216n16
Ribicoff, Abraham, 193–194
Richardson, Bailey v., 133–138, 140

268 | Index

Richberg, Donald, 78, 87–88
Rill, James, 110
Robinson, Edward, 51
Rockefeller, Nelson, 139
Rockefeller Foundation, 47
Rodale Press, 160
Rogers, William, 166, 167, 176
Roosevelt, Franklin Delano: Alcoa, 94; AMA investigation (1938), 95; antimonopoly message, 87–88; antitrust enforcement, 78, 80, 88, 89; Black nomination to Supreme Court, 81; brain trust, 78; Byrnes vacancy on Supreme Court, 94; controversial nominations, 81; *Folklore of Capitalism*, 78; Johnson (Lyndon) and, 153; *Looking Forward*, 78; Pound (Ezra) on, 166; Reed nomination to Supreme Court, 81; reelection (1944), 144; Rutledge appointment to Supreme Court, 109, 112; TA and, 77, 78, 109, 111–112, 113; TA's opinion of, 79, 80; TNEC, 88–89; Truman and, 130
Roosevelt, James, 92
Roosevelt, Theodore (Teddy), 70, 173
Rubber market, 107–108
Rutledge, Wiley, 109, 112

Sandburg, Carl, 166, 167
Saturday Evening Post (magazine), 32, 99–100
Schechter Poultry Corp. v. United States, 56, 80, 98
Schlegel, John Henry, 47
Screen Writers Guild, 150
Second Circuit appeals court, 94, 101, 105, 113, 139
Secondary boycotts, 104
Securities and Exchange Act, 54

Securities and Exchange Commission (SEC): commissioners, 231n54; Douglas (William), 89, 126, 231n54; Fortas and, 126; TA and, 64, 87; TNEC, representation on, 89; Wolfson and, 195
Senate National Defense Committee, 107
Senate Patent Committee, 107
Senatorial prerogative, 113
Seventh Circuit appeals court, 100
Seymour, Charles, 139
Sheen, Fulton, 170
Shenefield, John, 110
Sherman Act (1890): anticompetitive conduct overseas, 94; Douglas (William) on, 98; mergers and acquisitions, 105–106; passage of, 10; TA on, 84, 85, 112
Sixth Amendment, 143
Slosson, Mrs., 25–26
Slosson, Preston, 25
Social sciences, 51
Social Security Act, 54
Sociological jurisprudence, 14
Socony-Vacuum v. United States, 98
South Bend (Indiana), 92
Special Equipment Co. v. Coe, 117–118
Spock, Benjamin, 191
Springfield (Illinois), 21
Standard Oil of Indiana, 33
Standard Oil of New Jersey, United States v., 107
Star of the East, 170, 171
Stern, Gerald, 1, 34–35, 173, 176, 200
Stevenson, Adlai, 79–80, 172
Stevenson, Coke, 153–155
Stone, Harlan Fiske, 94
Stone, I. F., 148
Stone, Julius, 60

Sturges, Wesley, 64, 65
Summers, Hatton W., 89
Supreme Court. *See* United States Supreme Court
Swanson, Gloria, 145
Symbols, 51–52
Symbols of Government (Arnold), 50–61; aim, 51; argument in, 51–59, 169; critical reception, 59–61, 73–74; *Folklore of Capitalism* and, 65, 69, 72; Katzenbach and, 61; legal realism, 52; origins, 50–51; TA's view of, 75; Veblen and, 76

TA. *See* Arnold, Thurman
Taxation (public and private), 70–72
Temporary National Economic Committee (TNEC), 88–91, 105–106, 182
Ten Commandments, 146–147
Tenth Circuit appeals court, 113, 114
Texas Senate primary race (1948), 153–155
Thayer, James Bradley, 15, 18
Thomas, Norman, 185
Time (magazine), 109, 188
TNEC (Temporary National Economic Committee), 88–91, 105–106, 182
Tobacco industry, 105, 194
Tort law, 46
Treasury Department, 78
Trotsky, Leon, 73
Truman, Harry: Executive Order 9835, 131; Johnson (Lyndon) and, 153; loyalty program, 131–132, 137, 141, 147, 159; McCarthyism, 130–132; Roosevelt (Franklin) and, 130; Senate National Defense Committee, 107; on Standard Oil's agreement with I.G. Farben, 108; TA and, 107, 122, 170; Truman Doctrine, 130–131
Tugwell, Rexford, 78, 79, 109, 127, 188
Turner, Don, 190
Turner, John, 40, 43–44
Twain, Mark, 13
Tydings, Millard, 142

Union Pacific Railroad, 4–5, 6, 7, 30, 215n9
United States, Abrams v., 120
United States, Appalachian Coals v., 80
United States, Ethyl Gasoline Corp. v., 99
United States, Schechter Poultry Corp. v., 56, 80, 98
United States, Socony-Vacuum v., 98
United States, Williams v., 238n19
United States Department of Commerce, 89–90
United States Department of Justice, 64, 78. *See also* Antitrust Division
United States Department of the Interior, 127, 148
United States Department of the Treasury, 78
United States Supreme Court: antitrust indictments against labor unions, 105; *Bailey v. Richardson*, 137–138; Black nomination, 81; Byrnes vacancy, 94; caseload, 15, 161, 164; collective deliberation, 161, 166; craftsmanship of opinions, 161–162; Douglas (William) and, 111; Fortas and, 173, 183–184, 194–196, 239n31; Hart's critique of, 161–166, 186; Jackson and, 111; justices' time, 161; Murphy and, 111; Reed nomination, 81;

United States Supreme Court (*Cont.*)
Roosevelt (Franklin) and, 81,94, 109, 112; Rutledge appointment, 109, 112; TA and, 64, 75, 81, 96, 99, 137, 159
United States v. Hutcheson, 105
United States v. Lattimore, 141–143, 185
United States v. Pullman Co., 124–125, 159
United States v. Standard Oil of New Jersey, 107
United States v. Univis Lens Co., 99
U.S. Court of Appeals, Second Circuit. *See* Second Circuit appeals court
U.S. Court of Appeals for the District of Columbia. *See* D.C. Circuit court
U.S. Court of Appeals for the Tenth Circuit, 113, 114
University of Chicago Law Review, 75
University of Wisconsin Law School, 45
University of Wyoming, 7, 11, 31, 38, 181
University of Wyoming College of Law: Arnold (C. P.) and, 199; Arnold (Carl) and, 37, 41, 200; Arnold (George) and, 37, 200; highest rated law school, 199, 249n1; TA and, 114, 199
Univis Lens Co., United States v., 99

Valparaiso University speech, 186–189
Vanderbilt, Cornelius, 188
Variety (newspaper), 144
Veblen, Thorstein, 73, 76, 77
Vieth, Bud, 173
Vietnam War, 28, 188
Villa, Pancho, 23

Voltaire, 100
Voltaire and the Cowboy (Gressley), 2

Wabash College, 9, 11–12
Wald, Patricia, 141, 143, 172
Waldrop, Frank, 170
Walker, Esquire v., 119–121, 158
Walker v. Popenoe, 119
Wallace, Henry, 78, 127, 130
War Manpower Commission, 132
Warren, Earl, 140, 188
Warren, Francis E., 216n16
Warren, Frederick, 7, 24
Washington, D.C., 64, 65, 200, 232n73
Washington Post (newspaper): Ferrar case, 144; owner, 170; representation for admitted Communists, 149; TA's letter to editor, 185; *Washington Times-Herald,* 102, 172
Washington Star (newspaper), 81, 144, 188
Washington Times-Herald (newspaper): editor-in-chief, 170; Ferrar case, 144; Patterson ("Cissy") and, 169; TA anecdote in, 174–175; *Washington Post,* 102, 172
Water softeners, 117
West Virginia Bar Association, 42
West Virginia Law Quarterly (journal), 42, 50
West Virginia University College of Law, 37–44
White, Byron, 156
Wickersham Study, 47
Williams v. United States, 238n19
Wilson, Woodrow, 12, 24
Winston, Harry, 171–172
Wiprud, Arne, 121, 124, 240n6
Wister, Owen, 7
Wolfson, Louis, 195–196

Women's rights, 7–8
Woodruff, Robert, 29, 151–152
Wyoming: anti-Catholic activity, 37; cattle industry, 215n9; Democrats in, 9, 30; Great Depression, 30; iron triangle of Wyoming legal practice, 33; Ku Klux Klan in, 37; Militia Contingency Fund, 35–36; openness, 216n17; Republicans in, 7, 8, 9, 30, 216n16; settlement/development, 4–8; Standard Oil of Indiana in, 33; statehood, 10, 216n26; TA on, 38; Union Pacific Railroad, 215n9; women's rights, 7–8
Wyoming Cattleman's Association, 10
Wyoming House of Representatives, 30–31
Wyoming State Bar Association, 9, 21
Wyoming Stock Growers Association, 7
Wyoming Supreme Court, 35–36

Yale Law Journal, 49, 63, 99, 125
Yale University Law School: Arnold (Carl) and, 37; chorus girls, 63–64; Clark (Charles) and, 39, 43, 45; Douglas (William) and, 45, 46, 48; faculty, 45; Fortas and, 63; Hamilton and, 125; legal realism, 14, 45, 101; Lerner and, 63; Moot Court of Appeals (Thurman Arnold Moot Court), 49–50; Reich and, 163; TA and, 43–50, 62–65, 68, 77, 101
Youngdahl, Luther, 143, 158

Zlotnick, Bailey v., 116

About the Author

Spencer Weber Waller is Director of the Institute for Consumer Antitrust Studies and Associate Dean for Faculty Research at Loyola University Chicago School of Law. He has written widely on antitrust, international law, and baseball. He lives in Chicago, Illinois, with his wife, Laura Matalon, and their daughter, Jordan, all lifelong Cubs fans.